ZHUANGZI AND EARLY CHINESE PHILOSOPHY

This is comparative philosophy at its best. It is an object lesson in its own thesis, challenging the closure of exclusive interpretive judgments with the ingenuity of more productive, insights and discernments. From the purchase of a range of familiar Western interpretive strategies, Coutinho goes beyond dichotomy to promote a third position: penumbral thinking. In a word, penumbral thinking is an attempt to exploit the always attendant indeterminacy that honeycombs determinate vocabularies as an open and bottomless source of increased meaning.

-Roger T. Ames, Professor of Philosophy, University of Hawaii

The Daoist philosopher Zhuangzi (also known as Chuang Tzu), along with Confucius, Lao Tzu, and the Buddha, ranks among the most influential thinkers in the development of East Asian thought. His literary style is humorous and entertaining, yet the philosophical content is extraordinarily subtle and profound.

This book introduces key topics in early Daoist philosophy. Drawing on several issues and methods in Western philosophy, from analytical philosophy to semiotics and hermeneutics, the author throws new light on the ancient Zhuangzi text. Engaging Daoism and contemporary Western philosophical logic, and drawing on new developments in our understanding of early Chinese culture, Coutinho challenges the interpretation of Zhuangzi as either a skeptic or a relativist, and instead seeks to explore his philosophy as emphasizing the ineradicable 'vagueness' of language, thought and reality.

This new interpretation of the Zhuangzi offers an important development in the understanding of Daoist philosophy, describing a world in flux in which things themselves are vague and inconsistent, and tries to show us a Way (a Dao) to negotiate through the shadows of a 'chaotic' world.

Ashgate World Philosophy Series

The Ashgate World Philosophies Series responds to the remarkable growth of interest among English-language readers in recent years in philosophical traditions outside those of 'the West'. The traditions of Indian, Chinese, and Japanese thought, as well as those of the Islamic world, Latin America, Africa, Aboriginal Australian, Pacific and American Indian peoples, are all attracting lively attention from professional philosophers and students alike, and this new Ashgate series provides introductions to these traditions as well as in-depth research into central issues and themes within those traditions. The series is particularly designed for readers whose interests are not adequately addressed by general surveys of 'World Philosophy', and it includes accessible, yet research-led, texts for wider readership and upper-level student use, as well as research monographs. The series embraces a wide variety of titles ranging from introductions on particular world philosophies and informed surveys of the philosophical contributions of geographical regions, to in-depth discussion of a theme, topic, problem or movement and critical appraisals of individual thinkers or schools of thinkers.

Series Editors:
David E. Cooper, University of Durham, UK
Robert C. Solomon, University of Texas, Austin, USA
Kathleen M. Higgins, University of Texas, Austin, USA
Purushottama Bilimoria, Deakin University, Australia

Other titles in the series:
Buddhism, Knowledge and Liberation
A Philosophical Study
David Burton

Zen Buddhism and Environmental Ethics
Simon P. James

Comparative Approaches to Chinese Philosophy
Edited by Bo Mou

An Introduction to Yoga Philosophy
An annotated translation of the Yoga Sutras
Ashok Kumar Malhotra

Zhuangzi and Early Chinese Philosophy

Vagueness, Transformation and Paradox

STEVE COUTINHO
Towson University, Maryland, USA

ASHGATE

Published by
Ashgate Publishing Limited
Gower House
Croft Road
Aldershot
Hampshire GU11 3HR
England

Ashgate Publishing Company
Suite 420
101 Cherry Street
Burlington, VT 05401-4405
USA

Ashgate website: http://www.ashgate.com

British Library Cataloguing in Publication Data
Coutinho, Steve
  Zhuangzi and early Chinese philosophy : vagueness, transformation
  and paradox. – (Ashgate world philosophies series)
  1. Zhuang zi
  I. Title
  181.1'14

Library of Congress Cataloging-in-Publication Data
Coutinho, Steve, 1963-
  Zhuangzi and early Chinese philosophy: vagueness transformation
and paradox / Steve Coutinho.– 1st ed.
      p. cm. – (Ashgate world philosophies series)
   Includes bibliographical references and index.
   ISBN 0-7546-3730-1 (alk. paper)
  1. Zhuangzi. Nan hua jing. 2. Philosophy, Taoist. 3. Philosophy,
Chinese. I. Title. II. Series.

BL1900.C576C68 2004
181'.114—dc22
                                                        2004011994

ISBN 0 7546 3730 1

Printed and bound in Great Britain by MPG Books Ltd, Bodmin, Cornwall

...from western Zhou to Qin and Han, China followed a winding course of development.... The more than five centuries of the eastern Zhou era were the longest period of disunion in the whole of Chinese history, but China did not dissolve into separate entities, and no insurmountable barriers or fences separated the various states of lords. The intercommunication and movement of people, the merging and diffusion of cultures, and the strategic activities, allegiances, and subjugations of the rulers—these enabled the whole of China to maintain organic ties among its parts, as in a game of *go*....

Li Xueqin, *Eastern Zhou and Qin Civilizations*.

Contents

Preface

There is growing interest among experts and amateurs, Sinologists and Sinophiles alike, in the philosophy of the ancient Daoist thinker Zhuangzi (also known as Chuang Tzu). This book, I sincerely hope, will have something of interest to say to both. It is my firm belief that philosophy, no matter how rarified and technical, should make every attempt to communicate outside the walls of its discipline, and that, if worthwhile, it should make a difference to people's lives. The reader who browses casually through this book will notice unfamiliar signs, logical symbols and Chinese characters. These are technical details included solely for the convenience and benefit of scholars, and for those who read Chinese. They should not pose a serious obstacle for the general reader, but hopefully will pique their curiosity.

Western academia is in crisis. Post-colonial disillusionment with an imperialist past has led to a widespread rejection of the traditional ideals of rationality, truth, and progress. It is commonly thought that if one does not embrace a radical scepticism or relativism, then one must be an absolutist with imperialist designs. I do not accept the terms of this dichotomy. The extremists on both sides, I believe, have overlooked a pragmatic middle ground: one that rejects foundations without being nihilistic, and that accepts plurality without being relativistic. Such a position tends to be too radical for the conservatives, and also too conservative for the radicals. Perhaps if they abandon their dichotomous modes of judgment, they will be able to appreciate the value of the middle ground.

This book is an exercise in the cultivation of this middle ground. I aim to explore a philosophy that rejects the absoluteness of dichotomies, with a hermeneutic and pragmatic method that is rooted in the fertile soil of this middle ground. Through the course of my studies in the Department of Philosophy at the University of Hawai`i, situated itself half way between 'east' and 'west,' I have become convinced of the practicality, necessity, and the productivity of occupying this middle ground.

A note on grammar: The reader will notice my use of an odd grammatical form, the singular 'they.' Children find themselves automatically drawn to the singular 'they' to avoid sexist language. I have elected to follow their example. I resort to 'his or her,' which I consider to be a far uglier solution, only when the singular 'they' solution breaks down, as for example in the reflexive.

Acknowledgments

There are three people whose contribution to this work it is impossible to quantify. It certainly cannot be judged by the number of references that I make. Yet this book would be incomplete without acknowledging the enormous debt of scholarship I owe them. The first is A. C. Graham, whose pioneering work on the later Mohist *Canon*, and on the *Zhuangzi*, has made possible my own modest contribution—even if I do urge it to grow in new and unanticipated ways. The second is David McCraw, who has infected me with his passion for the ancient Chinese language, and whose linguistic insights have trickled into my own work in ways I could not hope to enumerate.

Most importantly, the 'omnipresence' of Roger Ames is clear to anyone who knows how to read the traces. I like to think of Roger's approach to comparative philosophy as constituting the 'field' within which my own research has developed its own characteristic 'focus.' Without Roger's depth of insight into hermeneutic issues concerning western interpretation of classical Chinese texts, my thoughts on Chinese philosophy might have been complicated, but they would have remained superficial. And without Roger's patience, generosity of spirit, and guidance, I could never have accomplished the hermeneutic task I had set myself.

I would also like to make a special note of thanks to Ray Cardillo of the Center for Instructional Assistance and Technology at Towson University. His untiring assistance enabled me to overcome the many technical problems (e-gremlins and cyberdemons) that conspired to stand in the way of the completion of this book.

CHAPTER ONE

Vagueness: 'East' and 'West'

The *Zhuangzi* is without doubt one of the richest and most intriguing among the world's philosophical texts, and so one would expect the field of Zhuangzi studies to be immense. Yet Laozi and Confucius, Augustine and Aquinas, Wittgenstein and Heidegger attract far greater attention than this mad man of Chu, leaving him in the shadows to wallow in the mud. Perhaps this is because he is such a madman, perhaps because he is too playful: his games take us far beyond the familiar into realms that verge on the grotesque. Perhaps it is also because his writing is extraordinarily difficult to decipher, in part because of its historical and cultural difference, but also because his text is 'self-consciously' semeiotic, playing with the very conditions of meaningfulness that it discusses. For these reasons, it is not obvious what reading strategies may appropriately be brought to the text. Was Zhuangzi writing an analytic text, or a deconstructive one? A religious text, or a philosophical one? A political text or a spiritual one? He tells stories, paints vivid pictures: but are these to be understood literally, figuratively, allegorically, metaphorically? If figuratively and metaphorically, how reliable are twentyfirst century western readings of these ancient images and metaphors? The obstacles to understanding may thus appear insurmountable: in the next two chapters I pursue a more detailed exploration of the problems and methods of interpretation. Yet, with even a superficial reading one senses that this text is deep with human significance. Even if we do not fully understand, we can see that important issues are being addressed with great sophistication and extraordinary skill. Our immediate impression is that this work will repay a profounder contemplation, and that an effort to unravel its complexities will be richly rewarded.

The *Zhuangzi* is an extraordinarily complex text. Interwoven amongst its many strands, there are to be found elements that remind us of a sceptical attitude, other elements that hint of relativism, others still that seem inconsistent with both of these. There is much that is highly reminiscent of Mahayana Buddhist idealism; other aspects resonate deeply with the *sunyavada* of Nagarjuna, or seem to anticipate the development of Zen. Now, when we first come across any strange and perplexing phenomenon, our natural tendency is to want to make it less strange by magnifying what seems most familiar. It thus becomes tempting to read the *Zhuangzi* by assimilating it to familiar philosophical doctrines. But a hasty application, or imposition, of such philosophical categories may not necessarily be of the greatest help. Indeed, the practice of looking for what is familiar may well have the unintended consequence of covering over the deeper import of ideas that are difficult to follow precisely because they are unfamiliar. The second chapter, for example, entitled *Qi Wu Lun,* 齊物論, 'Discussion on Smoothing Things Out,' reflects at length on issues concerning knowledge and language, but it bears little resemblance to a western treatise on epistemology or philosophy of language. For this reason it would be wise to refrain from a too hasty classification of the text as 'epistemology' or 'philosophy of language.' Moreover, in this same chapter we find, juxtaposed with paradoxes about language and knowledge, a definite existential mood: tired musings on the contingency and apparent futility of living and dying. Is this 'existentialism' or 'philosophy of language'? Or is it some bizarre hybrid: linguistic existentialism? At some point it becomes clear that forcing our familiar categories in an attempt to clarify the unfamiliar only results in making the text more confusing. It is without doubt instructive, and indeed indispensable, on our first approach to identify similarities with familiar schools and concepts, if we are to find a way in to an appreciation of the text. But as a next step, we must then be sure to notice where the similarities end, and to pay great attention to where and why the incompatibilities arise: this should curtail any tendencies we have to impose our preconceptions on what may turn out to offer something unexpected.

Recently, in the west, there has been some growth of interest in passages of the *Zhuangzi* that are concerned with human knowledge and understanding. What have drawn the greatest attention are aspects of the text that display a tendency toward some kind of relativism on the one hand, and those that display a contrary tendency toward some kind of scepticism on the other. A. C. Graham, following the traditional interpretation of the Jin dynasty commentator Guo Xiang, presents Zhuangzi as emphasizing the radical equality, and equal acceptability, of all things, all differences, and all perspectives.[1] This has been expressed in western interpretations through the language of radical relativism. Indeed, one might say that the received interpretation of Zhuangzi

---

[1]   A. C. Graham, *Chuang-Tzu The Inner Chapters: A Classic of Tao.* See also chapter four below.

is that he is a radical relativist. Paul Kjellberg and Lisa Raphals,[2] perhaps out of a sense of dissatisfaction with this interpretation, seek to re-read the text from another standpoint. Beginning with a thorough appreciation of the philosophies of the ancient Sceptics, such as Sextus Empiricus, they engage in the painstaking process of finding, collating, and interpreting parallels from the *Qi Wu Lun*, and other chapters. In this way, much light is thrown on aspects of the text that resonate with the epistemic attitudes of these western philosophers.

I propose to explore another possibility; one that I sincerely hope does not attempt to force the philosophy of the *Zhuangzi* into a preformed 'ism,' or into an *ad hoc* combination of such 'isms.' This does not mean that I attempt to approach the text from its own cultural point of view: this, alas, is clearly impossible. I have not been inculturated into that context and so cannot presume to read from it. Indeed, the philosophical and interpretive devices I use are utterly western, and I make no apology for this. Since I am a product of western culture attempting to understand a culture that is 'Other' to me, there is no possible alternative. Nor, on the other hand, do I claim to 'reconstruct the original meaning.' This, alas, is also impossible! For a genuine reconstruction of the original context of meaning would require that I perform the impossible task of erasing my own context of interpretation: my own historical, cultural, linguistic and philosophical context, and also that of my readers.

Between these two extremes—that of forcing the text to conform to my own preformed conceptual constructions, and that of attempting to uncover the original thought behind the text—there lies another possibility. I must start from my *de facto* starting position. I cannot but start from my cultural, philosophical background, but I can take care not to *hastily impose* my cultural categories and methodologies, not to insist that if I cannot force a text or a tradition of thought into my preconceived moulds then it could not possibly make sense. Of course, my starting position itself is not necessarily self-contained or well defined. Indeed, the starting position of some people is already multi-cultural, fragmented, inconsistent, and in process of construction! I suspect that this is true of all of us to a greater or lesser degree. Instead, I start from my inevitable starting point, however complex and unfinished it is: but then I must be willing to shift my position, I must be open to unexpected changes. I must be especially open to the possibility

---

[2]   *Essays on Skepticism, Relativism, and Ethics in the* Zhuangzi, edited by P. J. Ivanhoe and Paul Kjellberg.

that there may be *deep* differences even in modes of thinking: pre-suppositions, basic concepts, cardinal associations, and funda-mental metaphors, perhaps even structural relations between ideas. But the deepest differences are the hardest to see: so, I must be *on the lookout* for signs of difference, and I must *welcome* them. I must not allow my belief in a common human bond to blind me to whatever differences there may be, no matter at what level.

There is a growing tendency to express impatience with the postmodern call to reclaim the voice of the Other, or rather, to allow Others to reclaim their own voices, to allow those voices to be heard on their own terms. 'Otherness' has become a catchword, a standard tool for critique of the 'tradition.' There is, however, a danger of exoticizing the Other: objectifying and distancing 'it' as a fascinating object of curiosity. There is also a danger of Othering the Other, of excluding the Other precisely by categorizing it as 'Other' (with a capital 'O')! While these are important cautionary reminders, it does not follow that we should universalize without any sensitivity to difference whatsoever. Besides, I think it is far too early to be yielding to any expressions of reactionary impatience. We have not even begun to understand humanity in all its difference, and already we are getting tired of it. Being open to difference is painful and difficult, and indeed sometimes dangerous—but it is a necessary task, and an ethical responsibility, even with something so apparently trivial as interpreting a text.

Now, the reading that I explore emphasizes a number of intriguing passages that are not usually taken as central to the philosophy espoused by the *Zhuangzi.* 'A discourser has a discourse, but what is said is exceptionally indeterminate.' 'Using a horse to show that a horse is not a horse, is not as good as using a non-horse to show that a horse is not a horse.' 'If we wish to affirm what we deny and deny what we affirm, nothing is as good as illuminating it on the grindstone of nature.' These passages are usually understood by subordinating them to the parts of the text that have a more relativist, conventionalist, or fallibilist feel. My reading shifts these passages from the periphery to the center, and thereby produces a very different understanding, one that displaces the hints of relativism and scepticism with a very different sensibility. These passages suggest a very sophisticated attitude toward language, one that has *strong resonances* with the most recent of twentieth century linguistic theories. It is these resonances that I wish to exploit, not, I hope, by imposing the western ideas on the text, but by *sounding the textual material simultaneously and listening for the overtones.* Thus, my aim is not to unmask the real Zhuangzi as a deconstructionist, or has having discovered concepts of vagueness, open texture, and family resemblance. Unfortunately, for purposes of stylistic convenience, I find that I must often resort to this sort of direct attribution. Thus, I talk quite freely about Zhuangzi's aims, thoughts, and intentions! But the 'imputations' implied by such language go quite against my explicit intentions, and I urge the reader to make appropriate emendations: to read my apparent attributions not as direct attributions, but as *hermeneutic explorations*. Dichotomies and indeterminacies, clearings and penumbrae, as they appear from the standpoint of transformation: these will be both the tools and the materials with which I shall attempt to fashion my alternative interpretation. But, while sounding these traces through the text, I urge the reader to listen carefully for the clashes and the dissonances, and to struggle to understand what kinds of *deep differences* might be responsible. If vagueness and open texture somehow resonate deeply in these ancient Chinese texts, and yet at the same time seem somehow artificially imposed and jarring, I suggest the following hypothesis: this paradoxical state might be a sign of differences at the deepest levels of significance, structural differences at the very heart of the webs of understanding.

A prerequisite to interpreting any text is to place it in its historical, cultural, and philosophical context. The particular elements of context that one emphasizes will shape the possibilities of interpretation. If one emphasizes the Confucian context of early Daoist texts, for example, this leads to the familiar reading of Daoism as essentially a critical response to Confucianism. I choose instead to place greater emphasis on the philosophy of the Mohists, in particular the concurrently developing philosophy of the 'later' Mohists. Zhuangzi makes quite explicit reference to their concepts, especially when expressing his most complex and enigmatic ideas about language. The later Mohists articulate some very clear conditions of linguistic evaluation. Their attitude, I shall argue, is one that asserts a dichotomy of values, variously characterized as acceptability, *ke* 可, and unacceptability, *buke* 不可, or affirmation, *shi* 是, and rejection, *fei* 非. One might, as we shall see, characterize it as an attitude of '*bivalence*.' The word 'bivalence' is a term of art from logic: it refers to the existence of two and only two mutually exclusive values, Truth and Falsehood. What I am calling an attitude of bivalence is one that sees in the world, or imposes on it, such mutually exclusive dichotomies. Dualistic worldviews, then, are typical products of an attitude of bivalence. The later Mohists, I argue in chapter five, quite explicitly claim that any assertion must be either affirmed or rejected, it must either be acceptable or unacceptable; it must be one or the other, and it certainly cannot be both. It can thus easily be seen to be an expression of an attitude of bivalence. The Mohist discourse of *shifei*, affirmation and rejection, acceptability and unacceptability, plays a pivotal role in the philosophical discussions of the second chapter of the *Zhuangzi*. For this reason, a deeper understanding of the more complex passages devoted to Zhuangzi's reflections on *shifei* thinking requires a closer and more sustained investigation of the significance of affirmation and rejection in the later Mohist *Canon*. Moreover, the reflections on linguistic evaluation of the later Mohists also take place within their own context: the philosophical thinking of Mozi and the early Mohists. We will thus acquire a deeper understanding still by tracing the roots of such dichotomous thinking back to the political theorizing of the early Mohists. When placed in this context, new aspects of Zhuangzi's concern with language begin to surface, and their significance can in turn throw light on other aspects of Zhuangzi's philosophy.

The Mohists were the first among the Chinese thinkers to value simplicity and clarity in expressing doctrines and values. They took simplicity and clarity to new levels in the iterative structure of their arguments, and in their insistence on the importance of clearly determined dichotomies. Zhuangzi, in contrast, sees language as extremely open and unsettled—although words do say something, what they say is extremely vague, profoundly unsettled. We find a further indication of this when Zhuangzi suggests that we should affirm what we reject and reject what we affirm. Indeed, he gives us this advice as a direct response to the dichotomous thinking espoused by the Mohists. He also gives us a very cryptic piece of advice with regard to affirming what we reject: 'Using a horse to show that a horse is not a horse, is not as good as using a non-horse to show that a horse is not a horse.' A. C. Graham valiantly tries to throw light on this baffling passage by interpreting it as a reference to the conventional nature of language: if we simply switched linguistic terms and called a cow 'horse' we could show that a horse is not a horse.[3] Unfortunately, this does not strike me as a very insightful or interesting philosophical claim; it is at best an infantile word game, and it does not succeed in showing how it is possible for a horse not to be a horse. I hope to show that following up the leads of dichotomousness and bivalence as expressed in the later Mohist *Canon* yields the possibility of a new and more persuasive direction of explanation.

---

[3]   A. C. Graham, *Chuang-Tzu The Inner Chapters: A Classic of Tao.*

For this new explanation I introduce some of the ideas concerning determinacy and indeterminacy that have been influential in contemporary western philosophy. There are several different kinds of indeterminacy of language that have been explored in twentieth century philosophy, and indeed one that has been known, but marginalized, since the Stoics. Quine and Wittgenstein have put forward interesting and influential ideas on the nature of meaning, and specifically on its indeterminacy: Quine's naturalistic rejection of *a priori* knowledge and analyticity depends on an understanding that what we can know is constrained by an openness or indeterminacy in what we mean; Wittgenstein's excursions into the ill-defined borderlands of our concepts epitomize a philosophical methodology that eschews essences for family resemblances, and clustering (and re-reclustering!) concepts. The positivist philosopher Waissman's metaphor of porosity, or open texture, can throw light on the connection between Zhuangzi's concern for indeterminacy and vagueness and his tendency toward imaginative exaggeration. The Stoic interest in vagueness and sorites paradoxes provides a link between the thought of Zhuangzi and the spatio-temporal paradoxes of Huizi. These are some of the strings that will be sounded while we peruse the text: and we shall listen for where it resonates in sympathy. But, even if we find the resonances persuasive, we must not be hypnotized into imagining that we have discovered what the text 'really' says: we must also pay close attention to where we force it to ring out of tune.

In keeping with the spirit of pluralism and indeterminacy, I do not attempt to prove the 'truth' of my reading through detailed refutations of alternative readings. Such an endeavour seems clearly misplaced when dealing with texts as rich and fertile as the *Laozi* and the *Zhuangzi*. This, however, is not to adopt an irresponsible (though, alas, all too popular) relativism with regard to the meaning of the text, but arises out of an acknowledgment of two undeniable facts. The first is that the *Zhuangzi*, as is generally the case with classical Chinese texts, leaves its own meanings open. It is a text that is suggestive, indirect, using allegory and metaphor among other tropes to hint at the ideas it both conceals and conveys. And it is through the exploration of these allegories and metaphors that we shall uncover the clues, hints, and traces of what I believe to be more formative and pervasive significances. Indeed, classical Chinese philosophical works in general are as much works of poetry as they are explorations of ideas, and the use of poetic techniques involves the exploitation of tropes such as polysemy, ambiguity and metaphor. This is especially true of Daoist texts such as the *Laozi* and the *Zhuangzi*. It is thought by some that merely acknowledging the openness of meaning is to open the floodgates of nihilism, scepticism and relativism. Such a worry is, however, unfounded. Acknowledging openness of meaning is not a *carte blanche* permitting random interpretation that defies all constraints. Allowing ambiguity, vagueness, and metaphor to function, as we indeed do in ordinary everyday language, as well as in poetry and literature, is by no means tantamount to an 'anything goes' relativism. Vague, ambiguous, and metaphorical language can function *as* vague, ambiguous or metaphorical *only* if there is some degree of constraint upon possible interpretation. Indeed, it is impossible for meaning to lack all determination whatsoever, for this would fail to differentiate meanings from one another, and result in meaninglessness. Indeterminacy is a matter of degree and becomes a threat only if taken to extremes.

The second fact that favors a more open approach to interpretation is that the evidence to which we may appeal for uncovering the concerns and doctrines of Chinese philosophical texts of the earliest period is, to say the least, sparse. When a text is indeterminate, knowledge of its context can help to delimit possible and probable meanings, and to make (provisional) judgments that set aside certain readings as improbable. Much of the problem in reading a Zhou dynasty text is that its deliberate indeterminacy is multiplied by an exasperating indeterminacy of context. Such a problem will be familiar to scholars of ancient Greek philosophy, as it also occurs in the interpretation of the earliest stage of Greek thought—the fragments of the pre-Socratics. When so much of the context itself remains unknown or indeterminate, the semiotic task turns in on itself, producing higher order problematics of interpretation, requiring us to attempt to engage in the apparently circular task of reconstructing elements of cultural and textual context from the evidences within the text itself! Such a task, despite the apparent circularity of the reconstruction, ought not to be ruled out as altogether impossible. Umberto Eco, in *Semiotics and the Philosophy of Language*, demonstrates in his reading of the *Song of Songs* that the significances of what he calls an alien 'cultural encyclopaedia' need not be viewed as hermeneutically irretrievable.[4] One might think of these contextual values and significances as leaving their traces in the fragment in the way that a hologram is able to do, although unlike a holographic image, our reconstruction of such cultural significances must always remain to a very high degree tentative and hypothetical, and always

---

4   Umberto Eco, *Semiotics and the Philosophy of Language*.

incomplete.[5] Given these two manifestations of openness and indeterminacy, of text and of context, it seems clear that though we may work hard to produce persuasive readings, it is both naïve and irresponsible to suggest that we can establish with finality *the* unique definitive reading, or refute decisively the alternatives with which we have little sympathy.

Having established some background and touched on some methodological issues, I shall now briefly introduce the contrast with which I approach the early Chinese texts: dichotomy and penumbra, or clarity and vagueness. I shall highlight the significance of clarity and distinctness in the western tradition with a brief historical sketch. This sketch is admittedly an oversimplification and something of a caricature, but its purpose is very modest. The aim is not to provide an exhaustive account of all the variations in attitude toward clarity and vagueness of all the various philosophers who constitute the western tradition. Rather, the purpose is simply to outline a general cultural tendency. The claim is to establish only that clarity and determinacy have been and continue to be idealized throughout the western tradition, while vagueness and indeterminacy have been seen as obstacles to those ideals. There have indeed been exceptions, philosophers who have reacted strongly against the presuppositions behind these ideals, but they serve only to make more emphatic and dramatic the central and formative role of clarity in western thinking.[6]

Now, judgments of similarity and difference have applicability only from within some context of judgment. Things are similar or different only with regard to some specific characteristic, or from some particular context of comparison. One who loves the colour red may take crimson and vermillion to be vastly different, but to a person comparing them with green and blue, the differences become less significant than their similarities. The same goes for cultural and philosophical comparisons: Locke and Hume would be seen as standing at opposite ends of the philosophical spectrum to a specialist in early British empiricism, but when their ideas are compared with the philosophies of Heidegger and Jaspers,

---

5   The phrase 'tentative and hypothetical' has something of a realist ring. In chapter two, however, we shall see that this is not a matter of having discovered what the text really means.

6   For a more thorough investigation into the historical tendencies of western and Chinese philosophical thinking, see Hall and Ames, *Anticipating China: Thinking through the Narratives of Chinese and Western Culture*, and also, *Thinking from the Han: Self, Truth, and Transcendence in Chinese and Western Culture*.

their similarities far outweigh their differences. When the philosophies of the western tradition are compared with those of the Chinese tradition, not surprisingly we encounter the same phenomenon. When a judgment is made from within the tradition, it is the contrasts between the claims and doctrines that show up as significant; when one judges across traditions, previously hidden similarities begin to emerge. Comparing the western tradition with early Chinese philosophy, differences of philosophical temperament, aim, and method, become quite prominent. It becomes quite evident that the ideals of clarity and distinctness, for example, did not exert the same kind of force on the method, style, and content of Chinese philosophy. One simply does not, for example, find continuous dialectical argumentation aimed at the most rarified levels of conceptual analysis and clarification, as one does throughout the history of western philosophy.

The Contest of Clarity and Vagueness

Vagueness, indeterminacy, penumbras of uncertainty and even inconsistency are very disturbing phenomena. They epitomize the antithesis of everything philosophers desire, and the negation of everything that philosophy ought to strive for. It is a commonplace that the project of philosophy involves the search for, among other things, clarity, understanding, and truth. Indeed, William James saw fit to define the very practice of philosophy as 'the uncommonly stubborn attempt to think clearly.' Vagueness, however, seems to pose an obstacle to the achievement of these ideals. We identify vagueness with confusion, uncertainty, and as a psychological failing rather than as an independent and ineradicable phenomenon with which we are obliged to come to terms. When we criticize one another for being vague, it is such confusion and uncertainty that we attack, and we demand clarification, explication, and specification as remedies. We are unwilling to take seriously, or grant much respect to, thoughts that evidence carelessness and confusion. In this way, philosophers have tended to dismiss or devalue not only what is vaguely expressed, but also the phenomenon of vagueness itself as an object or theme of investigation. The phenomenon of vagueness has in recent years been attracting interest among analytic philosophers, and it is almost invariably the 'problem' of vagueness and the problems that it causes that attract attention. Just as we seek to diminish any effect of vague expressions through procedures of clarification, explication and disambiguation, so at a metalinguistic or philosophical level such techniques are brought to bear on vagueness itself, sometimes with the ideal of abolishing vagueness altogether, but always with the hope of dissolving the logical problems and paradoxes to which it gives rise.[7]

Among the pre-Socratics, the philosophers of the Eleatic tradition—whose origins have been linked to the 'mystery cults' of central Asia—Parmenides, Pythagoras, and perhaps Xeno, rejected the uncertainties, indeterminacies, and contradictions of the temporal world of flux in favour of a 'spiritual' realm of eternal, unchanging, self-consistent truth. And even Heraclitus, who saw the world not as substantial but as an 'ever living fire,' acknowledged that the flux flows and transforms according to a guiding principle of proportion: *logos*. For Socrates and Plato, following the mystico-mathematical tradition of Pythagoras, the goal of the philosopher was the pursuit of the celestial, spiritual realm of Ideal Forms, whose essence stands in absolute purity and clarity, and this was to be achieved in no small part through the dialectical practice of conceptual clarification and deductive argumentation. Despite the heckling of some dissenting voices, most notably the Sophists, the Greek tradition thus set western philosophy on a course shaped, in large part, by what I shall call an 'analytic' attitude: one defined by the search for definition, essence, clarity, and deductive validity, and conversely by the demand for the eradication of vagueness, ambiguity, and indeterminacy. It was often accompanied by an explicit devaluation of poetry, myth, and metaphor as obstacles to the attainment of truth, even if the philosophers who devalued them felt free to make use of them as

---

[7]   Timothy Williamson has been a staunch defender of the epistemic view of vagueness, according to which vagueness arises out of ignorance. According to this extremely counterintuitive view, there is a precise, but unknown, number of hairs, the loss of which turns a non-bald person into a bald person, and similarly an exact height at which a person becomes tall! See his book, *Vagueness*. See also his article, 'Vagueness and Ignorance,' which is reprinted in Rosanna Keefe, *Vagueness: a Reader*.

Kit Fine has championed a supervaluationist theory of vagueness, which proposes a semantics for vague terms that aims to solve the logical problems to which vagueness gives rise. Supervaluationist theories appeal to the notion of sets of 'precisifications' or 'sharpenings' of vague terms. For each sharpening the extension of the term is divided into two distinct sets (that of the term and that of its complement). A basic sentence with a vague predicate is then said to be 'super-true' (or 'super-false') if it turns out true on all sharpenings; otherwise it is neither true nor false. For a full discussion of the supervaluationist approach, see Kit Fine, 'Vagueness, truth and logic,' which is also reprinted in *Vagueness: a Reader*.

rhetorical devices. The Hellenistic period likewise followed the same analytic attitude, favouring deductive argument, definition, and theoretical clarification, as can be seen both in the argumentative method and the systematic development of logical theory of the Sceptics and Stoics. Even in the religious thought of the medieval period, Scholastic theodicies and *logical proofs* of the existence of God exemplified paradigmatically the purposes of deductive and definitive thinking. Clarity of definition and validity of logical deduction are still highly valued tools in much of the work of recent theology and philosophy of religion.

With the flourishing of the Renaissance, however, we run into an interesting phenomenon. The symbolic, alchemical, and indeed 'correlative' thinking of this period provides a salient and significant—and too often neglected—countercurrent to the overall trend that I have been sketching. Allegory, myth, and metaphor become central tools of philosophical reflection, whose aim is to uncover deeper and yet deeper levels of cosmological and spiritual significance. With Descartes, Spinoza, and Leibnitz, the rational and logical discourse of consequences, following the model of the mathematical sciences, again took hold of the reins of philosophy, and even the empiricists, though they abandoned the model and methods of mathematics for acquiring knowledge of the world, nevertheless maintained the need for definition, disambiguation and precision in the formulation of that knowledge. Kant and Husserl in the Continental tradition continued the Rationalistic search for essences, necessities, apodicticities, and at present in the English speaking world, philosophical analysis seems to have become in many ways definitive of all philosophical thinking.

This is not to say that there has been no assertion of the 'subaltern' voices throughout the history of western philosophy. Indeed, the most vociferous of those whose concern it was to establish the 'right method' for philosophical thinking, were speaking out against the threat, real or perceived, of those who did not believe in the efficacy or necessity of such thinking. Sceptics, relativists, sophists, nihilists and irrationalists pervaded Plato's world, the medieval world of the Christian, Jewish and Islamic philosophers, the worlds of Descartes, Kant and Husserl, and in recent times, following in the footsteps of Nietzsche, voices like these continue to hound those who still profess to believe in the ideals of Modernity. In a less extreme vein, the pragmatic philosophies of the late nineteenth and early twentieth centuries, rejecting some basic presuppositions of the tradition, attempted to make do without foundations, without certainties, and without necessities, and since the second half of this century the naturalistic philosophies of Quine and Wittgenstein have done much to reshape the presuppositions even of analytical philosophy. In the Continental tradition, Heidegger's phenomenology rejected the conception of Being as *ousia*—'substance' or 'presence'; and the influence of the subsequent tradition of French intellectuals on the humanities is causing some degree of alarm in the more conservative philosophy departments. What emerges from this reading of the history of western ideas is that the tradition is characterized by a tension between the *dominant* ideals of clarity, essence, and truth, and the dissension of those who refuse to conform.

In contrast, the explicit ideal of theoretical clarity and precision and the need to eliminate all traces of indeterminacy have never exerted a comparable influence on the style and method of Chinese philosophical reflection. One does indeed find the Confucian doctrine of the rectification of names, *zhengming* 正 名, Xunzi's development of this doctrine, the paradoxes of Huizi, the treatises of Gongsun Longzi, and the canons of the later Mohists. But, I maintain that the significance of these in the Chinese tradition is very different. It does not amount to what I have called an 'analytic' attitude, and to the extent that anything like an analytic attitude emerges in the Chinese tradition it does not maintain a deep influence on the methodology of the dominant modes of Chinese philosophy.

Confucius' concern for the rectification of terms is one of the first examples that come to mind of a concern with clarity of language in the Chinese tradition. In Book 13, chapter three, of the *Analects* Zi Lu asks Confucius what is the first thing he would attend to if he were to entrusted with the government of the state of Wei, he replies that the most pressing and important matter is nothing other than the 'rectification of terms'![8] This might, at first blush, be mistaken for a concern with precision and accuracy in one's definitions. But a closer look at Confucius's explanation reveals not an abstract concern, but a pragmatic one. If names and titles are not correct, then people will be confused about the proper mode of conduct, and affairs and duties will not be reliably accomplished. Rather, one must live up to the expectations and honours of one's own title, and bestow titles and evaluative terms on others appropriately and according to merit. Zhang Dainian[9] points out that Confucius is very careful to evaluate people with the

---

8   *The Analects of Confucius: A Philosophical Translation*, translated by Roger Ames and Henry Rosemont.

9   Zhang Dainian, *Key Concepts in Chinese Philosophy*.

most appropriate title: distinguishing 'renown' from 'excellence,' 'benevolence' from 'sageliness.' Now, this is indeed a concern for a kind of clarity: it is the clarity of *disambiguation*, and of choosing the most appropriate term from a number of synonyms. But this pragmatic concern with disambiguation is quite distinct from the theoretical concern with an abstract, pure, precision that characterizes the 'analytic' attitude that I have identified as distinctive of much of the western tradition. I shall take up this theme again in chapter five.

Now, Xunzi continues Confucius' concern with the rectification of terms in a chapter given that very title, and his concern lies within the same pragmatic context: that of bringing social harmony to the community.[10] Although he is generally opposed to the doctrines of the Mohists, Xunzi agrees with them that social harmony requires uniformity, and uniformity requires conformity. He agrees that diversity is a source of disorder, and results only in social disruption. And he especially disapproves of linguistic diversity.

Now, Xunzi explicitly characterizes *zhengming* in terms of clarity, *ming* 明, and distinction, *bian* 辨, *bie* 別. But this concern with clarity and distinctness is of a very different kind from that of the analytic attitude that I have characterized as motivating the dominant western philosophical tradition. Looking more closely at the differences provided by the context and by the details, we see a very different kind of 'clarity' and 'confusion' that are at stake. Firstly, Xunzi is most worried about the confusion caused by *using terms incorrectly*, by *abandoning traditional usage*, and by *proliferating new terms* without respect for tradition. It is the multiplicity of new terms, and of the new ideas and values that they express, and the resultant ambiguity that is the prime source of confusion, not a vagueness or indeterminacy in the meanings of those terms. Xunzi is concerned about the new ideas that are beginning to spread: especially the very un-Ruist ideas of the later Mohist *Canon*, the Daoists, and the so-called 'Logicians.' Instead of relying on the established usage of established ideas, these thinkers invent new terms, sometimes to express old ideas, sometimes creating new ideas. They cause even greater confusion by putting terms together in paradoxical and contradictory ways: that is, in ways that contravene established usage. Xunzi believes that if this is allowed to escalate, the result can only be confusion, disruption of fluent communication and, thereby, social disorder. It is

---

10   Hsün Tzu, *Basic Writings*, translated by Burton Watson.

especially important that evaluative terms maintain their integrity, so that people may also not be confused about what is virtuous and what is not.

Now, Xunzi goes out of his way to provide some clarifications of terms that he considers to be of vital importance, those pertaining to 'humanity': *xing* 性 nature, *qing* 情 emotions, *xing* 行 conduct, *zhi* 知 understanding. But, if we look in detail at the definitions that Xunzi provides, we notice that they are not definitions at all. The kinds of 'definitions' that Xunzi provides are more like glosses, brief characterizations that aid understanding, but do not expend much effort at clarification. The very first gloss provides a perfect example: 'That by which life is so, call it "*xing*".' 生之所以然者, 謂之性. Such a gloss certainly does not provide anything remotely resembling necessary and sufficient conditions for the application of terms, and no time is spent on a dialectical refinement of the definitions through a consideration of varied examples and counterexamples. Moreover, Xunzi's glosses rely on terms that are far from transparent, and he sometimes even defines terms in a circular manner with reference to themselves. This is true of his glosses on *zhi* knowledge, and *neng* ability: 'The means of knowing in a person, call it "knowing".' 所以知之在人者, 謂之知. He sometimes gives two glosses for the same term (as he does with *xing* 性, *neng* 能, and perhaps *zhi* 知), the second using the term itself in its own gloss. Now, given that this occurs in the context of a discussion of the pressing need for 'rectification of terms,' it is thus exceptionally clear that whatever is meant by this phrase, it cannot be a call for the articulation and refinement of precise definitions.

Although Huizi is counted among the 'Logicians' we have nothing left of his philosophy but a few dialogues with Zhuangzi, and a series of paradoxes. Neither of these is sufficient to demonstrate anything resembling what I have called an analytic attitude. Gongsun Longzi's *Bai Ma Fei Ma*, 'A white horse is not a horse,' treatise, however, I think does exhibit something like an extended discussion concerned to explore in detail the necessity of a certain kind of distinction: between what a thing is and how it is described. It is notable, however, that Gongsun Longzi's work, his concerns, and his methods, have little to no influence on the dominant concerns and methods of Chinese philosophical thinking.

The later Mohist *Canon* is another example of a tendency toward something like an analytic attitude. I shall take up a detailed consideration of the later Mohists in chapter five. For now I shall simply note that as with Xunzi, even if there is a need for some kind of clarity, this is not the kind of perfect abstract clarity that requires refinement through dialectical argumentation, but even at its most abstract remains rooted in pragmatic concerns. And as with Gongsun Longzi, the subject matter and motivation for this style of thinking rapidly fell out of favor, and remained lost and forgotten for close to two thousand years.

Joanne Birdwhistell[11] has suggested that the commentarial tradition of later periods might be thought to exemplify a concern for disambiguation of possible meanings of classical texts. Certainly, it is true that the traditional commentaries not only provide glosses, explications, and interpretations of the traditional texts, but also register disagreements over interpretations, and responses to other interpreters and commentators. But, as with Confucius and Xunzi, this is a concern not with *vagueness* as such, but with *ambiguity*, a different linguistic phenomenon altogether. And, again, it must be kept in mind that this disambiguation did not take the form of extended dialectical refinement of the terms and claims in question. Moreover, the commentaries themselves, the disagreements recorded, and the reasons given, are often highly condensed and obscure, and, as often as not, cause more confusion than clarification. Finally, if the commentators were concerned with clarifying possible ambiguities, this concern never entered into reflective philosophical discourse as a thematized distaste, or explicit rejection, either of vague language and expressions, or of the phenomenon of vagueness itself—as indeed has been the case in western philosophy since its very beginnings.

Now, it is far from my intention to suggest that the ancient Chinese did not argue, that they were not rational, or that they never saw fit to make clarifications. Arguments, clarifications, explications abound in Chinese texts. What it does mean is that reason giving, argumentation, and clarification, have had a different philosophical significance from that of the west. They are practiced always within a context of pragmatic concerns, and not with the aim of a perfect, abstract, objective precision. One will struggle in vain, for example, to find in the philosophical repertoire anything resembling the endless striving after truth and clarity through the dialectical refinement of definitions from the continual adducing of examples and counterexamples. And, in particular, one will be hard pressed to find the explicit theoretical assertion of clarity, distinctness, argumentation, and truth as the goals of philosophical inquiry.

---

[11]   In a personal communication, at the Society for Asian and Comparative Philosophy conference in Honolulu, 1998.

It is, however, my particular contention that in the Daoist thinking of Laozi and Zhuangzi, there is a recognition and appreciation not only of ambiguity, but also of something like the kinds of vagueness and indeterminacy that have been the scourge of western philosophy. Vagueness is not regarded with suspicion, but is simply an acknowledged characteristic of the world around us, and the paradoxes it engenders are not treated as logical puzzles to be solved by analysis and distinction making, but instead are treated as embodying insights, meditation on which will deepen our understanding of the way of things. According to the *Laozi* the outer boundaries of the outer regions are always unsettled: *tiandi* and *dao* are without bounds, without limits, perhaps finite, but inexhaustible. In the *Laozi* then, it is the outer boundaries that are called into question. In the *Zhuangzi*, it is the inner boundaries that are the focus of deconstruction, or dissolution: there is a recognition that the 'whole' is not a monotone uniformity, but is itself a pluralistic congeries of differences. Each region melts into the next in a series of interdiffusing clines of culture, value, and way of life. As one ventures away from home, differences build upon differences and the similarities and familiarities gradually dissolve. Yet the natural way is to make room for a plurality of ways: each region can coincide with others without universalization, and can thus respect the differences that go to make up the whole. There is no battle for control of the whole by imposition of the individual and parochial. Differences blend and jostle together at the intersections, without worrying about exactly which side of the 'divide' anything belongs to.

Overview

In the next chapter, I establish some social and historical background for understanding the context in which Zhuangzi flourished, and also for understanding the socio-cultural signifi-cance of the discussion of boundaries, dichotomies, transformation, and penumbrae. Chapter three raises important interpretive issues, and explores attitudes towards the determinacy and indeterminacy of interpretation of several methodologies. The issues of indeter-minacy of meaning raised are themselves directly relevant to the discussion in the *Zhuangzi* of the indeterminacy of meaning! Chap-ter four introduces the philosophy of the Mohists, a philosophy whose attitudes towards simplicity, clarity, and 'dichotomy' form the philosophical material that the *Zhuangzi* redefines and 'deconstructs.' Chapter five introduces a very specific kind of indeterminacy—'vagueness'—and attempts to abduce the significance of vagueness for understanding the processive Daoist world view as expressed in the *Laozi*. In chapter six, the significance of vagueness is extended to incorporate the phenomena of open texture and family resemblance. The role of the imagination of continuous transformation, and the construction of 'anomalies' (hard cases, penumbral cases), in opening the texture of meaning, give a sense to the vastness of roaming beyond the boundaries of the *Xiao Yao You*. Finally, chapter seven attempts to draw together these elements in a detailed reading of the central passages of the *Qi Wu Lun*: explaining why we should want to affirm what we deny, and how to find a horse that is not a horse!

All translations are my own. The problems of relying on literary translations, imbued with the translator's own interpretation, for philosophical purposes are well known to scholars of Ancient philosophy. One cannot of course produce an uninterpreted translation, but a philosopher can at least attempt to minimize interpretive flourishes that go too far beyond the more central and explicit meanings, and can also draw out any plausible peripheral significances that may be of philosophical relevance.

CHAPTER TWO

Zhuangzi:
Text, Author, Context

The text in historical and cultural context

The *Zhuangzi* is a work of philosophical literature that rarely resorts to literal, straightforward language. At first sight, it appears to be an eclectic and rambling concatenation of fables and musings, myths and parables, some ponderous, some humorous. It is, moreover, not easy to discern what moral might be intimated by the fables, or what might be the import of the musings. This is in large part because the style of the *Zhuangzi* has no surviving precedent in the Chinese philosophical tradition. We are not sure how to read this style of writing because it is the first of its kind, or at least the earliest extant example. In the works of Confucius, Mozi, or Mencius, myths and histories may be alluded to in the interest of illustrating a doctrine, but they are not composed afresh as a philosophical medium. It is tempting to claim that Zhuangzi was thus the originator of this new mode of writing. I find it more tempting to speculate that this style may have its roots in a tradition of thinking through narrative that would have been characteristic of Chu, the region of China that appears to have been the home of Daoist culture. Given the richness and complexity of the text, this lack of stylistic precedent makes it extraordinarily difficult to read and interpret with any great confidence.

For a philosopher trained in the Anglo-American tradition these characteristics make the text appear less than philosophical. It is a commonplace among analytic philosophers that a philosophical text is concerned with making literal claims and demonstrating their truth through deductively valid arguments. But if, after a sustained immersion in a text such as the *Zhuangzi*, one judges that it is indeed philosophical, one is forced to call into question such a conception of philosophical thinking: whether there is, or ought to be, a difference between literary and philosophical methodology; whether philosophers are, or ought to be, always concerned with formal justification of the truth of their claims; whether their claims ought to be interpreted as claims to truth at all; whether the meaning of the text ought to be clear and transparent; whether the reader has any significant role to play in creating and developing that meaning. Even for a philosopher trained in Continental styles of philosophy, which are quite familiar with literary modes of philosophical thinking, the cultural distance of the text still renders it highly enigmatic. Even if we are comfortable with reading philosophical ideas through literary tropes, the specific reading strategies required and the cultural thinking styles expressed in this particular text still remain quite unfamiliar.

Now, a text may be read in any of a variety of ways, but there is one type of reading that is of particular relevance here. This is a very particular kind of academic or 'scholarly' reading, an historically oriented reading that aspires to understand the past as much as possible on its own terms, situated in its own context, while minimizing distortions incurred by imposing inappropriate preconceptions. If this is our tentative goal, then our interpretation will be bound by certain parameters. This at the minimum includes the historical period, the local culture, and most specifically the production of the text. By this I mean not just the person (or people) believed to have been primarily responsible for the text (its 'author' or writers), but even the most specific conditions of its production: whether for example it was dictated to a scribe, or written as notes prior to some form of public speaking, or taken down as notes afterwards; whether it was intended to clarify and popularize the essential thought of the master, or rather as a secret and impenetrable framework only for the initiated; and indeed, whether it was collectively recorded as the doctrine of a school or as the work of a single individual. We would also, ideally, need to understand the class, the background, the concerns, and purposes of the writer or writers in order to further delimit the parameters of interpretation. This requires us to be familiar not only with the intellectual climate in which they engaged, but also with the social, economic, and religious structures within which they lived and functioned.

These structures imbue words with significance, sometimes directly if a direct reference is made, sometimes indirectly by supplying the metaphors that the writer takes for granted, and does not think to explain. The more we learn about the context, the better we are equipped to solve potential problems; the better we are able to understand the cultural associations, the historical references, the literary devices employed in the text; the better we are able to understand the ways in which the text might have been interpreted by its contemporaries, and most importantly, the ways in which it might have been interpreted by its own author. Of course, this is not the only way, nor even the best way, of reading any text; but it is a way that is of interest at least to a certain type of academic scholar, whether philosopher or historian. These issues will be taken up again in more depth in the next chapter.

All this, however, lands the academic reader of the *Zhuangzi* in a quandary, for we have a relatively minimal knowledge of the history and culture of the Eastern Zhou period in which he lived, and so we have, comparatively speaking, very little information about the context and production of this text. We have to make do by piecing together scant evidence to construct a hazy context. With regard to the production of the text, we can surmise that a significant part of the writing of the text would in all probability have been done by Zhuangzi himself. The style of the writing is very distinctive—the individuality of Zhuangzi's own voice is unmistakable. Moreover, the conciseness of the classical Chinese written language, *guwen* 古文, makes dictation highly unlikely. We can also see directly from its form that the *Zhuangzi* is essentially a *written* work, sometimes making allusions and associations through the visual form, the structural constituents, of the characters, as well as through the usual poetic techniques that exploit associations of sound. In order to be able to write such a sophisticated work, Zhuangzi would have had to have come from an educated, and therefore aristocratic, class. Of course, this is not an established fact, merely a conjecture, but it is one that provides a social context within which to interpret Zhuangzi's discussion of social issues.

The Author: Zhuang Zhou 莊周

We may make further hypotheses concerning background and context from clues scattered within the text: references, allusions, associations; and we also have some scant information about Zhuangzi himself recorded in the *Zhuangzi* itself, and from a few other sources. It is clear from references that Zhuangzi makes in the *Inner Chapters*, and from his own technical terminology, that he was writing with a background consisting of at least three distinct influences: Laozi, the Mohists, and the Ruist tradition of Confucius. There was, for a while, some uncertainty about the relative dating of the *Laozi*. A. C. Graham was a supporter of the tendency to place him at a later date, after Zhuangzi. The recent excavation of a *Laozi* text at Guodian in 1993 dating to around 300 BCE places it squarely within the life of Zhuangzi, if not before.[1] The presence of passages in the *Inner Chapters* that imitate the style and feel of the Laozi, I believe, also corroborates the traditional dating. Some more obscure references suggest a possible acquaintance with the writings of the young 'logician' Gongsun Longzi, and some familiarity with his contemporary Mencius. There are also copious references to certain kinds of 'spiritual' practices, perhaps 'mystical,' 'meditative,' or 'shamanistic,' but since these are the earliest extant references historically available,[2] we do not have any prior context within which to interpret them in such a manner as to throw light on the *Zhuangzi* itself.

Now, the *Zhuangzi* itself contains stories about its own author, and would thus seem at first sight to provide an invaluable source of information about him. Unfortunately, those stories are not quite so straightforwardly reliable as they may appear. Firstly, there are very few such stories, and they are very brief. Moreover, they have the same air of fabular narrative that pervades the *Zhuangzi* as a whole. If I am not mistakenly imposing an inappropriate cultural judgment, I would suggest that they do not have the tone of factual description, but are quite evidently concerned with conveying, or illustrating, a moral. Thus, while they tell us about the values and ideals of the school who propagated the tales, it is not clear how much they tell us about the actual career of the historical figure who inspired them. They occur mostly in the chapters written by what Liu Xiaogan refers to as the School of Zhuangzi (chapters 17, 18, and 20), rather than in the *Inner Chapters*.[3] It is interesting to note that the moral conveyed by this picture of Zhuangzi expresses the philosophy of what Liu refers to as the Anarchist chapters. Perhaps this shows a greater continuity of thought between Zhuangzi, his followers, and the Anarchists.

These anecdotes give a vivid impression of an impoverished but imposing character. He lives in a wretched state, residing in a small alley, weaving sandals for a living. His neck is scrawny, his complexion sallow. He wears a patched garment made of sack cloth, and shoes tied with string. At one point he becomes so desperate that he is forced to beg for food, albeit unsuccessfully, from the Marquis of Jianhe. Despite his lowly circumstances, however, he is

---

[1]   See Ames and Hall's recent translation, *Daodejing: 'Making This Life Significant,'* and also Robert G. Henricks, *Lao Tzu's Tao Te Ching.*
[2]   Jordan Paper, *The Spirits are Drunk: Comparative Approaches to Chinese Religion.*
[3]   Liu Xiaogan, *Classifying the Zhuangzi Chapters*, translated by Donald Munro.

often courted by kings and princes who recognize his worth and his capacities (his *de* 德), and want to employ him in a position of great power. We are not told how they know of this, whether it is because he somehow has a reputation for good government, or simply from the charismatic power, *de* 德, that he exudes. He always refuses, not politely, but with an insolence that puts his life at risk. This portrayal of truculent refusal has a dramatic impact, and the moral of these stories is clear. No matter how dire his circumstances, he would never stoop so low as to accept a position in office in a time of corruption.[4] And though he lives in poverty at least he lasts out his years, enjoys himself doing as he pleases.

These stories certainly ring true to the spirit of the *Inner Chapters*, and the exaggerated caricature of the parable is quite consistent with Zhuangzi's own distinctive narrative style. Moreover, the character portrayed is very much in keeping with the company of outcasts who find their home in Zhuangzi's own imagination. However, one senses that the purport of the stories is not to make a record of historical facts, but to illustrate a moral, to exemplify the virtues held as ideals by the followers of Zhuangzi. It seems doubtful to me that any ruler concerned with governing a state would turn to a person who, by his own description, puts himself outside the bounds of social convention, and who has no concern for mundane power. Thus, it is not clear to what extent we should take these stories as indicating the actual conditions of Zhuangzi's living circumstances. Nevertheless, even if the writers were not motivated by a need for some kind of accuracy of detail, this does not mean that the stories are simply fabrications. Rather they may be understood as readings of the life of the master in terms of the ideals he taught and embodied—and in this sense *true to* his life and values. This, at least, is how I suggest we might overcome the dichotomy between fact and fiction, history and fantasy. If we assume that these stories were inspired by Zhuangzi himself, then we might speculate that he must have been a figure outside the bureaucratic norm. Though educated and of a privileged class, he

---

4   Note the similarity with the Confucian scholar, who must also refuse office in a time of corruption. The Confucian scholar comes forward when the way prevails, and retreats when it is obscured. Note also the contrast with the idealism of the Confucian, who sacrifices his political career and lives in poverty, but always in accord with the exigencies of *li* 禮, propriety, and *yi* 義, appropriateness. The Daoist, in contrast, feels no great need to furnish his retreat with such social paraphernalia, but seeks instead to learn from what remains when the impositions of civilization have been held at arm's length.

was not wealthy. He was an unconventional, bohemian figure surviving on the borderlines, negotiating his way through the interstices of an organized, structured world. To borrow a metaphor from Deleuze, he was a 'nomad' wandering through the city, intrigued by the complexity, intricacy, and obstinacy of the structures, yet always aware of their contingency and fragility.[5]

Sima Qian, the Grand Historian of the Han dynasty, paints a very different portrait from that given by the school of Zhuangzi. He tells us that Zhuangzi held a minor official position as a public employee at Qi Yuan, 'lacquer garden'. We cannot be sure whether 'lacquer garden' is an actual orchard of lacquer trees in which he worked, or simply the name of a district. Nor can we tell from this brief description exactly what post he held, or what were his duties.[6] According to Sima Qian, Zhuangzi was born in the middle of the period of the Warring States (*ca* 369 BCE) in a village called Meng 蒙 in the state of Song[7] 宋, over a century after the death of Confucius, and more than sixty years after the death of Confucius' chief critic, Mozi. He was educated, at least in part, in the intellectual culture of the central plains, a culture that was characterized by ideological rivalry between the Ruists and the Mohists. The Ruists, the 'gentle/genteel' ones, were the scholars, teachers and propagators of the tradition, and by the time of Zhuangzi they had become identified with the followers of Confucius. [8] The Mohists, the followers of Mozi, were the chief opponents of the Ruists. They came from a lower social stratum and were highly critical of what they perceived to be the extravagant

---

5   See Gilles Deleuze, *A Thousand Plateaus: Capitalism and Schizophrenia.* Deleuze's metaphor of the nomad has been taken up by Rosi Braidotti in *Nomadic Subjects: Embodiment and Sexual Difference in Contemporary Feminist Theory,* to describe the modes of thinking of those who inhabit the margins, the boundaries between cultures. Gloria Anzaldúa's *Borderlands: La Frontera* illustrates vividly the multilingual, pluriform flexibility of nomadic language and thinking (whether or not she would consider herself to be a 'nomadic subject').

6   Zhuang Wanshou, in *Zhuangzi Shilun,* presents a very interesting study of the term *yu* 虞, which appears to be the name of some kind of animal guardian. In the ancient times these were taken to be 'spirits,' sometimes themselves having animal or part-animal form.

7   Sima Qian: *Shi Ji, Laozi Hanfei Lie Zhuan,* quoted in Tu, Youguang.

8   The term Ruist strictly speaking refers to the teachers of the Zhou tradition. Fung Yu-lan, in *Selected Philosophical Writings of Fung Yu-lan,* (pp. 620—631), distinguishes between the Ruists as professional teachers and the subsequent philosophical school of the same name, of which Confucius was in all probability the first representative.

elitism of the Ruists. They seem to have constituted some kind of cult, guild, or brotherhood, of artisans and warriors, who had developed a distinctive and remarkable system of culture and values. Though the *Mozi* vents a great deal of energy criticizing the Ruists for their elitism and extravagance, and though the bulk of Mohist writing tends to be dull and repetitive, there are moments in which a certain degree of education and literary competence can be discerned. There are copious quotations from the *Shijing*—the *Classic of Poetry*—and places where the text itself becomes rich, dense, poetic. We must thus be careful not to fall so easily into the trap of pigeonholing the Mohists as uneducated dullards who had no understanding of, or appreciation for, the history and tradition of Zhou. Although the Daoists are often portrayed as rejecting the Confucian way of moral self cultivation, it was I believe the worldview of the Mohists that was a primary target of criticism. We shall examine in detail the ideas of the Mohists in chapter three.

Whatever we make of Sima Qian's portrayal of Zhuangzi as a petty official, the dates that he gives of Zhuangzi's life give us a great deal of information about his intellectual environment. As we have seen, Zhuangzi was born into an intellectual climate fuelled by an antagonism between the Ruists and the Mohists. We can also see that he must have been an almost exact contemporary of the Confucian thinker Mencius (371—289). Given that they were contemporaries, it is odd that neither seems to have had much to say about the other. Zhuangzi makes what appear to be several covert references to Mencius, but Mencius does not reciprocate. From the *Zhuangzi* itself we can see that Zhuangzi was a close friend of the paradox-monger Huizi (380—305), fragments of whose writings survive only in the final chapter of the *Zhuangzi* as a series of logical paradoxes. Although they had vastly different temperaments, they engaged often in debate, whether logical or rhetorical, and when Huizi died, Zhuangzi lamented that he had lost the one person he could engage masterfully in the art of language. When Zhuangzi himself died at the grand old age of 84 (following traditional dates), Mencius' Confucian rival Xunzi had himself become an established scholar, in his thirties or older, respectful, but critical, of the old man of Chu. Xunzi criticizes Zhuangzi for what he perceives to be his onesided obsession with *tian* 天, the natural that goes beyond the human, at the expense of his understanding of *ren* 人, the human, which Xunzi understood as constituting, and being intimately constituted by, *wen* 文 'culture' and *wei* 偽 'artifice.' Gongsun Longzi, whose fascination with problems of intending and indicating has bestowed on him the modern title 'Logician,' was thirty four years old.

Zhuangzi was a writer of consummate skill and sophistication, and indeed the *Zhuangzi* is considered by some to be one of the greatest pieces of Chinese philosophical and literary writing. His style contrasts dramatically with the technical and jargonistic dullness of the Mohists. One might make a comparison with Continental styles of philosophical writing as contrasted with the more down-to-earth style of the typical analytical philosopher. Though one must keep in mind, when making all such comparisons, that the *differences* between the counterparts are often more instructive than their similarities. Zhuangzi's writing is vibrant and imaginative, his style echoing the noise and color of the art of Chu. He himself is quite aware that his style may well appear excessive, and indeed that his imagination at times ventures so far from the ordinary and everyday that it verges on the unintelligible. Most remarkable is the breadth and range of his style and subject matter, his multi-faceted expertise. Even within the confines of the *Inner Chapters* we find story-telling, myth-making, poetry, logical dexterity, political advice, mystical discipline, shamanism, spirit journeying, philosophizing about language. Sometimes the connections between these are readily intuitable. But more often than not the journey through the text is a passage through unfamiliar and disjointed terrains, a ride that leaves one at the same time confused and exhilarated. After the deepest contemplation of where one has been and what its significance might be, one is not necessarily any clearer about what has happened. One has to wait for the experience to interpret itself—somewhat as a dream suddenly becomes meaningful and obvious.

There are some scholars who insist on performing conceptual analyses of these writings on the grounds that if they are philosophical—and worth their philosophical salt—they ought to be susceptible to such analysis. Now, while conceptual analysis is an important philosophical tool, we must be careful not to force its use inappropriately. Conceptual analysis is appropriate where a text makes a philosophical claim explicitly through propositions that express their meaning as literally and clearly as possible, and through arguments that aim to demonstrate their conclusion with varying degrees of plausibility (or even necessity). Since Daoist texts do not function within the context of such a conception of philosophy such analysis at one's first interface with the text seems forced and inappropriate. Conceptual analysis becomes appropriate if and when one manages to isolate literal propositions and demonstrative arguments. Until then, one must seek out the aid of other philosophical, literary, and interpretive methods.

Chu culture[9]

The village of Meng, in which Zhuangzi was born, was located in the southernmost part of Song, in the 'borderlands' one might say between Song and Chu 楚, between the central plains and the south. Wang Guowei[10] points out that, according to Lu Deming, the Pu River, in which Zhuangzi was said to have fished, was in the territory of Chen. By the time of Zhuangzi's birth, Chen had itself become a feudality of Chu. Thus, in looking for a context within which to place Zhuangzi, we would do well to invest some time and interest in the culture of Chu. What is to be gained by identifying the 'locus' of Zhuangzi's philosophy in this way? I do not mean to suggest that geography determines ideology. Neither do I believe that local culture determines ones beliefs. However, I do believe that one's cultural environment is an important factor in one's intellectual development. Such circumstances of placement can often help to unravel mysteries of the motivation of a philosophy. Thus, the meeting place, or the borderlands, between the central plains and the state of Chu will provide the liminal setting for the development of Zhuangzi's particular 'liminal' style of Daoist thinking.

Recent excavations from Hubei and Hunan have been unearthing masses of evidence about the culture of Chu, and have given rise to the new historical field of Chu Studies, *Chuxue* 楚學. We now know something about the food, the clothing, the housing, the social arrangements, and about the arts and aesthetic sensibility of Chu. Some of this knowledge of the culture of Chu provides an invaluable framework within which to place the text. Zhang Zhengming,[11] the historian of Chu, contrasts the *Xia* 夏 culture of the south that was centered around the Yangzi River, with the *Hua* 華 culture of the central plains that had its home in the Yellow River basin. This difference, as he traces it, eventually becomes manifest in the two great schools of the Chinese

---

9   For a more complete discussion of the history and culture of Chu, see Zhang Zhengming, *Chu Wenhua Shi*, Song Gongwen, *Chuguo Fengsu Zhi*, Pi Daojian, *Chu Yishu Shi*, Tu Youguang. *Chu Guo Zhexue Shi.*
10   Quoted in Tu Youguang, *Chu Guo Zhexue Shi*, p.345.
11   Zhang Zhengming, *Chu Wenhua Shi.*

tradition—Daoism and Confucianism. A mere glance at the artifacts of Chu from the Warring States period, reveals remarkable differences in mood between the culture of the central plains and that of the south. When the most representative works of the central plains are juxtaposed with the most distinctive pieces from Chu, the aesthetic differences become quite pronounced. The feel of the artworks of the central plains tends to be solid, grounded, imposing, awe inspiring: as is befitting their ceremonial function. The pieces of the Zhou hark back to the art and tradition of the Shang, and gain their authority and power through this association. They often have intricate angular patternings based on recurring involutions of the 'taotie' monster motif. These patterns balance the solidity of the forms with a moving energy. But when these works are placed side by side with characteristic works from Chu, they take on a comparative sense of restraint. The ceremonial pieces of the south are exuberant and extravagant. They have a relative lightness, elegance, and refinement. Pulses of energy writhe and whirl even through the merely geometrical, and the intricate angular taotie motifs of the north become softened and flowing, like tongues of flame, wisps of smoke, swirls of water. A vivid naturalism pervades the representation of all kinds of birds and beasts: deer resting, fawns playing, birds strutting. Scenes of fishing and hunting, or of villagers gathering fruit and crops or playing in the open air, abound as decorations on pottery, while fantastic beings, dragons and phoenixes, and the shamans who controlled them adorn silk fabrics that themselves come in a vast array of qualities, thicknesses, weaves, and styles.

There are some who are not entirely convinced that there is such a thing as the culture of Chu. Firstly, it appears to create an artificial boundary between areas that were really quite fluid in terms of their geopolitical identity. In doing so, it seems to overlook the extent to which Chinese culture has a continuity and coherence throughout the different states and through history. And lastly, and most critically, it does not adequately account for the difference in time period between the artifacts typical of Zhou, and those from Chu. The artifacts that typify Zhou culture generally come from the central plains during the Western Zhou (before 700 BCE); those that are taken to typify Chu culture, do indeed come from regions dominated by Chu, but they also generally date to the Eastern Zhou (after 700 BCE) Thus, it is suggested, the difference in style might just as well be attributed to development over time, as to differences between cultural regions.

While this is possible, this explanation does not give a convincing account of why such artifacts are found only in the southern territories, and not in the central plains. It also does not adequately account for the distinctiveness of style. By associating the new styles of artifacts with other elements of Chu culture—food, clothing, religion, philosophy—an extraordinarily coherent and persuasive picture of a distinctive southern culture emerges. If there really were no such thing as Chu culture as evidenced by these artifacts, one is at a loss to explain how this illusion arises. Thus, while the temporal difference is important, this should not be allowed to overshadow the significance of geographical location. It is true that the evidence is not decisive, but it is not as ambivalent as it might at first seem. Moreover, the claim that there is a *distinctive* culture associated with Chu is not at all equivalent to the claim that the culture of Chu is *distinct from* those of surrounding regions. As we shall see in our investigation of vagueness and of boundaries, that there were no sharp boundaries between Chu and the central plains does not entail that there could be no distinctive differences. Here is a simple analogue: there are no sharp boundaries separating orange from yellow, and yellow from green, yet each colour, without being distinctly separated from the others, nevertheless maintains its own distinctive 'identity.'

Chu philosophy[12]

Like the society of the central plains, Chu was also an agrarian society relying on an understanding of seasonal change. Nevertheless, while agriculture, nature and the seasons may have exerted some influence on the thinking of the central plains, in particular the philosophy of the *Yijing*, they seem to have been of the *most fundamental* significance for the thinking of the south. The Daoists based their philosophy on their observations of the natural environment: they observed the astronomical cycles of the heavens, *tian* 天, and the seasons, *shi* 時; they also closely watched the behavior of the nature spirits and ancestral spirits, *shen* 神, and *gui* 鬼. This close attentiveness to the behavior of the 'natural' environment provided the key to understanding the world and how to live in it. This orientation toward the processes of nature is exemplified in the philosophy of Laozi, the first philosophical text that can be identified with the culture of Chu. One of the central concepts of this philosophy is that of the way, *dao* 道 of nature, *tian*

---

[12] For an extended discussion of the styles of thinking associated with Chu, see Tu Youguang, *Chu Guo Zhexue Shi.*

天, its subtleties, *xi* 稀, *wei* 微, *miao* 妙, secrets, *xuan* 玄, *ji* 機, powers, *de* 德, *ji* 機, and energies, *qi* 氣. Reflection on natural processes was the means by which the sage gained philosophical insight—a thorough and penetrating understanding, *tong* 通, of all change. In this way they observed a polarity of cyclical movement, a dynamism of forces, which eventually came to be understood through the metaphors of *yin* 陰 and *yang* 陽.

Yin and *yang* are metaphors derived from images relating the movement of the sun to the faces of a mountain, the bright side, and the shady side. In some places and at some times the earth and air are baked in the sun, *yang*; in others, they are drenched in the shade, *yin*; and always there is some gentle transition toward one direction or the other. The characteristics associated with these provide powerful metaphors for the interpretation of all processes and of all things. The shady side of a mountain tends to be wet, green and fertile, cool, dark, and cloudy, soft, and yielding; the sunny side tends to be hot and bright, clear, and dry, hard, dusty, and firm. By association and extension, other things, qualities and pairs of qualities become associated with these two—thus weak and strong, receding and progressing, rest and movement become interpreted in terms of *yin* and *yang*.[13] Of course, the culture of the central plains was not without its own ideas about nature and change. The Great Commentary to the *Zhou Yi*, or *Book of Changes*, was a repository of insight that rivaled, if it was not influenced by, that of the Daoists. It differed quite significantly in its preference for the evaluative order of *qian* 乾 over *kun* 坤—counterparts of *yang* and *yin*, but associated primarily with the hierarchical pairs of heaven and earth, father and mother, male and female, high and low, leading and following.[14]

Now, the ideas of the early Daoists also exhibit an unmistakable predilection toward process, as has been well documented. The fundamental terms of Daoist thinking that are philosophically most

---

[13] For an extraordinarily rich discussion of the social significance of *yin* and *yang* in early China, see Marcel Granet, *La Pensée Chinoise*. At the same time, I must register my disagreement with his sociological explanation of *yin* and *yang* in terms of male and female roles in an agricultural society. It seems that the more natural and plausible direction of explanation is that masculine and feminine qualities are interpreted in terms of the associated qualities of *yin* and *yang*, than that the two sides of a mountain are interpreted as male and female. See also, Granet's *The Religion of the Chinese People*.

[14] Indeed, it seems to me that Granet's account of *yin* and *yang* succeeds much better as an explanation of the ideas of *qian* and *kun*.

significant—what we might call Daoist 'categories'—instinctively avoid the substantial: *dao* 道, *yin* 陰, *yang* 陽, and *qi* 氣, are metaphors that contrast starkly with the western categories of 'substance,' 'property,' and even 'relation,' insofar as the former have an explicit temporal sense that the latter lack. [15] '*Dao*,' for example, as the way or *ways* of the natural world, has a strong primary sense expressing modes of action and modalities of behavior, which is not captured in the conception of an underlying substance, or an atemporal form. As a fundamental category, it places emphasis not so much on *what entities are* as *how processes occur*; it expresses the manner of changes, rather than the 'Being of entities.' If we understand *qi* as the substance, matter, or stuff of which things are made, then we are in danger of losing the dynamic sense of the energy that pulses through these changes, and of which apparently stable 'things' are merely temporary congealings. *Yin* and *yang* ought not to be understood simply as properties of things, since in doing so we lose their primary sense as *phases* in the cyclical development of things. In this way the highly temporalized world view of the early Daoists presents an interesting and instructive counterbalance to the predominantly substantialist ontologies that have been characteristic of much of traditional western metaphysics.

The Daoist understanding of the cyclical transformation of the seasons, of the heavens, and of the earth is encapsulated in Zhuangzi's philosophy in the metaphors of the *grindstone of nature, tianni* 天倪, and the *potter's wheel of nature, tianjun* 天鈞. Both wheels revolve about an empty space, *wu* 無, through which passes an invisible axis, *shu* 樞. The function of the potter's wheel is to build things up, that of the grindstone is to wear things down. The activity of nature consists of cycles of wearing down and building up: the great clod is thrown on the potter's wheel, is shaped into the myriad forms, which are ground down by the very same wheel only to be transformed into yet other forms. The Pole Star and the axis of the earth become metaphors for the center of balance, the center of stability around which the cyclical transformations take

---

15   Note that there is a problem here with linguistic terminology: concepts of process, indeed the very term 'process' itself, when expressed linguistically, must be nominalized, if they are to stand as subject or object terms. This in itself however should not be allowed to obscure the fact that they are very different in kind from concepts of substance. For an overview of process philosophies, see Nicholas Rescher, *Process Metaphysics, An Introduction to Process Philosophy*.

place inexhaustibly, *wuqiong* 無窮: transformations from nothing, *wu* 無, to something, *you* 有, and back to nothing 無.

One aspect of the concept of *tian* 天, nature, can also be expressed in the classical Chinese language as *ziran* 自然, spontaneous, and this latter idea is thus of crucial importance to understanding Daoist thinking. Tu Youguang, in his account of the history of the philosophical thinking of Chu, takes this phrase 'literally,' and interprets it as equivalent to a modern subject predicate phrase, *ziji ru ci* 自己如此 'itself like this.'[16] In translating *ziran* this way, Tu's intention is to emphasize the role of 'the self' 自己, or rather of the *individual*, in Zhuangzi's philosophy. Thus he interprets this concern with nature, that is characteristic of Daoist thinking, to be indicative of a type of individualism. Tu contrasts this with the collectivism of philosophies associated with the central plains. I am not persuaded by this attempt to read such a relativistic individualism into the meaning of the phrase *ziran* 自然. There is indeed a strong element of *pluralism* in Zhuangzi's version of Daoist philosophy—'the ten thousand things transform themselves, the ten thousand breaths are not the same,' *wan wu zi hua, wan chui bu tong* 萬物自化，萬吹不同—and this pluralism does indeed arise out of a profound respect for difference. Zhuangzi continually warns us about the dangers of parochialism, of imposing our own particular ways of doing things on others. But such a pluralism does not require a 'metaphysics' of individual entities each striving to preserve its own identity, any more than does Confucius' sensitivity to the appropriateness of response in each context.

On the contrary, I shall argue, in chapter five, that it is the Mohists who come closest to espousing such an individualist metaphysics. The Mohists are, among other things, a military group, and this lends an unmistakable colouring to their understanding of social groups. They see a social group as a collection of individuals, each postured defensively against potential encroachment and subjugation from the Others. Zhuangzi, I shall argue, rejects this view and urges us to abandon such an aggressive/defensive posture, to let go of such restricted identities, and instead to recognize that self and Other are already mutually interdiffused.

The strongest associations of the phrase *ziran*, however, do invoke the idea of non-acting, or non-interference, *wuwei*, 無為, a term that describes the spontaneous activity of the natural world,

---

[16]   Tu Youguang, *Chu Guo Zhexue Shi.*

and in human terms implies actions that are not rigidly constrained by fixed preconceptions. My own preference in terms of translation is for acting 'without artifice,' *wuwei* 無偽. The word '*wei* 偽' is a cognate of '*wei* 為': it is contrasted with '*zhen* 真,' 'genuine,' and often has the sense of 'fake' or 'false.' Etymologically, it is composed of *wei* 為 'activity' with a person radical, *ren* 人. It is thus that which is produced through human artifice. As the Confucian philosopher Xunzi will come to use it, it becomes a positive term referring to the achievements of human culture. Thus, if we emphasize this latent sense, *wuwei* becomes action that does not *impose* artificial constraints, but that senses and *follows* the tendencies of things, events and processes. It works with the natural changes of things as closely as possible, minimizing the effort necessary to bring about certain states of affairs. Thus, *ziran* suggests the multiplicity of tendencies and spontaneities to which we must be sensitive if we are to function skillfully in our worldly interactions.

Zhuangzi or the *Zhuangzi*?

When working with a text that is named after its author the question inevitably arises as to whether one is explicating the author or the text. In the case of the *Zhuangzi*, the extant text is all that we have available to us of the author himself. We have no independent access to the author except through the extant text, and so we cannot treat the question as entirely clear cut. Indeed, this remains the case, as Derrida would urge, even with living writers: even in the case of a living writer *any communicative expression* whether written or spoken, or even thought, constitutes an 'inscription' or 'text.' The radical distinction between the original idea that remains clear and evident to the author, and the expression of that idea that must be interpreted, is thus dissolved. To the extent that there even could be anything like an 'original idea' (a *transcendental signified*), it too must be interpreted.[17]

---

17   Note that this is *not* a scepticism or relativism about meaning, but a *holism*, and a holism that incorporates open texture in such a manner that the whole always remains open, always grows, develops organically. According to this understanding, since meaning is always open, there can be no final meaning—but that there can be no final meaning does not entail that there is no meaning at all. Nor does the indeterminacy of meaning entail a radical relativism. Indeed a thoroughgoing relativism of meaning is incompatible with the indeterminacy thesis! If one sees the indeterminacy as lack of final decision between alternative perspectives, then insofar as

However, this does not entail that we can make no sense whatsoever of the distinction between 'text' and 'author.' We may indeed make a pragmatic distinction that corresponds to the distinction between *the extant text* and *the text with which the writer would have responded if confronted with a possible interpretation.* When interpreting the text as *extant* text we are concerned with exploring its possibilities without regard to how the writer would have responded if confronted with our interpretation. One may thus completely disengage the text from the context of its production, and read it within the hermeneutic context of one's own cultural background. On the other hand, one might allow one's reading to be constrained by the text's own textual context, or by its cultural context, or by its historical context, and so on. Finally, one might insist that one's reading must be one that the writer would have approved of if somehow given the opportunity of being confronted with it. Note that this case is not as straightforward as it may seem, since the writer is confronted with the same hermeneutic problematic as we when confronted with our textual representation of our interpretation! There is also the epistemological problem of what could justify our claim to know that the author would agree with our interpretation. Nevertheless, it is this final ideal interpretation that those who believe they are discovering the claims of the 'author' believe themselves to be discovering. I remain sceptical that there can be such a thing as *the* interpretation with which the author would uniquely agree if confronted with it, but still accept that such an idea may function as a regulative ideal for one possible, and very valuable, type of interpretative methodology.

When we no longer have access to the living writer or to the living context of the writer, discovering the claims of the author becomes practically impossible—and entirely impractical even as a regulative ideal. We are left with some form of interpreting the text within the constraints of its context, or rather, what we understand of its context. This is our situation with respect to the *Zhuangzi.* Thus, I shall not even consider the problem of discovering what Zhuangzi really meant. Nor, on the other hand, am I interested in simply imposing a modern interpretation on the text without respect for its own context. Instead, I shall devote my energies to developing an interpretation of the text, the *Zhuangzi,* that is as responsive as I can make it to its textual, historical, and cultural background. I would hope that if Zhuangzi himself were somehow

---

each perspective maintains a determinate resolution there will be no perspective that preserves indeterminacy. If the indeterminacy is to be preserved then it cannot be resolved by deciding on a perspective.

per impossibile to come across this interpretation he would find it rich, intriguing, and not entirely implausible.

Problems of interpretation will be taken up in greater detail in the next chapter, but there is an issue about distinguishing text from 'author' that must be briefly taken into consideration. The Chinese approach to authorship has been very different from that of the modern west. The writer to whom a Chinese text is attributed is not necessarily a single individual who is the creator and owner of the ideas. The emergence of a text is a cooperative production that often continues after the death of the 'author' and that may even start before the contribution of the particular individual to whom the text is attributed! Much of the text attributed to Zhuangzi, for example, was produced long after the death of Zhuangzi, and was written by people who did not necessarily identify that strongly with the core of Zhuangzi's philosophy. Guan Feng,[18] Takeuchi Yoshio,[19] Ye Guoqing, Zhang Hengzhou and Luo Genze,[20] have all concerned themselves with the problem of classifying the chapters of the *Zhuangzi* according to the schools that produced them. Liu Xiaogan and A. C. Graham[21] have, independently of one another, also taken up the same investigation. Despite frequent differences of opinion there is, surprisingly, a great deal of agreement with regard to the classification of major portions of the text. It is generally agreed for example that the historical Zhuangzi was in all probability the author of the first seven chapters, which have come to be known as the *Inner Chapters*, while the rest, divided into the *Outer* (8-22) and *Miscellaneous Chapters* (23-33), is taken to have been written by followers, and others, from the time of his death to at least the founding of the Qin empire.

The *Outer* and *Miscellaneous Chapters* can be thought of as falling into three general groups: the school of Zhuangzi's followers and disciples, a Laozian school of anarchists, and the Huang-Lao school. Liu considers chapters 17 to 27 and chapter 32 to have been written by the closest of Zhuangzi's followers; he calls the school the *Shu Zhuang Pai* 述莊派, the 'Transmitter School.' Graham agrees that chapters 17 to 22 were written by Zhuangzi's followers, but considers the remaining chapters to be a mere 'ragbag'

---

18   Guan Feng, *Zhuangzi Neipian Yijie he Pipan.*
19   Takeuchi Yoshio, *Rooshi to Sooshi.*
20   The results of these last three are summarized by Liu Xiaogan. Liu also provides a useful summary of the work of Guan Feng and Takeuchi Yoshio.
21   Chuang-Tzu: *The Inner Chapters: A Classic of Tao.* See also, 'How Much of *Chuang Tzu* Did Chuang Tzu Write?' reproduced in *A Companion to Angus C. Graham's 'Chuang Tzu: The Inner Chapters,'* edited by Harold Roth.

collection of random fragments.[22] At any rate, these chapters retain much of the focus, character, and style of the *Inner Chapters*, and often contain elaborations and developments that do not over-stretch the fabric of the text. As a record of the interpretations of those 'closest' to the thought of Zhuangzi, they thus provide an invaluable resource for the academic interpreter of Zhuangzi who wishes to take into account the textual context of Zhuangzi's philosophy.

The second group consists of chapters eight to ten and the first part of chapter 11, and chapters 28 to 31. Liu considers these to be the work of a single school of Anarchists, followers of a philosophy more closely related to that of Laozi. Their thought and style is highly distinctive and immediately recognizable. They believe in simplicity of life, of moving away from the noise and clamor of 'civilization.' They praise the state that is small, in which there is no authority that belongs to leaders invested with superior powers. And they seek to enable people to last out their natural years by nurturing and protecting their natural capacities, *xing* 性.

Graham considers these chapters to belong to two slightly different schools: chapters eight to 11a come from the hand of an individual he calls the Primitivist, while chapters 28 to 31 he believes to be records of the followers of Yang Zhu. Now, a difficulty with this last attribution is that chapters 28 to 31 do not make any reference to Yang Zhu at all. Graham is very well aware of this difficulty, but he claims that there is a very good reason for this. He points out that at that time the name of Yang Zhu was not well respected: rightly or wrongly, he had acquired a reputation for a distasteful form of egotism. The school of that time had not yet come to be associated with the name of Yang Zhu, and so for strategic reasons may well have preferred to distance themselves from his name, if not from his teachings.

However, when one considers the doctrines and style of these two sub-groups, the similarities between them seem to outweigh the differences, and it seems to me that at most they ought to count as two branches of the same school. Graham points out that chapters eight to 11a contain criticisms of Yang Zhu. But the explanation that Graham uses to explain the lack of reference to

---

[22]   Graham's analysis largely follows that of Guan Feng. Liu is critical of Graham, taking him to be a mere follower of Guan, whom he criticizes as merely regurgitating the Communist party line. But whether Guan was following the party line or not, his research can be evaluated independently of his politics. Indeed Graham does not appear to be simply following Guan, as Liu suggests, but quoting him with approval.

Yang Zhu in chapters 28 to 31 surely serves just as well to explain the criticism of Yang Zhu in the other chapters. Because of Yang Zhu's bad reputation, the writers of those chapters chose to distance themselves more vehemently by criticizing Yang Zhu explicitly, rather than just avoiding mention of his name. We can avoid this difficulty altogether by refraining from making the attribution in the first place: then no problem arises about the lack of reference, or negative reference, to Yang Zhu in these chapters.

As for the remaining chapters, from the second part of chapter 11 to chapter 16, and chapter 33, these are ascribed by Liu to the Huang-Lao school. The beginnings of the Huang-Lao school date from the end of the pre-Qin period to the western Han. It is a very eclectic school, drawing from popular religion, and the philosophies of Legalism, Laozi, *yinyang* cosmology, and a motley array of others. For this reason, Graham refers to the school as the Syncretists. Its own name traces its origin to the figures of the mythological Yellow Emperor *Huangdi* 黄帝, and Laozi. But the school is so eclectic that it is no more closely connected to the thought of Zhuangzi than to any of the other philosophies from which it draws.

If so many of the *Outer* and *Miscellaneous Chapters* did not arise from the hand of Zhuangzi himself, must we then dismiss them? Does this mean that they can have no relevance to our project of interpreting Zhuangzi's text? Not at all. Some chapters develop and expand on ideas that were raised in the *Inner Chapters* and thus provide an interpretive context for the *Inner Chapters*. These would include the Anarchist chapters and those of the School of Zhuangzi. Others develop new ideas, not all of them having any evident or necessary connection with Zhuangzi's distinctive ideas. We may, then, consult those chapters that develop themes outlined in the *Inner Chapters*, and thus explore the ideas as they were understood by the followers and disciples of Zhuangzi. Ideas from the Huang-Lao syncretists lie far beyond the central regions of Zhuangzi's philosophizing, and so are unlikely to figure in the elaboration of my interpretation—the further away from the Zhuangzian homeland the lesser the likelihood. What lies too far beyond the horizon of the *Inner Chapters*, what takes us to a place from which it is rendered foreign, will have no claim to enter into our interpretation.

CHAPTER THREE

Interpretation: Problems and Methods

Hermeneutic problems

As interest in Zhuangzi grows in the west, interpretations of the *Zhuangzi* begin to compete, each apparently attempting to demonstrate what Zhuangzi really thought, what Zhuangzi actually believed, what he rejected, and what he was really trying to do. Some say that Zhuangzi was a 'relativist'; others, that he was actually some kind of sceptic, perhaps a 'methodological sceptic,' 'or a linguistic sceptic.' Some argue that Zhuangzi had an epiphany, a 'conversion experience'; others, that he rejected 'Reason,' or that he was an 'anti-Rationalist.' As rival claims develop concerning the real meaning of the text, we become acutely aware of the problem of interpretation. What exactly does it mean for us to read and understand an ancient text from an ancient culture? And not just an ancient culture, but also a distant one, one whose history is far removed from the development of our own. We in the postmodern west look back from the vantage point of the twentyfirst century, shaped by the histories of our ideas, by the history of western religions, science, theology, and by the slow and steady development of philosophical concepts and methods. When we turn to ancient China, we do not simply look back over time, we also gaze across toward a different stream of historical development, expressing itself in and through distant languages and less familiar modes of discourse.

When we are told that Zhuangzi believed that claims to knowledge of 'the external world' are not justified, or that he was an 'anti-Rationalist,' we have to wonder how exactly these attributions are to be understood. Conceiving of the world as 'external' and in need of 'epistemic justification' did not become a widespread presupposition, even of mainstream western philosophy, until the seventeenth century. The problem was not taken for granted as an obvious concern, but was explicitly articulated and argued for by Descartes at great length. It arose as a natural outgrowth of the development of the mathematical and natural sciences, and from the confrontation with religious authority of these rival claims to knowledge during the Enlightenment. Can we simply impose such historically conditioned presuppositions on texts written with a different historical, cultural, and textual context? When we make such attributions, what do we succeed in understanding, and what remains hidden, or covered over? How do these impositions promote our understanding? And, equally importantly, to what extent do they hinder our understanding? Can we simply assume that 'knowledge,' 'the external world,' or 'rationality' are universal concepts? Can we simply ignore their historical evolution and development, and claim that they exist in the same form in all peoples everywhere? What is gained, and what is lost, by denying the historicity and cultural specificity of these ideas? When we impute a belief with a modern western content and vocabulary to an ancient Chinese thinker such as Zhuangzi, we have to wonder how he himself could have framed such a belief. What early Chinese history of philosophical ideas would provide him with an equivalent philosophical vocabulary? These concerns lead me to wonder whether such *direct* attributions of modern beliefs are appropriate at all, and this in turn leads to some deeper, more fundamental questions of methodology. What exactly is it that we are trying to do as interpreters of this text? Are we trying to reach the hidden thoughts of the author? Are we trying to reconstruct what he really must have been trying to say? And if so, is it really possible to abandon the linguistic and cultural context in which it was embedded, and restate those very same thoughts in a modern context and vocabulary? Or, if it is not, do Zhuangzi's ideas remain forever inaccessible? Or, does interpretation then just become a free for all?[1]

Now, if we start by accepting the notion of the indeterminacy of meaning, then the idea that there can be a single correct meaning begins to look naïve and implausible. Quine's notion of the indeterminacy of meaning, as argued for in his paper 'Two Dogmas of Empiricism,'[2] and developed in *Word and Object,*[3] has become the basis of the naturalistic tendency of contemporary analytical

---

[1] Perhaps we can read into the text anything we like so long as it can be made to appear compatible with *the words*? But this, far from offering a solution, merely opens up a whole new problematic with its own distinctive questions: 'compatible with *which* words—the classical Chinese, or an English translation? And if we mean an English translation, then which translation? And again, why not German, French or modern Mandarin?'

[2] W. V. Quine, 'Two Dogmas of Empiricism.'

[3] W. V. Quine, *Word and Object.*

philosophy. To condense Quine's argument, meaning is not the kind of thing that can have identity conditions because meaning is not a thing. If this is correct, it is not possible even in principle to rephrase the exact meaning of a text in other words: since meaning has no identity conditions, there can be no such thing as 'the exact meaning' of a text. Furthermore, once we have let go of the idea that there must be a well-defined meaning underlying and expressed by the text, it becomes easier to let go of the presupposition that there can be only one correct understanding. This is especially true of a text that is as explicitly open and polysemic as the *Zhuangzi*. Only the naïvest of readers could assume that they have discovered the one true meaning of his words, or if they have not discovered it that it is there waiting to be discovered, as though Zhuangzi himself would have experienced no difficulty, made no mistakes, and never have changed his mind, in expounding the more abstruse passages of his own work.

But if we reject such a realist conception of meaning, aren't we left with just scepticism or relativism? Either there is no meaning at all, or the text can be read to say anything you want it to say. Not at all. The extremes of scepticism and radical relativism are not the only alternatives to a naïve realism. It is only with a dualistic, dichotomous, all or nothing attitude that these appear to be the only alternatives. But if we reject this dichotomous mode of thinking, then we are able to see that in the vast space between these extremes there are indeed many more moderate and sensitive ways to proceed. There are pluralist, pragmatist, and indeterminist attitudes of several varieties, all attempting to construct a middle ground, humble but livable dwelling places for the seeker of understanding. Unfortunately, from the perspective of a dichotomous thinker, such pluralist and indeterminist attitudes are often mistaken for either a scepticism or a radical relativism about meaning—though it is a curious fact that this misunderstanding occurs less when the ideas are presented in analytical overalls than when decked out in Derridean *haute-couture*. Derrida is regularly accused, despite incessant denials and arguments to the contrary, of being a sceptic, relativist, nihilist, and even charlatan, while Quine, one of his accusers, maintains his own rejection of meanings and essences with relative impunity.

But the claim that there is no single exact translation of any text is not tantamount to the sceptical claim that there is no correct understanding, nor is it equivalent to the relativistic claim that there are no incorrect understandings. On the contrary, to say that meaning is indeterminate is to say that the boundaries and possibilities of any *correct* understanding are left, to a greater or lesser extent, open. The possibilities that are open at any point in time have greater or lesser plausibility, many may have equal plausibility, and many more have none whatsoever. That there are better and worse readings of the text is something that even the radical relativist acts in accord with in practice if not in theory. But, conversely, that what makes an interpretation better or worse is how close it gets to some fixed and determinate original meaning is a claim that is highly contentious and highly dubitable, if indeed it makes any sense at all. What makes such a doctrine seem plausible is a certain naïvety about the social and historical conditions of meaningfulness, not to mention a certain forgetfulness about the vagueness and indeterminacy of what is meant in the first place.

This raises the question: what are the criteria by which we may judge one interpretation to be better or worse than another? Of course, there are always criteria to which one can appeal in order to justify one's judgment: historical sensitivity, linguistic sensitivity, closeness to the text, coherence, and so on. These criteria arise from our situatedness. We are already situated within contexts of interpretation; we already interpret, and evaluate interpretations, according to these kinds of criteria. Such criteria are for the most part not explicit, nor are they necessarily clear or well-defined, and they may be clarified and formalized in different ways that are not necessarily internally consistent, nor mutually compatible. But, no matter how we choose to explicitly articulate and formalize our intuitions, it must be admitted in the final analysis, that the plausibility of an interpretation is ultimately a matter of *recognition*. In Wittgensteinian terms, interpretation can be thought of as a 'language game' that we learn to play by total immersion. We learn the standards by being thrown into the game and playing as others do. The procedures have no absolute foundations, but if we do not fall in with the practice we cannot succeed in communicating. Thus, even the most radical sceptic must still communicate as others do, if they are to succeed in expressing their disapproval of the established procedures. And the most radical relativist will not be understood by others if they do not at first express themselves by adopting the prevalent mode of discourse, however arbitrary it may seem.

Now in actual practice, recognition of the plausibility of an interpretation is primarily immediate and intuitive, with justifications in terms of coherence, historical sensitivity and so on constructed, if at all, after the fact. But this does not mean that the intuition is arbitrary. We all have an interpretive capacity that we need in order to function at all: we interpret our experiences, the world around us, our natural environment, our social environment, our political situation—not only when we interpret the words people speak, the words we read, but when we read people's emotions, intentions, motivations, when we sense that someone is unhappy, or that someone is being less than fully honest. We interpret the weather conditions outside, and 'inside' we interpret our own behaviour and physiological conditions; we interpret facial expressions and body gestures. Indeed, we are never not interpreting—to use Peirce's terminology, we dwell in *semeiosis*, and in the language of Heidegger, our fundamental mode of comportment toward Being is *hermeneutic*—and we are always having our interpretive powers tested, honed, refined by their successes and failures. Again, I need to reiterate, success and failure are not incompatible with indeterminacy and pluralism: there may be more than one way to be successful, and a successful interpretation need not itself be well defined. This becomes more evident the more we are engaged in interpreting the human, the social, the ethical, political, emotional, psychological—in short, the more we engage in the activity of interpreting the interpreting activity of the interpreters themselves!

Intuition, then, is a natural capacity, and a 'good' intuition is trained by extensive experience, and draws upon extensive knowledge. Note that though the judgment is intuitive this does not entail that it is merely subjective. The judgment of an expert has been schooled by, and takes place within, a community of experts, though there is no guarantee of univocity of opinion even within the most cohesive of communities. Different schools may endorse different judgments, and differences of opinion may arise even within one and the same school. All the same, the differences are not trivial or arbitrary: differences of opinion may coexist and be equally worthy of respect, though the respect accorded any school should be a function of the extent to which its experts live up to the criteria of expertise. At the most ideal, and perhaps unattainable level, a good interpreter of a philosophical text will have a complete array of historical, textual, linguistic data at their disposal, as well as a familiarity with a vast variety of philosophical concepts and systems, and extensive experience in interpreting different kinds of texts, under the guidance of those acknowledged to be experts in the art of reading. This situates interpretation and its evaluation within a cultural tradition, but it does not necessarily confine it thereby, since there is always the possibility of opening oneself up to training in other traditions.

Perhaps rather than simply thinking in terms of 'better and worse' interpretations, we might do well to talk instead of richer and thinner interpretations, rewarding, intriguing and superficial understandings, appropriate and inappropriate, plausible and implausible readings. Such evaluative terms reduce the temptation to think of interpretation exclusively, since they are themselves open terms that can be applied in many ways. Perhaps, then we can strive to create rich, rewarding, intriguing interpretations that are sensitive to history, culture, language, context, and we can judge readings accordingly. Of course, it must be remembered that all interpretations and judgments thereof are always provisional, never final, but always awaiting further refinement or revision.

Clearly then, although I adopt an academic stance and engage in an academic interpretation, I certainly do not mean to suggest that there is only one way of reading a text well, that we may read a text well only according to a fixed set of academic criteria. On the contrary, there are many purposes that a reading of a text may serve. One may read an ancient Chinese text for personal inspiration, or for linguistic analysis; one may read it as a religious text, as a philosophical text, as an historical text: one may read it as an existential phenomenologist, as a structuralist anthropologist, or as a postmodern poet: and this does not begin to exhaust the possibilities. Paradoxically, even the most deliberate misreading of a text may have some value. It is a common strategy among those trained analytically to read an ancient text (whether Chinese, Indian, or Greek) as though it were engaged in a dialogue with a twentieth century analytical philosopher of language or mind, while ignoring all elements of the text that do not fit this mould.[4] Yet, while this is a clear case of anachronistic misreading, it cannot be denied that this has often led to the most fruitful and scholarly results. Again, an historian, or historically oriented philosopher, motivated by a desire to understand a text from another culture without imposing anachronistic ideas, would do well to take Gadamer's advice and reflect on the purposes and presuppositions of their methods of interpretation, and on the extent to which they are striving to remain sensitive to linguistic, cultural and historical context. Of course, language, culture, and history are not simply given, but are themselves part of what is to be interpreted. We read them from the text, and we read the text in their light: the interpretation of each, text and context, shapes and redefines the interpretation of the other in an endless *pas de deux*.

Now, I claim that vagueness plays a central role in Daoist philosophy, and that a rich and fruitful reading of the *Laozi* and the

---

4   The analytical approach to Plato, for example, explores him as a thinker engaged in the dialectical process of refining definitions, while ignoring the mystico-religious context without which the purpose of this dialectical process cannot be understood.

Zhuangzi results when one explores the significance of transformation on the unsettling of boundaries. But I do not claim to have discovered that vagueness was the real topic of Zhuangzi's philosophy, or that his intention was to try to convince us that our meanings must always remain vague. Thus, I would prefer to avoid making such claims as: 'Zhuangzi *believed in* the ubiquity of vagueness' or 'Zhuangzi *intended to demonstrate* the inadequacy of the Mohist belief in bivalence.' The telepathic air of such pronouncements makes us (or ought to make us) extremely uncomfortable, as should the direct imposition of modern western philosophical concepts as the content of Zhuangzi's beliefs and intentions. Besides, the literary and poetic complexity of these Daoist texts makes such reductionistic readings highly implausible. But, as I have already pointed out, it is extraordinarily difficult and tedious to sustain such a 'hermeneutic *epoché*.' And so, I do indeed end up having to express myself in such direct attributions of propositional attitude. But this is merely a matter of stylistic convenience, and should not be taken to contravene my most basic hermeneutic stance. *What* then is my claim? Vagueness, and its significance for a world understood as process, is indeed *a significant and productive hermeneutic possibility* for these texts, perhaps even central—provided a text can have more than one center. But to isolate the ubiquity and inescapability of vagueness as Zhuangzi's major doctrine, and to turn the stories and fables into arguments for this as the conclusion, is, I believe, to stretch the literary fabric of the text beyond its 'natural' capacities. Even if I succeeded in identifying such an explicitly stated doctrine, I would still need to work hard at understanding its significance within its own literary, cultural, historical, and philosophical contexts.

The *Zhuangzi* is a web of tightly knotted paradoxes and perplexities that force one to engage in the continuous process of raveling and unraveling, weaving and reweaving the texture of one's understanding. The textual fabric sustains a variety of patterns: a form taken up in one part affects the form taken in another, and there is never complete closure as to what those forms might be. However, that the text is flexible does not mean that it cannot be overstretched. For this very reason we should be alert to the tendencies of the text, sensitive to when it is being overworked, and when it is beginning to rip or fall apart. That the wildest images may be superimposed on the palimpsest of the *Zhuangzi* is undeniable, but this is all the more reason for us to be alert to the ever present danger of obscuring what we had wished to bring to light. Now, when interpreting any text, the very act of bringing to light must at the same time be a covering over—when we fill in the details of one of the many possible readings, what is covered over are the very gaps that are the conditions of the possibility of other sustainable elucidations. This is especially true when dealing with a rich, poetic text that is a multivalent fusion of half-expressed suggestions. But, it is possible for the obscuration to go too far. When the texture of the interpretation begins to determine its own development regardless of the extent to which this tugs and pulls against the warp and weft of the text, this is when our interpretation has begun to shroud the texture of the fabric that we are attempting to make sense of.

The problem of how to interpret the *Zhuangzi* turns out all too often to be indistinguishable from the problem of how to translate the text. Complicating things still further, questions about how to translate the text also turn out to depend intimately on how to interpret it. This problem is especially acute when it comes to the interpretation of the more obscure passages. The strength or plausibility of an interpretation of a particularly difficult passage will depend on the plausibility of the translation of that passage. Thus, one cannot justify an interpretation *solely* by relying on a favourite translation. And the same holds the other way too: one cannot justify a translation *solely* by relying on one's favourite interpretation. This adds a peculiar twist to the problem of the hermeneutic circle, but there is no reason for it to lead us into a vicious circle. It does, however, have two important consequences: the first is that our interpretation must always seek to be responsible to the original text; the second is that while our translation must remain sensitive to matters of philosophical interpretation, it cannot presuppose some *fixed* interpretation. The plausibility of one's translation, if it is to be persuasive, ought not to depend on a prior acceptance of some specific interpretation. Of course, there will be some passages where this is unavoidable. This is especially the case where the text becomes particularly obscure. In such passages, translation generally proceeds by reading the obscure passage in the light of one's preferred interpretation. For this reason, one ought to avoid presenting such passages as evidence in favor of that interpretation. Certainly, I am not saying that such passages have no persuasiveness whatsoever. If, for example, the passage is not easily translatable in light of a particular interpretation, that would count as evidence against that interpretation. But, if one is trying to present persuasive evidence to an uncommitted reader, it is advisable to steer as clear of such controversial passages as possible.

We may start reading a text with some preconceptions about its content or purpose. Indeed, we have no choice: to read is to start with a language, with a background, with opinions and attitudes, however thin or ill-defined we believe them to be. One may deliberately choose specific and explicit presuppositions: we may choose, for example, to follow a traditional reading, or to follow a new one. Or we may plunge in blind, constructing hypotheses as we go. At some point, we will have the beginnings of a working interpretation. The question then arises: How do we proceed from here? How do we know when to maintain, modify, develop, or change our reading? Again, there are indeed criteria by which to judge whether it is appropriate to maintain or change an interpretation: coherence with the rest of the text, coherence with historical and social circumstances, for example—though these criteria are not necessarily explicit or quantitative. And again, even in those rare cases where the criteria are explicit, the final arbiter must be the honest intuitive judgment of one who has familiarity with the available evidence, and a wealth of experience making such judgments—the judgment of an expert.

All this makes the problem of how to remain responsible to the text a pressing one. Some minimal guidance might be provided by keeping in mind an heuristic distinction between what I shall call *reading out* from a text, and *reading into* a text, between being *open* to the alterity of the text and sensitive to what it is struggling to offer, and *forcing* upon it what we ourselves find familiar and reassuring. There is of course no hard and fast distinction, nor any hard and fast definition; the two horns of the dilemma are indeed themselves so gnarled and intertwined as to be in places indistinguishable. Nevertheless, by constantly keeping in mind this kind of distinction, one can at least aim as an ideal toward openness and sensitivity, while being alert to where one might be reading too much into the text. In some cases, of course, it will be all but impossible to avoid reading in some apparently extraneous sense, especially where the context of significance of the passage has been lost. Moreover, in order to understand anything at all of a text one must start from some horizon of interpretation.[5] One must first choose from among the most appropriate starting points that are

---

5   This insight though attributed to Gadamer, can be traced back through Heidegger to Husserl's notion of the sense-giving phase of all intentional acts—all experiences must be taken up actively by consciousness in an act of interpretation, a sense is bestowed on the experience. Further experience will either be in accordance with the interpretation or will require that the interpretation be modified. Every sense bestowal itself takes place in the context of an horizon of understanding—what one might construe crudely as a set of background presuppositions.

available, but then one must be always prepared to alter, to modify, or even to radically transform the gestalt that prefigures one's understanding. Nevertheless, in deciding between alternative readings, it is always possible, and advisable, for us to ask 'Which of these are more sensitive, and which seem more forced?' Reading-in is not in itself objectionable, since all readings are not simply 'extracted' from the text, but also, to a greater or lesser extent, imposed upon it. At all events, we need to be acutely aware of how we read, of the extent to which we impose extraneous presuppositions, and *we must above all be willing to acknowledge that these extraneous presuppositions may well turn out to be inappropriate.* When reading the *Zhuangzi* this has the dizzying effect of a hermeneutic roller-coaster ride: but if responsibility to the text is any part of our aim, we must be ready for a bewildered understanding. Echoing Zhuangzi's words: when he speaks freely, we must listen openly.[6]

Methods of Interpretation

What are the methods that are available to a philosophical interpreter? I identify below several approaches to interpreting a text: phenomenological, analytical, semeiotic, hermeneutic, structuralist and poststructuralist, all of which play a greater or lesser role in my reading of the *Zhuangzi.*

Phenomenological [7]

There are as many phenomenological methods are there are phenomenologists. Husserl, Heidegger, Sartre, Merleau-Ponty, Gadamer, and arguably, Derrida, all have their own distinctive styles of phenomenology, but even if there is no one thing that their philosophical methods all have in common, it can be argued that there is still a family resemblance, with some members of the family

---

6   予嘗為女妄言之，女以妄聽之. I have toned down the mood of Zhuangzi's advice. More literally, he says 'I shall try to expound it wildly for you; you thus heed it wildly.'

7   See Edmund Husserl *Ideas: General Introduction to Pure Phenomenology.* For an excellent introduction to Husserl's phenomenology, see Jean-François Lyotard, *Phenomenology.* For a discussion of the application of the phenomenological method to the humanities, see Erazim Kohák, *Idea and Experience: Edmund Husserl's Project of Phenomenology in Ideas.*

resembling one another more closely than others. For my purposes, I am thinking primarily of the phenomenological methods of Husserl, Heidegger, and of phenomenological anthropologists. I consider Gadamer below as a hermeneuticist and Derrida as a poststructuralist. The purpose of the phenomenological method for Husserl and Heidegger is, at least in part, the uncovering of fundamental presuppositions. It is essentially a technique of first person reflection on the functioning of our understanding in such a manner as to reveal the limits and parameters, the necessities and possibilities, of that understanding. A phenomenological description is one that uncovers the deepest significances of the various aspects of our experience, regardless of whether these significances have any objective validity. Indeed, the purpose of phenomenology, as Husserl conceived it, is to investigate these structures as the conditions of the very possibility of objectivity. We do not start with a conception of 'objectivity' but discover how objectivities are constructed in our understanding.

Phenomenology so conceived is a transcendental enterprise aiming to discover the most fundamental constitution of human consciousness, in the case of Husserl, or the 'existentialia' of 'Dasein,' in the case of Heidegger. Phenomenological anthropology is purged of these transcendental presuppositions, and allows for a variety of possible 'phenomenologies.' In anthropology, the phenomenological approach to another culture would require absorption of the researcher into that culture so as to enable them, ideally, to engage in a first person reflection on that culture. The anthropologist attempts to describe the significances of the culture under consideration from within its own worldview, from its own self understanding, and without imposing the anthropologist's own culturally specific presuppositions. The phenomenological approach is in part a reaction against the traditional hegemonic conception of anthropology as a scientific enterprise—the objective observation and analysis of 'exotic' cultures from the superior perspective of western science. Rather than exoticize the 'Other' as an object of scientific curiosity, the phenomenological anthropologist aims for a deeper understanding by respecting the role of the other culture as self interpreting. The phenomenological anthropologist aims to describe the people of another culture as they describe themselves, and hopes to enable us to understand them as they understand themselves. Ideally, the phenomenological anthropologist would attempt to internalize the language, to become a part of the community, rather than to pretend to be an external, impartial, pure observer. If this ideal of complete absorption can never be realized, the anthropologist in practice collaborates with an inside interpreter/translator. Though to be an interpreter/translator one must be not only an insider but also an outsider, already different in this fundamental way from one's own kin.

With an ancient culture then we reach an impasse, for there is no way we can immerse ourselves in the culture as a living environment. All that remains are written documents and artifacts that survive only as signs and shadows of their former significances. We have to do our best to read from (and impose on!) these inscribed remains an understanding, not just of the ways of thinking, but of the most fundamental characteristics of the ways of thinking of these ancient cultures. Husserl's first person reflection requires the technique of variation in imagination: we, as living meaning-bestowers, reflect in imagination on the way in which we actively construct our understandings. With an archaic lifeworld we have access only to the actual variations and possibilities that remain as inscribed traces of that culture. And of the language all that we have access to is the actual associations of words, ideas, images and contexts as preserved in the ancient documents. However, we can still aim to immerse ourselves in these texts, and in the project of deciphering their traces. A thorough familiarity with the texts, and internalization of those associations, will enable us to conduct *some* degree of phenomenological reflection on the possibilities as they have been 'frozen' in the extant documents. That is to say, an appreciation of some of the most basic modes of understanding of that ancient culture can arise from a thorough familiarity with the actual associations that are preserved in the texts, which in turn gives one the beginnings of a sensitivity to the kinds of things that are possible and not possible in that lifeworld.

Analytical

Analytical philosophy is a useful, rigorous and extremely powerful tool, characterized by the clarification of concepts, removal of vagueness, ambiguity and metaphor, and the following through of claims to their logically demonstrable consequences.[8] Many

---

8   Incidentally, analytical philosophy is in fact much closer to Husserl's conception of phenomenology than most practitioners realize. The method of demonstration of possibilities and impossibilities through thought experiments and counter-examples is a close parallel to Husserl's method of eidetic variation in imagination for the uncovering of invariant forms. See Gilbert Ryle, *Collected Papers*. Volumes I & II. See also Michael Dummett, *Origins of Analytical Philosophy*. An important difference between the analytical and phenomenological methods, however, is that the post-

philosophers hope to discover the truth about things, by thinking clearly about our concepts and drawing logical conclusions from them. They aim to express as literally and clearly as possible a claim as to the way things are, or as to some necessary truth about the way things are, and through the medium of arguments designed to persuade the reader that the most rational thing to believe is the author's claim about the way things are. The techniques of analytical philosophy are refinements of some of our natural thought processes: conceptual clarification and logical argumentation, presupposing objective truth, and deductive validity. Such techniques are perfect for engaging with and evaluating a text that has the same aims.

Now, such techniques are powerful indeed, but they are sometimes confused for the whole of philosophical thinking—as though one were to take *trompe-l'oeuil* verisimilitude for the whole of painting, or fine engraving for the whole of sculpture. These are all important techniques within the practice of each art or discipline, but it is naïve in the extreme to confuse them with the entire thing. Philosophical analysis is such a potent and mesmerizing tool that it can on occasion blind us to the fact that it may not *always* be the most appropriate tool for the job. It is inappropriate for example to treat a text that gives a rhetorical presentation of its world view as though it were arguing for the logical necessity of its claims. It is again inappropriate to argue literally against a text that makes its claims metaphorically (that is, to take the metaphors literally). It is inappropriate to diminish the significance of metaphor in a philosophical text that primarily expresses itself metaphorically, as though a metaphor is simply a rhetorical stand-in for a more literal expression. It is perhaps most importantly inappropriate to treat a text from a distinctively different philosophical context as though it had the same concerns, values and presuppositions as a twentieth century article written in an analytic mode. When confronted with such an 'alien' discourse, it is surely wise to be open to learning the strategies of reading and thinking that define the particular discourse, which may or may not turn out to be of an analytical nature.

Husserlian varieties of the latter allow the possibility of a plurality of phenomenologies, and thus of phenomenological analyses as they would be carried out by a different culture.

Semeiotic[9]

Charles Peirce was in all probability the first thinker to investigate the *formal structure* of interpretation, and to notice the ubiquity of this mode of understanding. His name for the dwelling of human being in interpretation was '*semeiosis*.' Semeiosis is the ever-present process of the reading of signs, codes, and symbols, that constitutes our relation to our environment. The logical form of the interpretation of signs is neither deductive, as in mathematics, nor inductive, as in statistics, but what Peirce called 'abductive' (at one time 'retroductive'). Abduction is a mode of thinking that has three distinctive characteristics: one is confronted with a set of phenomena, clues, signs, evidence or data; one is situated in a context of knowledge and experience which one brings to the phenomena; and finally there is the abductive step itself, in which one seeks to fit the phenomena into the context of one's knowledge and experience. There are many ways to bring the phenomena into conformity with one's background knowledge, but one aims ideally, of course, for the best possible fit. In fact, abduction is commonly defined as 'inference to the best possible explanation.' However, though an abduction is ideally the best explanation, it is not necessary that the diagnosis, solution, explanation, or interpretation actually be the best in order to count as an abduction. Moreover, it is also possible there is more than one best fit. Abductive arguments proceed by guesswork, and hypothesizing.

Successful abduction requires accumulated knowledge, extensive experience and a lively imagination. We start with a mystery, a perception, a text; these provide the 'evidence' consisting of a small number of clues, or traces. We then use our imaginations, informed and constrained by our extensive experience, and accumulated knowledge to construct an explanation, an interpretation. This is the mode of thinking performed by detectives in solving mysteries, doctors in making medical diagnoses, and scientists in constructing hypothetical explanations. It is also the manner in which we live as communicative beings: we listen to the words of others, we read the texts of others, but we also read the gestures, behaviors, facial expressions, and silences of others—and of ourselves—as well as the signs of the environment around us, and of our own bodies.

---

9 For an enjoyable excursion into this method of reasoning, see Eco and Sebeok, *The Sign of Three: Dupin, Holmes, Peirce*. For a more technical discussion, see K. T. Fann, *Peirce's Theory of Abduction*.

There is one possible implication of this way of thinking about textual interpretation that I would like to avoid. If one assimilates interpretation too closely to scientific explanation, this might give the impression that one is identifying some thing that left behind traces of its presence, the cause of those traces. If one conceives of meaning in this naïve realist way, then any abduction will be either right or wrong: one has either identified the correct interpretation or one has not. The meaning of the text is an objective entity that one must discover, by inferring it from the evidence. Again, my own philosophical sympathies lie with Wittgenstein, Heidegger, Quine, and Derrida: meanings are not mysterious but objective *entities* the existence of which is to be inferred. Rather, the kind of interpretation that is involved in textual abduction is one that is stripped of any presuppositions of unity and determinacy: that there can be, and must be, only one correct well-defined answer. Indeed, it is the unending *processes* of understanding—*noesis, hermeneusis, semeiosis*—that are phenomenologically the most basic. At the same time, I also wish to avoid the opposite tendency, that of a radically relativistic view of meaning, according to which no interpretation can be taken to have any advantage over any other interpretation, so that all interpretations must be considered equally applicable. Between these two extremes lies a more pragmatic and pluralist notion that allows for a ranking of interpretations as more or less plausible, more or less supported by the evidence, and that allows several interpretations to have equal plausibility. It also allows several mutually incompatible interpretations to have equal plausibility without requiring us to choose between them. Note that this notion also allows that some interpretations may reliably be ruled out as implausible.[10] The view of meaning presupposed by such a notion may be thought of as anti-essentialist.

Rather than an 'all or nothing' view, that sees the issue as right or wrong, and the evidence as pointing one way rather than the other, I suggest that it would make more sense to see the strength of the abduction as indicating the degree to which the theme abduced *informs* the text. That is, the strength of the abduction does not indicate the probability with which we may have

---

10   The criteria of plausibility by which interpretations are ranked are simply those by which we are naturally disposed to interpret our 'world' insofar as we are hermeneutic beings, beings whose being it is to dwell in semeiosis. Such criteria are not necessarily explicit, nor need they be expressible as a set of rules: they may rather be intuitive and paradigmatic, proceeding by *phronesis*.

found the correct explanation, but rather the extent to which this sense (among others) is sustained by the text from within its context. Meaning, on such an anti-essentialist view, is a matter of degree, and thus is itself a penumbral phenomenon: meanings do not have precisely defined identity conditions—they are indeterminate. Indeed, several distinct meanings, even incompatible meanings, may be coinstantiated to varying degrees. Rather than simply being present or absent, significances are sustained or sustainable by the linguistic, historical, textual and contextual evidences. There is indeed a further question of which of these significances the author would be inclined to recognize as coinciding (to varying degrees) with his or her 'intentions,' but there is no reason to suppose that this question itself has a determinate answer.

Thus in interpreting, one notices the extent to which patterns of evidences and interpretations may be overlaid, the extent to which they coincide. But since one can never have a complete and decisive set of evidence—the very idea of a complete set of evidence for an interpretation, one that establishes it with finality, is incoherent—there can never be a complete overlapping of patterns. And one ought never to claim with confidence that there is only one best fit. Indeed, there may be several mutually contradictory best fits. Now, there is a genuine and interesting issue concerning the 'author's intentions' but this ought not to be taken as the singular goal of interpretation. As we have seen, concern for such authorial authenticity requires that one's interpretation account for all of the available relevant evidence—which includes evidence about the historical, literary, economic, social conditions, evidence about language, about linguistic usage, and so on. Thus, if one is engaged in the search for what one believes to be the author's own interpretation of their own work, then one must pursue those readings that may be sustained by the more complete set of evidences composed of the text situated within its historical, social, cultural context. This, however, still does not rule out the possibility of a plurality of distinct, and even mutually incompatible, readings.

In chapter four, I engage in an explicit abduction of the significance of vagueness in the *Laozi*. The formal structure of the abduction is as follows. In general, if characteristics α, β, ... γ are identified as distinctive of some concept ϕ, then this semeiotic method will allow one to take each of the characteristics α, β, ... γ as a 'trace' of ϕ. A trace in the ordinary way of speaking is a sign, an indication, a clue left behind, evidence that something has passed by. In our sense, a textual trace of ϕ is a characteristic that may be

taken as linguistic evidence that indicates the degree of relevance of
ϕ to the text, or the plausibility of associating ϕ with the text. Thus,
one may *abduce* the relevance of ϕ in any text that is concerned,
explicitly or implicitly, with characteristics $\alpha, \beta, \dots \gamma$. The more of
these traces that are found to be associated with the text, the
stronger will be the abduction. Moreover, if $\alpha, \beta, \dots \gamma$ are found, on
investigation of ϕ, to be interrelated in certain characteristic ways,
then one's abduction of the relevance of ϕ will be stronger to the
extent that similar interrelations may be discerned in the text in
question.

Hermeneutic[11]

The particular virtue of the hermeneutic approach, especially as
advocated by traditional practitioners such as Schleiermacher, is its
recognition of the role that the historical and cultural conditions of
the production of the text plays in its meaning. According to
Schleiermacher, the goal of interpretation is to understand, through
a methodically guided process leading to a moment of empathetic
insight, the original meaning of the text as the author would have
understood it. Indeed, since one is bringing to consciousness the
historical conditions of which the author was but dimly aware, for
being immersed within them as unspoken presuppositions, and
also making explicit their implicit connections and implications, one
can be said to understand the text better than its own author. I
have already argued that such a notion, of a single well-defined
meaning behind the text, though it has its value, is extremely naïve.
Nevertheless, I concede that one may, if one wishes, adopt this
presupposition as a methodological research strategy. If one does
attempt this, then in order to discover that original meaning, one
must understand not only the writer and their topic, but also their
situation, life, background, their hopes and fears, their religious
beliefs, their cultural presuppositions, their relation to other
cultures and societies of the time, and so on. Of course, not all of
this information is relevant to interpreting every passage, but as
much as possible of this information must be gained if we are to
understand the context within which every passage has its place.
Moreover, such concerns may affect one's methodology even if one

---

[11]　See Gayle Ormiston and Alan D. Schrift, *The Hermeneutic Tradition:
from Ast to Ricoeur*. See also Richard Palmer, *Hermeneutics: Interpretation
Theory in Schleiermacher, Dilthey, Heidegger, and Gadamer*, and David
Couzens Hoy, *The Critical Circle: Literature, History, and Philosophical
Hermeneutics*.

does not share the full-blooded realist metaphysics of the traditional hermeneutic.

Dilthey's philosophy is characterized by a tension between
such a realist conception of the meaning of the text, and an
historicist relativism that grounds understanding in the full and
rich '*experience*' of '*life*,' imbued with personal and social
'*significance*.' He believes that he is not committed to a full-blooded
historicism, because the life in which we are historically situated is
already endowed with reflective, critical tendencies that give it the
possibility of transcending its situatedness. For Heidegger, understanding is not just something we bring to particular acts of
communication, but is a structure of the being of *Dasein*.
Understanding is *Dasein*'s mode of comportment that constitutes its
being-in-the-world. His analysis of understanding reveals that it is
characterized by 'fore-structures,' grounded in our facticity, that
anticipate what is to be understood. Such fore-structures might be
thought of as prejudices that prevent objective understanding, but
Gadamer, following Heidegger, insists that these fore-structures,
derived from tradition, are essential to any mode of understanding.
What appears to be merely historically situated prejudice turns out
to be a necessary condition for the possibility of any interpretation
whatsoever. These fore-structures define the horizon of our understanding. Gadamer's brand of phenomenological hermeneutics,
following in the tradition of Dilthey, and of Heidegger's onto-
phenomenological hermeneutic of *Dasein*, attempts to overcome the
shortcomings of the traditional hermeneutic. It rejects the notion of
an originally intended meaning that exists independently of the
interpreter, and rejects a simplistic attitude toward universality of
human culture, and demands that we always remain sensitive to
the otherness of the culture being interpreted.

It is through shared fore-structures that we are able to
communicate with one another, and it is through clashes of fore-
structures that we are able to expand and merge our horizons.
Since horizons are always in the *process* of development, they are
themselves also *historically* conditioned and conditioning. This is
what makes possible a fusion of horizons. But this leads to a
problem for the comparative philosopher. We cannot assume a
continuous development of horizons of understanding. Our
horizons and those of the text we are trying to understand do not
necessarily share genealogies.

When a European philosopher attempts to understand
ancient Greece, or when a modern Chinese philosopher strives to
understand pre-Qin thinkers, it is an ancestral culture that they
are trying to understand. The ancient ideas have been formative in

the development of their own current language, culture and philosophy, and in some way have survived, albeit in a transfigured form. It is the genealogy of the familiar in the unfamiliar, the fusion of the ancestral and the modern that makes possible a productive communication over time. It is not that we re-create some 'original' meaning, but that the very meaning itself is still in process of construction—the horizons of the ancestral text are still live in some way in its descendants. But when the two philosophers exchange tasks, a radical change takes place.

With the comparative project, there is no comparable fusion of past and present horizons through a single historical tradition, and for this reason the alterity of the culture and philosophy to be understood looms larger still. But much of what Gadamer says about approaching an ancestral text still applies to the project of the comparativist:

> It is the tyranny of hidden prejudices that makes us deaf to what speaks to us in tradition....That is why a hermeneutically trained consciousness must be, from the start, sensitive to the text's alterity....The important thing is to be aware of one's own bias, so that the text can present itself in all its otherness and thus assert its own truth against one's own fore-meanings.[12]

This is a moral that Roger Ames and David Hall take very seriously: the comparativist cannot understand a text without fore-structures and presuppositions, and so what we must do is to become aware of which presuppositions we bring to an ancient Chinese text, and why.[13] But, they also point out that we do not come from a single, well-defined tradition: it may have a centre, but it also has many peripheries. When the text proves recalcitrant, we must be ready to bring forward and modify those fore-structures, find some from the margins and peripheries of our own culture that ease the process of understanding, and allow the text its own breathing space. Thus, rather than Plato and Aristotle, Descartes and Kant, Hume and Russell, rather than looking for truth claims and valid arguments, they suggest that we turn to philosophers who were explicitly critical of the presuppositions of that tradition: Nietzsche, Heidegger, Whitehead. Perhaps, we could be more adventurous still, and wander deeper into the margins of the western philosophical

---

12   Gadamer, *Truth and Method.*
13   See for example, Hall and Ames, *Thinking from the Han: Self, Truth, and Transcendence in Chinese and Western Culture,* and their *Anticipating China: Thinking through the Narratives of Chinese and Western.*

tradition, searching for resonances in the ideas and thinking styles of Thoreau, Eckhardt, Paracelsus, or pseudo-Dionysus!

Structuralist and Poststructuralist [14]

Structuralist anthropology aims to uncover systems of meaning, of signification, of different cultures. Following the structuralist doctrine of the French linguist, Ferdinand de Saussure, that all meaning is a function of structure, that symbolic elements derive their meaning from their place in a symbol system, structural anthropologists such as Lévi-Strauss interpret cultural significances by locating cultural artifacts in systems of difference. One gathers information about some facet of culture, being sure to understand the relative values and significances of the artifacts. One then arranges the artifacts in orders of cultural significance. Having done this for a variety of aspects of culture, one can then place these structures of significance side by side. A comparison of the similarities between the structures of significance will deepen our understanding of the culture under investigation. It was part of Levi-Strauss's structuralist *credo* that there are universal structures underlying all human cultures. So that cross-cultural comparisons of structures of significance will yield structures that underlie all of human culture. When we have discovered these, we will have found the structures that determine human significance in general.

Saussure's linguistic structures are abstract Platonic structures. Though meanings are defined by their place in a system, the value of each node in the system, at any point in time, remains determinate. Even though the material embodiment of the system changes over time, it is still possible for the values of the nodes in the system to remain constant. The material production of the phonemes may even transform into one another: the phonemes [b], [v], [f], and [p], may develop over time into the phonemes [v], [f], [p], and [b] respectively. But so long as the relations between the nodes remain the same, the abstract *values* of the phonemes, their role in the system, remain identical. This does not mean that it must remain constant. The system considered diachronically can change over time: the relative values between the nodes may remain the same, or they may vary. A change in one place affects the values of nodes elsewhere. For example, a phonetic system may also develop over time in such a manner that there is no simple correspondence

---

[14] See Saussure, *Course in General Linguistics*. For an excellent introduction to Structuralism, see Jean Piaget, *Structuralism*.

between the phonemes at the beginning and end points: the phonemes [b], [v], [f], and [p] may develop into [β], [ɸ] and [h]. In this case, it is not only the material forms that have changed, but because the relative definition of the nodes has changed, so have the nodes or values themselves. Saussure's claim is that the importance of linguistics lies in the abstract structure, and the abstract values, and not with the inconstancy of the material in which they are embodied.

Derrida[15] overturns this focus, and attempts to draw from this inconstancy of the material a much greater philosophical significance. He argues from Saussure's concept of structural difference to the deconstructive concept of 'differance.'[16] Or from the concept of iterability, and the necessity of the possibility of mistake/*catachresis* that he maintains follows from iterability, to the essential indeterminacy of meaning. Now, there is a question as to how strong this argument is, though it is by no means clear to me that the argument fails.[17] Nevertheless, what to me is *philosophically* important is not the strength of the argument (the intricacy and tightness of the logical stitches), but the power and plausibility of the position itself. What is important is the working out of the play of differance, both within the metaphilosophical enterprise of deconstruction and in the general application to understanding, and, most specifically for us, in the specific application to textual interpretation.

Deconstruction, as post-structuralist philosophy inspired by Derrida has come to be known, is not simply a critical philosophy, nor is it simply the uncovering of hidden assumptions. Most philosophical methodology involves criticism and the uncovering of assumptions. Rather, what distinguishes deconstruction as a philosophical methodology is that it aims to derail presuppositions of 'presence' or stability of meaning. It aims to undermine the claims of any text to have a determinate meaning, to have a fixed and final meaning, and demonstrates the impossibility of that

---

15   See Derrida, *Grammatology*, and *Limited, Inc.* For one of the best and clearest introductions to Derrida, see Henry Staten, *Wittgenstein and Derrida.*

16   It has become common practice to distinguish differance from difference by leaving it in French and pronouncing it with a French accent! At least part of Derrida's point, however, was that the words should be indistinguishable in pronunciation, thereby instantiating one case of the primacy of 'writing' over 'speech.' In keeping with Derrida's point then I urge the reader to make no difference in pronunciation between the two.

17   For a careful exposition of the logic of this possible entailment, see Samuel C. Wheeler III, *Deconstruction as Analytical Philosophy.*

closure by searching out and focusing on elements of significance of the text that remain outside of the writer's control. One can indeed *intend* to say something, and one can succeed in saying what one intends, but what one cannot do is to control and contain all possible understandings of what one says. Indeed, *in principle* one cannot know with complete closure all the ramifications, implications, associations, and developments of what one has said. Deconstruction is not simply the task of opening up readings, but of showing how readings that claim to be closed could not possibly be closed. Thus, since deconstruction is the move from apparent closure to openness, it does not make much sense to talk of deconstructing a text that acknowledges its own openness. Now, since the *Zhuangzi* is a text that acknowledges its own openness *par excellence*, a deconstructive reading of it would at best be redundant. Nevertheless, a post-structuralist understanding of meaning has great affinities with both my understanding of meaning, and with the treatment of language in the *Zhuangzi*, and thus provides a most appropriate background from which to approach this text.

CHAPTER FOUR

Xiao Yao You:
Wandering Beyond the
Boundaries

On Scepticism and Relativism

The interpretation of Zhuangzi as a relativist has a long and prestigious heritage. It can be traced back to the commentary of Guo Xiang, through the philosophy of the *Liezi*, and still further to the ideas of what Liu Xiaogan calls the *Shu Zhuang Pai*, the school of Zhuangzi's followers. Its most distinctive manifestation is in chapter 17, *Qiu Shui*, 'Autumn Floods,' in which the magnificent Yellow River flows down to the northern ocean and for the first time realizes that he can take himself to be the vastest of things only so long as he remains ignorant of what lies beyond his ken. Guo Xiang's commentary on the *Zhuangzi* can be thought of in large part as a development of this line of thinking through the ideas of individuality, particularity of nature, and radical equality. As we have seen in the last chapter, these ideas can be summarized in the concept of equality of all individual things, and by extension of all viewpoints. All things are what they are; they follow their own spontaneous 'thusness.' Each thing is individual; each individual is self contained, and is self-preserving; each requires a freedom to develop its own inner tendencies, and so must be accepted on its own terms. It can be seen how this radical individualism rapidly develops into a radical relativism. No judgments can be made over other things, because the other things over which one makes critical judgments have their own particular 'natures,' and thus their own particular standards by which they judge themselves to be acceptable. Moreover, according to Guo Xiang, it is wrong to try to change what something spontaneously is. Things, if left to work themselves out on their own accord, will work out in the way that is most appropriate for them. Everything is acceptable so long as it is left to its own devices. Thus, things and creatures *wu* 物 are equalized, *qi* 齊, insofar as none can be judged better or worse just for being what it is.

This is how Guo Xiang takes the moral of the opening chapter of the *Zhuangzi*, the *Xiao Yao You*, 'Wandering Beyond.' According to this interpretation, there are many perspectives, vast and small, each nested within the next in size, but they are all equal in value. None can sensibly be taken to be better than any of the others. The perspective of the giant migrating bird described in the very first story is no better and no worse than that of the little fledglings below. They both have their strengths and their weaknesses, and neither is to be judged for its failings. The small birds cannot fly high, they cannot fly for long, and they cannot fly great distances, but it is also true that the giant bird is incapable of flying without a great expanse of air beneath its wings. It is, moreover, oblivious to the goings on of the world beneath it, because it is unable to see things so small and so far away. All things in the world have their place, and the giant bird is simply another creature that may seem impressive from one point of view, but will show itself to be inadequate when other factors are taken into consideration. This, according to the relativistic reading, is the significance of the discussion of the vast and the small.

It makes sense, if one adopts this reading, to extend this evening out of things to an equalizing and relativizing of all doctrines. All doctrines, teachings, and evaluations are made from some point of view, and since all judgments between points of view must themselves be made from some point of view: there is no final ground, no ultimate arbiter, or in the words of Zhuangzi, 'no thing on which all things agree in affirming.' And so, it is claimed, Zhuangzi has no preferred teaching, indeed, no preferences whatsoever. It would follow that Mohism would be as good as Daoism, the Ruist official the equal of the Daoist sage. And indeed, to be consistent, an absolutist doctrine would be as good as a relativistic one.

The early followers of Zhuangzi, in chapter 17, the *Qui Shui*, 'Autumn Floods,' corroborate this reading. They take up this aspect of the *Zhuangzi*, which now becomes the central focus of their philosophy. In their words, the significance of the vast and the small is that 'measures have no exhaustibility': once one starts the process of expansiveness, one realizes that it need never stop. Everything that at one time seems vast and impressive will vanish from sight from a still vaster perspective. There is thus no ultimate arbiter of the vast and petty.

There are indeed several discernable tendencies in the Autumn Floods chapter, the most evident being that toward some form of relativism: there is no ultimate standard of the vast and the small, what appears vast from one perspective will appear small from a larger perspective, and what appears small from one perspective will appear huge from a perspective that is smaller still. It is notable that this form of relativism is still quite reasonable: it is not claimed that the large can appear small from a smaller perspective. What is acknowledged is a relativity, but it is not a reciprocal relativity. It is a graded hierarchy of measures. Nevertheless, a more radical claim is made when the potentially infinite nature of this hierarchy is taken into account. This more radical claim appears to take the form of a kind of nihilism: *nothing can be judged to have any value whatsoever* because any perspective from which something appears to have value will be superseded by a perspective from which it has little or none. They also insist that since all judgments of right and wrong must be made from some point of view, and since each viewpoint considers itself right and others wrong, so no judgments of right and wrong can ever be made. Not just that no judgments can be made with finality, but that the sage has transcended judgment-making altogether.

There is also, however, in this chapter, a brief acknowledgment of the pragmatic function of evaluations. While it is true that judgments have no absolute application, nevertheless, evaluations are always made from within some context and for some particular purpose. With this acknowledgment, the writers of the *Qiu Shui* are returning closer to their Zhuangzian origins. But there is, I believe, overriding all of these tendencies—the relativistic, the pragmatic, and the nihilistic—a deeper tendency. This is a sense that there is beyond the beyond, beyond the vanishing point, 'something' ancestral that can only be called a nothing. This extraordinary line of thinking is pursued still further in the *Liezi*, which again uses metaphors and images of vastness to point to a realm beyond the limits of our ordinary distinctions. These are wild, untamed places, reachable only in dreams and flights of shamanic 'ecstasy.' The measures of these 'places,' their space and time, have no comparison with our own. Zhuangzi, his followers, and Liezi, all three associate this wandering beyond with *wu* 無, in this context to be understood as involving a dissolution of boundaries. It is a thin, attenuated, empty place, described by Zhuangzi as *wusuo* 無所, no place, in which what one does is *wuwei* 無為, non-doing. Our actions from this view from nowhere can only be called non-actions. This ancestral nothing is perhaps identified with Laozi's *dao*.

To return to the *Zhuangzi*, the *locus classicus* for this interpretation in the *Inner Chapters*, apart from the discussion of the vast and the petty in the *Xiao Yao You*, is the response of Wangni, Royal Grindstone, to Nieque, Toothless, in the *Qi Wu Lun*:

民濕寢則腰疾偏死，鰍然乎哉？木處則惴慄恂懼，猿猴然乎哉？三者孰知正處？民食芻豢，麋鹿食薦，蝍且甘帶，鴟鴉耆鼠，四者孰知正味？猿猵狙以為雌，麋與鹿交，鰍與魚游。毛嬙麗姬，人之所美也；魚見之深入，鳥見之高飛，麋鹿見之決驟，四者孰知天下之正色哉？

If people were to sleep in a marsh, they would develop a deathly lumbago—but is this so of a fish? If they were to set up home in a tree, they would shudder with anxiety, fear and dread—but is this so of apes and monkeys? Of the three, which knows the right place to live?

People eat livestock; deer eat grass. Centipedes relish juicy maggots 甘帶; while owls and crows delight in rat flesh. Of these four, which knows the right taste?

Apes take apes for their mates; deer mix with deer; fish prefer the company of fish. Mao Qiang the courtesan is one whom people consider beautiful. Fish that see her dart into the deep; birds that see her flap up and away; and deer that see her break into a gallop. Of these four which knows the world's true beauty?

The first thing to be noticed is that as the literal story goes, there is nothing in it with which any philosopher, or non-philosopher, would disagree. It simply expresses common sense. No one would deny that it is bad for a monkey to sleep under water, and bad for a fish to sleep in a tree. To acknowledge this is not to be committed to a doctrine of relativism. Even the most die-hard of universalizing Realists would not deny the claims in question. The question then is to what extent is it appropriate to generalize the claim into a universal doctrine: all evaluations are right from their own individual points of view. Now, Zhuangzi is indeed drawing attention to the presupposition made by Toothless in the very form of his question: that there is something on which all creatures agree 子知物之所同是乎?. His examples show that we cannot make simplistic universal judgments and impose these on all creatures. Creatures have their own particularities, circumstances, tendencies and aims. It is simply ignorance of the way things are that would lead us to want to impose values universally without taking into account their appropriateness in appropriate circumstances.

Still, none of this amounts to a philosophical *doctrine* of relativism. Acknowledgment of such individual appropriateness is not what is usually meant by the philosophical doctrine of relativism. If this amounted to philosophical relativism, there would be no one who is not a philosophical relativist! What is usually meant by this doctrine is that *all* claims to objective judgment are really just claims from a particular point of view, and more significantly that *all* conflicting claims are *equally valid* since no judgment can be made between them. Those who attribute to Zhuangzi this strong form of relativism start from this recognition of appropriateness, and its dependence on context, and assume that this recognition necessarily leads to a radical relativism. But this stronger form of relativism does not follow from Zhuangzi's common sense observation of appropriateness. Since acknowledgment of context dependence is an acknowledgment of *relativity* to context, it may indeed be described as a kind of 'relativism.' One might call it a weak relativism, but since it would be next to impossible to find anyone who is not a weak relativist, the label is, philosophically speaking, useless. Useless, and misleading, insofar as it tempts us to slip from Zhuangzi's sensible understanding of the relevance of context to the questionable and pernicious doctrines of relativism that assert that nothing is better than anything else, that no way of life is better than any other, that no system of judgment can ever meaningfully be critiqued. That this cannot be the moral of the story is evident in it right from the start: *it is better* for fish to sleep under water; *it is bad* for them to sleep in trees. These are evaluative judgments that the story presupposes.

The central concept of Guo Xiang's philosophy, which he attributes to Zhuangzi through his commentary, is that of nature or naturalness. The word for nature in classical Chinese, as we have mentioned, is *ziran* 自然, 'so by itself,' or 'spontaneous,' and the significance of this term in Guo Xiang's philosophy is that although each thing is different, every individual thing is so of itself, and in this way all things are equal. To wander freely, to engage in non-action, is to allow things to be themselves of themselves. Nothing is better than anything else; there are only differences in kind. The Phoeng is no better than the sparrows, and the 'utmost person,' *zhiren* 至人, also is no better than the Phoeng, despite Zhuangzi's explicit account to the contrary. Indeed, if we are to take such a relativism seriously we would have to say that there is no distinction between the *zhiren* and anyone else, and therefore that there is no such thing as the *zhiren* or the Daoist sage. Thus, we end up with the unlikely claim that he does not value vastness, nor does he place any positive evaluation on the *zhiren* or the sage. However, we need only recall Zhuangzi's own comment on the difference between the great and the small (the *vast* and the *petty*) in order to refute this interpretation: 'What do these two creatures understand? Little understanding cannot come up to great understanding; the short-lived cannot come up to the long-lived.' Liezi can fly for fifteen days, the Phoeng can fly for six months, but the highest achievement is to have nothing to depend on—no self, no merit, no fame—and then there will be no limit to one's flight.

More recently, interpreters of Zhuangzi, have recognized the limitations of the relativistic interpretation of the *Inner Chapters*, and have instead focused on the similarities between what we may call his epistemic stance, and that of the Pyrrhonists of ancient Greece.[1] The *locus classicus* for this interpretation is again the exchange between Toothless and the Royal Grindstone:

> 齧缺問乎王倪曰：子知物之所同是乎？曰：吾惡乎知之！子知子之所不知邪？曰：吾惡乎知之！然則物無知邪？曰：吾惡乎知之！雖然，嘗試言之。庸詎知吾所謂知之非不知邪？庸詎知吾所謂不知之非知邪？

> Toothless asked Royal Grindstone, 'Do you know what creatures agree in affirming?' He replied, 'How would I know that?' 'Do you know what you don't know?' 'How would I know that?' 'All right then, do creatures have no knowledge?' 'How would I know that? Nevertheless I shall try to talk about it. How do we know that what we call knowing is not ignorance? How do we know that what we call ignorance is not knowing?'

In this exchange, the Royal Grindstone replies three times with the rejoinder, 'How would I know that?' This, perhaps, suggests something of an attitude of epistemic humility. Moreover, he adds, 'How do we know that what we call knowing is not ignorance? How do we know that what we call ignorance is not knowing?' Here we do indeed have a thought that expresses a doubt worthy of a sceptic. But it is significant that this speculation is not followed up at any great length. Besides, I believe that the import of *buzhi*, not knowing, is not simply ignorance, but a specific kind of knowing. It is a capacity to cope with and understand the world and to engage in it that lacks the specificity and articulation of explicit knowledge, and that indeed is the condition of the possibility of any explicit knowledge whatsoever. If this is so, then what appears to be ignorance is indeed a form of knowing, and what appears to be knowing becomes more like ignorance, in comparison. By focusing

---

1   *Essays on Skepticism, Relativism, and Ethics in the* Zhuangzi, edited by Kjellberg and Ivanhoe.

on the *yin* aspects of our epistemic (or, rather, 'phronetic') relation to the world, the hierarchy of explicit knowledge and tacit knowledge becomes overturned.

Now, there are other structural and functional similarities that can be discerned between the thought of the *Inner Chapters* and the ideas of the ancient Sceptics, concerning, for example, the relation between such epistemic attitudes and a state of emotional tranquility (*ataraxia*). But I am not sure that the similarities between the two are sufficient to outweigh the differences. The differences between the two are, I believe, great enough to make it misleading to call Zhuangzi a sceptic. I do concede that, once it is pointed out, the *family resemblance* between Zhuangzi and the ancient Sceptics is unmistakable, but it is, surely, at most a family resemblance of a distant relative.

Moreover, to the extent that Zhuangzi is cautioning epistemic humility, it is not scepticism as such, but the pragmatic attitude of *fallibilism* that he is recommending. It is important not to confuse these two. Fallibilism allows us to make judgments, indeed requires us to make judgments, so long as we hold them open to revision. Thus, a fallibilist can indeed make the assertion that it would be bad for a fish to sleep in a tree, or for a monkey to sleep under water. Indeed, the pragmatist requires us to make these provisional, situated judgments, since they follow from our experiences and context. This is exactly why Zhuangzi is able to make the claim to know that the fish in the River Hao are happy—despite Huizi's refusal to accept his right to make this claim. And it is indeed, exactly the reason he gives in response to Huizi.[2] Unlike the ancient Sceptics, Zhuangzi makes many knowledge claims—indeed, he makes several such claims, on which his argument depends, in the very passage in question: 'If people were to sleep in a marsh, they would develop a deathly lumbago,' 'If they were to set up home in a tree, they would shudder with anxiety, fear and dread,' 'Centipedes relish juicy maggots,' 'Owls and crows delight in rat flesh.' Zhuangzi does not shy away from claiming to know such things. The ancient Sceptics were careful to insist that such claims could be made only as appearance statements. Zhuangzi does not even hint at the distinction between an appearance statement and an objective statement, let alone insist that we confine all our claims to the former. Thus, while the investigation of the elements of scepticism in the *Zhuangzi* has thrown a great deal of light on certain aspects of Zhuangzi's philosophy, it is only a half light, and needs to be supplemented with an equally extensive investigation

---

2   *Wandering at Ease in the* Zhuangzi, edited by Roger Ames.

into the differences of significance between the two points of comparison.

Central themes of the *Inner Chapters*: Death, Boundaries and Vastness

The overwhelming mood of chapter two of the *Zhuangzi*, the *Qi Wu Lun*, 'Discussion on Smoothing Things Out,' and chapter six, the *Da Zong Shi*, 'The Vast Ancestral Teacher,' is existential. Life and death, the weariness of existence, the endless cycles of emotional turbulence: these are central problems that drive Zhuangzi's philosophical explorations. Zhuangzi places these cyclical processes in the context of the processes of nature and thus tries to gain an insight into such existential problems. But he is also preoccupied with language, evaluative language in particular: the language with which we affirm and deny, approve and disapprove, express our likes and dislikes. Since we use such linguistic contrasts to express our feelings, the issues of linguistic and logical distinctions are closely linked to issues of evaluative distinctions and emotional responses in early Chinese philosophy.

People, things, meanings, are all delimited by boundaries *feng* 封 : spatial boundaries, temporal boundaries, qualitative boundaries, boundaries of understanding. Human lives in particular are delimited by two temporal boundaries: the beginning of our lives, and the end. This tripartite temporal structure—of nothing 無, something 有, and nothing 無—is a motif that recurs throughout the *Zhuangzi.* The process of change from nothing to something is a process of emergence *chu* 出, that from something to nothing is an entering, *ru* 入 . Like a wave, we emerge into presence, into thinghood, and submerge into the ocean of undifferentiation. This submergence is considered to be a process of return—with Laozi it is a turning about, *fan* 反, and with Zhuangzi it is quite explicitly a returning home, *gui* 歸. But what the *Zhuangzi* draws our attention to is not just the endless cyclical process, but also *the boundaries themselves.* It draws our attention away from the 'things' delimited by them, and forces us to focus closely on the processes of transformation of the two transitions. By focusing closely on the transitions we become aware of the continuity between something and nothing: the sharpness and clarity of the boundary dissolves; the dichotomy becomes a penumbra. Things come into being over time, and go out of existence over time; things bring each other into existence and out of existence. Things even become one another: a chrysalis *becomes* a butterfly; a seed *becomes* a tree. By dissolving boundaries, by turning dichotomies that separate things into penumbrae that meld them, Zhuangzi turns our attention to the continuities, *yi* 一 that constitute the natural world as an interlocking web of cyclical processes. From such a vantage point, Zhuangzi hopes to temper our natural tendency to identify with the evanescent region between the two boundaries.

Zhuangzi's advice is to release the ties, attachments and dependencies, *lei* 累, by which we believe ourselves to be defined, to cease to cling to these limitations and boundaries of our selves, and to realize our continuity with what is radically Other by realizing that we are already other to ourselves. Zhuangzi's insight here is paradoxical: for it is only in recognizing our continuity that we gain independence! Dependence involves closing ourselves off by identifying strongly with some while rejecting others. Dependence ties us down to a fixed home, family, and body: it does not sufficiently recognize the fluidity and instability of these, with the result that we become unable to accept and cope with radical loss, *wang* 亡. Zhuangzi's metaphors for this process of expansive identification are those of 'vastness, *da* 大,' 'wandering, *you* 遊,' and this is to be achieved through an intense psycho-physical spiritual discipline the result of which he describes as 'harnessing the dragon and roaming beyond the four seas.'

The second major theme of the *Qi Wu Lun*, rivaling the theme of death in terms of the number of passages devoted to it—words, language, judgment, distinctions—is, despite appearances, not so different a theme after all. Indeed, it is the distinction between life and death that is ultimately at stake. Deeming, judging, and distinction-making of a certain sort, fail to realize the continuity of things insofar as they set hard and fast boundaries between them. A deeming, judging, or distinguishing that does not set such sharp boundaries is able to be more sensitive to the subtleties and intricacies that bedevil our everyday lives. Such a judging respects the lack of determination of word, idea and thing. As the *Zhuangzi* itself says, 'Words are not blowing. Words have what they say, but what they say is exceptionally indeterminate.' A fuller appreciation for the meaning of this kind of indeterminacy will require a meandering excursion through the cultures of the central plains, and through the state of Chu, with an occasional dramatic change of scenery: twentieth century Europe and America! We shall begin our journey with Zhuangzi's own free and easy wandering, after which we shall pay a visit to the early and later Mohists.

The following section is part translation, part commentary on the first chapter, the *Xiao Yao You* 逍遙遊 'Wandering Beyond.' The usual translation of this title is 'Free and Easy Wandering' or 'Carefree Wandering' and certainly in modern Chinese *xiaoyao* has come to have this meaning. There is, I think, a deeper significance that is missed by this translation, and that is the sense of *yao* 遙 'distance.' It is not just a careless or random wandering, but a wandering into the distance, over the horizons, or perhaps it is into the distance above, a distance that allows what was previously considered vast to diminish in significance.

Wandering Beyond: traversing boundaries, overcoming limitations

The first of the *Inner Chapters*, the *Xiao Yao You* opens not with dialogue, nor with a discussion of abstract concepts, but with Khaon,[3] a giant sea creature about which we are told scarcely more than its name. No sooner are we acquainted with this dark embryonic beast than it transforms into Phoeng, an equally colossal air spirit. We begin then, not simply with a sea creature, but with a *yinyang* metamorphosis of mythic proportions: Water to Air, Fish to Bird, Dragon to Phoenix, Darkness to Light. But this primordial Birth is not an easy one: Phoeng thrashes the water for three thousand leagues, kneading, lifting, rocking[4] and rising ninety thousand leagues upwards, and in six months is out of breath. Only when it has risen beyond the resistance of the winds and broken through the clouds is it able to embark upon its seasonal migration southward. Far below, tiny birds scoff and sneer at the

---

3   Kun 鯤—both this name and that of the Peng 鵬 are problematic to translate. My ugly and unpronounceable neologisms here need some justification. With 'Khaon' I attempt to preserve something of the sound and also the etymology of the Chinese. The phonetic radical on the right of the character, *hun*, evokes the idea of chaos. With 'Phoeng' I attempt to incorporate Lu Deming's suggestion that the Peng is in fact a *feng* 鳳— phoenix, while retaining something of the sound of the Chinese name.

4   The traditional reading of this line follows Lu Deming in taking *fuyao* 扶搖 to be a gradual pronunciation, 緩言 *huanyan*, for *piao* 飄 whirlwind. While I have no good reason to doubt the correctness of this reading, my translation emphasizes the literal meaning of the words, the impression of which, with three successive hand radicals, gives a strong feeling of exhaustive effort, a motif which is picked up again in the meditations on life and death in the second chapter.

gargantuan proportions of the monster above them. They have no conception of the significance of such vastness; they cannot begin to understand what lies so utterly beyond the confines of their mundane experience. Just as the morning mushroom or the summer cicada could not begin to understand the Dark Numen, *mingling* 冥靈, whose springtime lasts five hundred years, or the Chun tree whose fall lasts eight thousand years. This is not an elitism that despises the everyday, but an attitude of expansiveness that despises parochialism.

The small birds are the officials who wander within the realm of the four seas; the vast and solitary migrant bird is the recluse who wanders beyond the realm of the recognizable. Those within the realm include the Ruists who seek office, both to make a name for themselves and for their lineage, and also to bring the social realm into harmony. Note that this is not a direct rejection of the claims of the Ruists: they do indeed have their place. Rather, it involves a recognition that there is a broader perspective from which this place begins to seem inadequate. What was previously thought to be of the utmost importance is seen in new light as one's experience broadens. The great emperor Yao recognizes that it is not his own selfless devotion, but the non-interference of the recluse Xuyou that is responsible for the smooth functioning of the 'empire,' and wishes to cede the throne. But from Xuyou's vaster perspective there is no value in taking credit for allowing the kingdom to harmonize itself.

In the next story Jianwu questions Lianshu, relating to him the teachings of Jieyu, the madman of Chu. Grand and unorthodox ('vast and out of line'), terrifying and endless like the Milky Way, having little to do with human concerns. 'In the mountains of Maoguye there live spirit people, *shen ren* 神人,[5] whose flesh is like frozen snow.... They do not eat the five grains, but suck in the wind and drink the dew. They *straddle the cloud qi, harness a dragon, and roam beyond the four seas*. Their spirit congeals, keeping creatures free from disease and ensuring the year's harvest. I thought this crazy and would not believe it.' 'Of course,' Lianshu replied, 'the blind have no means to take in the sight of sophisticated ornaments; the deaf no means to take in the sound of bells and drums. Could it be that there is only physical deafness and blindness? The understanding also has them. Such person's

---

[5]   I take this in the plural, since it seems to me fruitful to take these as the same masters of the Maoguye Mountains mentioned further on.

teachings are ripe with meaning.[6] Such a person, such power, can embrace all things as one. When the world approaches disorder, who would wear himself out in service of the empire? Such a person! Nothing can harm them: though a great flood may reach the heavens, they will not drown; though a great drought may melt metal and stone, and scorch the mountains, they will not be burnt. Such a person's chaff and dust can mould a Yao or Shun—and who would dare so boldly to make of himself a servant of things?'

In many cultures, the shaman is one who engages in distinctive practices of a kind similar to those described in such passages,[7] who takes flight beyond the limits of the ordinary, and who thus has powers and capacities 德 that are useful to the community. The concept of the 'shaman' has had a rocky history in the discipline of anthropology. Mircea Eliade sought to distinguish shamans from mediums and mystics. But these categories have since proved to be less helpful than at first anticipated. It turns out that there far too many intermediate cases and problem cases for these distinctions to be of much use. There has more recently then been a tendency to use the word 'shamanism' as a blanket term for all these phenomena. Now, while there are no universal characteristics of all shamans, nevertheless there are some tendencies that stand out as quite distinctive. They are associated enough with shamanism to make the connection significant.

In many traditional ('premodern'/'precolonized') cultures, a shaman is often one who transgresses boundaries: between male and female, masculine and feminine; and traverses the boundaries between the human world and the spirit world, between the human and the natural environment. The shaman has often acquired a wealth of traditional knowledge, and personally acquired experimental knowledge, about the nature of things: plants, animals, people, spirits, and perhaps most importantly the 'propensities' of things,[8] their capacities to affect us and to affect the things around us. The powers or spirits of things are thus the domain of the medicine wo/man. This includes knowledge of the

---

6   由時女也 literally: 'like a timely woman.' Traditional readings make no good sense of this phrase. This metaphorical paraphrase of the literal reading however surely makes enough sense to avoid resorting to emendation.

7   Indeed, according to Jordan Paper, this passage constitutes the earliest reference to such practices in China. See his book, *The Spirits are Drunk: Comparative Approaches to Chinese Religion*.

8   François Jullien, *The Propensity of Things: toward a history of efficacy in China.*

seasons and medicinal properties of roots, herbs and other substances, and so the shaman is entrusted both with the ability to foresee a good crop and to maintain the health of the community.[9] The shaman may also be a skilful maker of things *zaozhe* 造者, an artist, and in early China, even metallurgist, responsible for transforming the world around them, while inspired by the spirits.[10] Jianwu's scepticism in the face of this story is much like our own, and through Lianshu's chiding of him, we are cautioned not to discount what may lie beyond the cultural limitations of our own understanding. Now, whether or not Zhuangzi had a religious belief in shamans and magicians,[11] the story functions powerfully at a metaphorical level. These two levels, the literal and metaphorical, are far from mutually exclusive, and this story constitutes an instance not only of the richness and polysemy of this text, but of a polysemy that is essentially indeterminate. What I wish to draw attention to is the metaphor of *flight*, or traveling beyond the limitations, and the subsequent capacity to 'harness the dragon.' To harness the dragon is to become a master of transformation, to be at home with the complexity and unwieldiness of things, to have the capacity to thrive without firm foundations.

The great sage king Yao, after journeying beyond the confines of the kingdom to the masters of the distant Maoguye mountains forgot all that he previously was honoured for. His previous worldly titles now diminished in significance. The Yao of this story had the capacity to learn from the unruly ways of these mountain-dwelling shamans. This was not just the humility that forces us to rethink when we discover other cultures and other ways of life, but was a recognition of the previously unrecognized value of their particular other 'way.' This other shamanistic way, we can surmise from the *Zhuangzi* and the *Liezi*, is one that demands that we let go of our preconceptions, diminish our sense of self-importance, and become open to learning from what is alien: nature, spirits, demons and dreams. It seeks to transcend parochial limitations in its search for a deeper understanding of the world and our place in it. At first, however, Yao was like the man of Song who decided to take his ceremonial headwear south and try to sell it

---

[9]   Mircea Eliade, *Shamanism: Archaic Techniques of Ecstasy*.

[10]   Chan Ping-leung, 'Ch'u Tz'u and Shamanism in Ancient China,' Ph. D dissertation.

[11]   Though he certainly does not approve of the particular form of shamanism practiced by the 巫 *wu*. It is in answering such questions that we see the need for a greater knowledge of the culture and beliefs of the writer of the text.

to the tribal people of Yue, convinced that they would immediately give up their primitive ways and adopt the superior culture of the central plains. But the people of Yue had their own customs of shaving and tattooing their heads and had no use for the ceremonial curiosities of their naïve visitor. The ruling house of the central plains, having a more institutionalized state 'religion,' was not likely to have looked with approval on the tribal beliefs and cultures of the south.[12] Zhuangzi can be read again as issuing a warning to those who have no patience with such beliefs that there are things to which our presuppositions make us blind. But more than this he is representing through the metaphor of the shaman, and indeed of the dragon, the 'nature' that lies beyond the 'city' limits. From within the confines of the city the world outside appears wild and unwieldy, but once we learn to let go of the structures by which we bind ourselves, we realize that the wildness and unruliness are an illusion. What appears to be chaotic and destructive in fact has an order of its own, and is not necessarily dangerous.

Lastly, there are two stories in which Huizi actually prides himself on his inability to deal with vastness! His attitude of ridicule echoes the fledglings' mockery of the giant bird whose dimensions surpass the limitations of their understanding. In the same way Huizi takes his inability to make sense of Zhuangzi's statements as evidence that they are nonsense. Huizi said to Zhuangzi, 'The king of Wei gave me the seed of a great gourd[13] and I planted it.... The gourd was vast indeed. I thought it was useless and smashed it.' In reply Zhuangzi tells a story about a family who made their living from traditional use of an ancient secret recipe. They were happy with their old and familiar ways, and so they never learned to make use of its other possibilities. The least imagination would have opened up new worlds for them. He then chides Huizi for being unable to think beyond the ordinary everyday uses of things, as though things could have none other than their familiar functions. A more genuine and thorough appreciation of things would be responsive to all the ways in which they relate to each other and to

---

12 For an investigation into the social structures within which shamanistic culture thrives, see Ioan M. Lewis, *Ecstatic Religion.* Chu was also a southern shamanistic culture, but was certainly not tribalistic. Indeed it appears to have been a highly complex and developed culture that nevertheless preserved its shamanistic roots.

13 The egg, the seed, the inchoate: the 'not yet determined'! On the significance of the imagery of the gourd in Daoist thinking, see Norman Girardot, *Myth and Meaning in Early Taoism: The Theme of Chaos, hun-tun.*

one's needs and purposes. The gourd may not have been suited to making bowls, scoops, and utensils, or even to making musical instruments, but it would have made a wonderful flotation device for drifting at leisure across rivers and lakes. The seeds of the gourd become a metaphor for the propensities of natural development, the vastness of the gourd a metaphor for unexpected turns of development, and the floating, drifting, meandering along the river a metaphor for accepting and being responsive to the openness in which we are enveloped.

Huizi also tells of a tree he has that is as monstrous and ugly as Zhuangzi's own teachings—and just as useless. Jianwu a little earlier was chided for making the same criticism of the ravings of the madman of Chu. In reply Zhuangzi describes the virtues of wildcats and weasels, each of which leads directly to its downfall. Parallelism of structure suggests to me that there is something missing from this story. The wildcats and weasels are small, sleek and swift, and this makes them extraordinary skillful and useful at catching rodents. But it is this very skill that makes them so 'useful' that also leads to their downfall, to their death in a trap. The giant yak on the other hand, because of its size is rendered useless—and here the story ends. The parallel is usually taken to be between the uselessness of the yak and the trapping of the wildcat. But this cannot be right. What was in question was the uselessness of words that are vast and out of line. The yak, like Zhuangzi's words, is vast and useless. Thus, the parallel we would expect, and one that we find in several other stories about uselessness, is that the yak, precisely because of its uselessness, is thereby able to preserve its life. Thus, though this tree is rendered useless on account of its ugliness, its virtue lies precisely in its uselessness. Because it is 'useless' it will never suffer the harm that results from being cut down for uses that are at odds with its own natural development. Thus, uselessness here is only apparent uselessness—what appears to be so from a conventional point of view. The art is to find a usefulness that goes beyond the limitations of conventional usage. For the tree itself survival is the major issue: how to preserve its life in a hostile environment. When survival is no longer an issue, the question becomes how to appreciate what things have to offer without thwarting their natural dispositions, how to work with them without exploiting them.

In these stories the theme that is consistently repeated is that of *vastness*. The significance of this vastness is in each case an expansiveness that goes beyond the limitations of the routine and the commonplace. The corner of the world that we become familiar with is not representative of what lies just over the horizon. Our mastery and familiarity with the daily grind is not enough to enable us to engage reliably with the differences and irregularities that are not far off. The commonplace and regular tends to be narrow and shallow and defensive of its limitations, proud of its self. To break the bounds of such petty identities is to go roaming beyond the restrictions that tie us down. Concern for gain, for prestige, for accomplishment and wealth as set by the social structures within which we function, while it has its value, is too contingent and limited to satisfy sufficiently, and too precarious to satisfy reliably. As one expands the limitations through which one is identified one becomes better able to drift with the current of the way, rather than exhausting one's energies fighting against it. One is also thereby released from the shackles of convention that constrain our choices: vastness is release from ties that condition us to accept social codes and structures as given and beyond critique.

The political and ethical ramifications of this attitude are not entirely clear. They certainly provide a critical force for the tradition to contend with, but it is not clear what values, if any, are to contain this wandering beyond the boundaries. Such an attitude, if allowed to get out of hand, can result in disastrous consequences: the aesthetics of violence espoused by the samurai is an example that immediately comes to mind. There are times when it appears as though Zhuangzi may be willing to take this attitude of openness to extremes, and the writers of the *Shu Zhuang Pai* and of the *Liezi* seem to take up and develop this line of thinking. However, while Zhuangzi provides no explicit safeguards to ensure that transcending social limitations does not justify atrocities, his attitude is in *fact* implicitly constrained by his own concern for human suffering. Indeed, Zhuangzi is evidently moved by a profound respect for people, especially those who are Othered and marginalized, those pushed beyond the boundaries of social respectability.

Nevertheless, if there is any validity to the doctrine of the indeterminacy of meaning, there is no guarantee that even an explicit constraint will succeed in ensuring the humanity of the *zhiren* 至人. Zhuangzi himself, I suggest, provides a model, a paradigm case, for us to intuit the implicit constraints of his 'nomadic' way. It is, as we shall see, the nature of all models, and also of all instructions, that they can not guarantee closure of application. In fact, it is not clear that guaranteed closure of application would necessarily be a good thing. After all, an open society must be capable of critiquing itself at the most fundamental levels. There is, unfortunately, no final, definitive answer to this dilemma. We can, nevertheless, at least attempt to make refinements, and to add more paradigm cases, in the hope of curtailing any tendency toward straying too far from the ethical and into the realm of the brutal.

Before we can begin our detailed discussion of vagueness and the penumbral we need to make an excursion into the philosophy of the Mohists. It is, indeed, the Mohist insistence on clarity, and distinctness of dichotomous boundaries that leads to the meditations on vagueness and boundarilessness in the *Xiao Yao You* and the *Qi Wu Lun*.

CHAPTER FIVE

Mohism: Clarity and Dichotomous Evaluation

The Philosophical Attitude of the Mohists

The development of logic in China is associated with the names of Huizi, Gongsun Longzi, and the later Mohists. These thinkers were fascinated by language, argument, correctness, and distinction making, and so have, somewhat misleadingly, come to be known in the west as Logicians and Sophists. This is an interest that is quite out of the ordinary for early China: one rarely finds contextless discussions of topics on a level of abstraction removed from obvious social applicability. Yet Gongsun Longzi, in the 'Discourse on Indicating Things' *Zhi Wu Lun* 指物論, engages in an extended exploration of the relation of indicating to what is indicated 指, and in the 'White Horse Not Horse' *Bai Ma Fei Ma* 白馬非馬 dialogue, of what is sought for *qiu* 求 to what is brought about *zhi* 致. The later Mohists expend a great deal of effort in developing what appears to be in part a lexicon of philosophical terms, and in part a detailed investigation of the structure of distinction making, and disputation over distinctions.

The later Mohists are often treated distinctly from their earlier forebears, but a fuller understanding of the significance of their claims about language and evaluative judgment results from situating their thinking within the context of early Mohist doctrine. In fact, I believe that it is best to treat the early and late Mohists as continuous rather than as two distinctly placed schools. After the death of Mozi the school split up into three factions, and continued to develop its ideas. This development would have been taking place before and during the life of Zhuangzi and would have reached its culmination after his death, in what we now know as the completed later Mohist *Canon*. The language of the second chapter of the *Zhuangzi* is littered liberally with later Mohist terminology, but the references are not easy to decipher. A thorough investigation of the context and principles of the later Mohist lexicon will give us a deeper understanding of Zhuangzi's response to their precepts.[1]

Hansen and Graham suggest that it was not Zhuangzi who was responding to the Mohists but they who were responding to Zhuangzi's critique.[2] For philosophical reasons I do not find this persuasive. As a response to a cogent critique, the later Mohist precepts are inadequate, since they are very simplistic, and as such demonstrate no deep understanding of Zhuangzi's central concerns. The Mohists simply reassert as philosophical dogmata the presuppositions of which Zhuangzi has given us reason to be suspicious. If they are responding to Zhuangzi, their response shows no evidence of having understood Zhuangzi's criticism. Moreover, it seems that Zhuangzi is using the already established terminology of the Mohists in order to make his points. Now, if the Mohists had been responding to Zhuangzi specifically, they would surely have said so directly. It would not be consistent with their style merely to allude to him, since they were too much opposed to suggestive language. Thus, even if we suppose that it was the Mohists who were responding to Zhuangzi, and not the other way around, Zhuangzi's critique remains unanswered and continues to provide a challenge to the statement of Mohist doctrine.

School

The Mohists constitute an extraordinary group, a mysterious guild or brotherhood of artisan 'logicians,' religious 'empiricists,' pacifist warriors. Their contradictory qualities would seem to make them worthy of Daoist respect, but their limited vision made them the object of Daoist ridicule and criticism. They were also utilitarians and merchants, and after their founding rapidly became the major rival of Confucianism in early China. But after a brief spell of about two hundred years, they simply vanished without a trace. Traditional dates place the founder of the Mohist school from 479 to

---

[1]   The question of balancing our understanding of the later Mohists, modifying the extent to which they are characterized as logical, precise, emphasizing clarity and distinctness, is work to be done in the future. For now the caricature can stand as a temporary foil against which to hone our understanding of the *Zhuangzi.* Further changes in our understanding of the later Mohists will of course result in future elaborations of our interpretation of the *Zhuangzi;* and, of course, further refinements in our understanding of the *Zhuangzi* will enable us to deepen our appreciation of the Mohist *Canon.*

[2]   See for example, Chad Hansen, *A Daoist Theory of Chinese Thought: A Philosophical Interpretation.*

about 368 BCE. He would thus have been the immediate successor of Confucius, and was the first of those recorded who rejected the way of the Ruists. There is a great deal of mystery surrounding the figure of Mozi. Graham points out that 'Mo 墨' is not a traditional Chinese family name. As a descriptive term '*Mozhe*' 墨者, 'the blackened ones,' may refer to carpenters or masons (whose hands were blackened, perhaps by the ink of the plumb line); or it may even have connotations of those who are marked by being branded as a form of punishment. At any rate, it appears that unlike the other *Zi* 子 Mozi did not come from the aristocracy, but from one of the 'lower' strata of society. In chapter 47 of the *Mozi*, King Hui of Chu refuses to grant an audience with Mozi on the grounds that he is a man of base origins, *jian ren* 賤人. In the *Lüshi chunqiu* chapter 21/5 Mozi introduces himself to the King of Chu as a 'commoner from the north' 北方之圖人. He may himself have been some kind of craftsman, since the Mohist school seems to have formed some kind of craftsmen's guild. As the Mohists were also soldiers, it may well have been a guild of artisans connected in some way with warfare. They may for example have been makers of weaponry, as one of the Mozi anecdotes suggests. They constituted an army of defensive strategists, whose aim was to defend the weaker against the aggression of the stronger. Their primary purpose, however, was to prevent conflict altogether. They were thus a guild or brotherhood dedicated to putting into practice their precepts of universal concern *jian ai* 兼愛 and non-aggression.

Though their conception of an ideal society differed from that of the Ruists, they shared much of the same moral language, if not the same values. As with the Confucians, Mozi's concern is with doing what is good for everyone, rather than what is good for oneself alone. This involves cultivating one's person: cultivating moral qualities as embodied by one's superiors, and most especially by the ancient sage kings: sincerity, filiality, considerateness, and so on. Unlike the Confucians, however, it also included frugality almost to the point of abstinence, mutuality *xiang* 相, and impartiality of concern *jian ai*. They rejected the Ruist notion that our love and concern should be greatest for our family and friends and diminish by degrees as emotional distance increases. They were moved by a vision of universal harmony, and at least of an equal distribution of 'welfare' if not of property, privilege, and power. Though they had leanings toward egalitarianism, this did not prevent them from believing in hierarchy and tradition. They were even familiar with the *Shujing* and the *Shijing*, the *Classic of History* and the *Classic of Poetry* beloved of the Confucians, to which they made frequent reference. They often appealed to the practices of the former sage kings in order to make their doctrines convincing. Indeed, appeal to the practice of the former sage kings was one of their three standards by which claims to knowledge are to be tested.

They were a deeply, and perhaps naïvely, religious group. Although they are sometimes described as superstitious, their concern with religion was primarily with institutional religion, the official state religion, not with local practices. There is no mention of any form of shamanism, for example, even when discussing ghosts and spirits. They promoted a state religion as did the Confucians, but they criticized the Confucians for excessive ceremony, and for what they perceived to be too strong an emphasis on the human, *ren* 人, and not enough on the intentions of *tian* 天, 'heaven/nature,' and *gui* 鬼, the ghosts and spirits. This brings to mind Xunzi's criticism of Zhuangzi for emphasizing *tian* at the expense of *ren*. But the Mohist concern with *tian* was very different from that of the Daoists. The Daoist reverence for *tian* was not a matter of fear of the punishment of the ghosts and spirits, but an appreciation for the spontaneous patterns of natural processes.

Given their ability to write, their knowledge of the *Shujing* and the *Shijing*, and their occasional dense and poetic passages, there can be little doubt that the Mohists were educated about the traditions of Shang and Zhou. Their emphasis on simplicity and straightforwardness, however, was very uncharacteristic of the Ruist aristocracy. In many ways, the Mohist insistence on simplicity, straightforwardness, literalness, and explicitness to the point of redundancy is reminiscent of a certain type of common sense philosophy, for which everything that is not clear should be made to become clear. Those who ascribe to such a view are impatient with the richness, ambiguity, and instability of language, and believe that anything that blurs the boundary between clearly defined opposites, has thereby transgressed beyond the bounds of meaningfulness, and has become dangerous. Such suspicions are not altogether without foundation: ambiguities and subtleties may be, and all too often are, exploited for unscrupulous purposes. But an awareness of ambiguity and subtlety also gives one a greater appreciation for the complexities and difficulties of real life, and a greater openness to the unforeseen.

We shall now examine the style and method of the early Mohists, and then investigate some of their basic values and presuppositions. We will then be in a better position to appreciate the social structures and philosophical attitudes that underlie the thinking of the later Mohists. We will also be in a better position to understand not only the logical import of Zhuangzi's suspicions with regard to the later Mohist doctrines about language, meaning, and argumentation, but also the more encompassing social and philosophical implications, and motivations of his alternative view.

Style

言無務為多而為智；無務為文而為察。

As for one's language: do not work to make it verbose, but to make it wise; do not work to make it literary, but to make it careful.

The Mohists are known for their disapproval of extravagance. Chapter 21 of the *Mozi*, 'On Moderation,' extols the virtues of usefulness. Usefulness is explained in terms of benefit to the ordinary people. Anything extraneous is wasteful; all elaboration and sophistication, since they are not of benefit to the people, are considered excessive. When the Mohists preach against music, they are not against the making of musical sounds as such, but against the wastefulness of the expenditure that is required for grand musical ceremonies. They disapprove of this expenditure because of the heavy impositions on the ordinary people that are required for the state to hold such ceremonies. It is not that they lacked aesthetic appreciation; it is rather that they did not see in what way the aesthetic constitutes a genuine necessity, or benefit to the people. This is because they measured benefit only in terms of basic human necessities: food, clothing, shelter and rest. Zhuangzi's predilection for the use of the useless can be construed in part as a response to this utilitarian functionalism of the Mohists. A flourishing life cannot be just a matter of acquiring basic necessities: laughter, play, creative excess are also an integral part of human fulfillment.

The same attitude can be seen in their linguistic style. Their inclination on the whole is toward simplicity; their writing, for the most part, is repetitive and lacking in sophistication. They say what they have to say, and then they say it again. They give several different illustrations, and then say it one more time. No beating about the bush; no playing with words. There is very little in the way of enjoyment of language; they conceived of luxuriating in the pleasures of language as wasteful. Yet it is strange that they did not think of their own repetitive and redundant style to be a kind of wastefulness. For a language as difficult to inscribe as classical

Chinese one would expect an appreciation for economy of words. Perhaps their judgment that such an expenditure of effort was necessary tells us something about how urgently they felt the need to persuade, and so how resistant their audience must have been to their doctrines. Perhaps also, as representatives of a working class, they had no literary context of their own in which to be writing. They wrote in opposition to the Ruists, but were not comfortable adopting the Ruist context which was alien to them. They needed to be understood, and they needed to persuade those who were unlikely to believe them. Hence their emphasis on laboring details, on repetition, on hammering the point home, until there could be no possible doubt as to the truth and obviousness of their doctrines.

Method

Their method of persuasion, unlike that of Confucius and unlike that of the Daoists, was argumentative. The arguments they produced were long and drawn out, formulaic to the point of redundancy. They assert claims, they provide grounds for these claims, and they expect us to be persuaded. They deny the claims of their opponents, and give grounds for rejecting those claims. Their argumentation displays an urgent need to persuade us of the right course of action by demonstrating the disastrous consequences of the various alternatives. They also hope to show us that our current practice may be inconsistent with our desires. They attempt to persuade us through explicit argument, laborious and repetitive, that the most profitable and useful, *yong* 用, course of action is to adopt their principles of action in all things, and that the best way to regulate a society or state is to follow their precepts. This startling new form of persuasion came from the earliest school of thought after Confucius.

Mozi's obsession with justification of his claims is very noticeable. 'How do I know that it is so?' Mozi repeats this refrain often, always concerned to show how he knows, to convince his audience that what he is saying is simple, obvious, and true. He identifies three modes of justification: authority, observation, and pragmatic results. 'Root it in the words and deeds of the ancestors. Source it in the eyes and ears of the people. Use it to see if it brings benefit to the people.' Often the grounds for his claims are historical, or pseudo-historical. He often cites the conduct of the ancient sage kings, claiming that they ruled according to Mohist precepts. In adopting this method of persuasion by example, the Mohists are in agreement with the more traditional style of argumentation of the Ruists. Often the evidence given in answer to the question 'How do I know that it is so?' takes the form of a 'practical logic.' They used imaginary thought experiments to discover the consequences of actions so as to establish not just the best particular course of action, but the best general policy of action. They set up hypothetical alternatives, and follow the consequences of each. One alternative leads to what we desire, the other to what we do not desire. From which they conclude that we ought to do that which leads to what we desire. They thus sought to persuade leaders of the social efficacy of their maxims:

> You desire *X*.
> Doing *Z* brings about *X*.
> Therefore you ought to do *Z*.

> You do not desire *Y*.
> Not doing *Z* brings about *Y*.
> Therefore you ought to do *Z*.

The consequences appealed to at first glance appear to be empirically tested consequences, but on closer inspection they begin to sound more like logical consequences: 'When the eminent and wise rule over the stupid and humble, there will be order; when the stupid and humble rule over the eminent and wise there will be chaos.' It is as though Mozi's real answer is 'It stands to reason, doesn't it?' Mozi thinks that the desirable consequences of his doctrines follow trivially, and thus do not require much in the way of sustained argument, or in the way of empirical testing.

But if the Mohist precepts are so trivially true, it is odd that so much time is spent establishing and reiterating them. Mozi uses the traditional form of parallelism of structure, but takes it to extremes. Parallel structure now becomes repetition of entire paragraphs: argument contexts are repeated several times in their entirety with substitution of relevant variables at each iteration. The Ruists, as exemplified by Confucius, did not waste time making details explicit. Their writing was condensed, and was meant to be understood only from within a certain social context. Mozi, in speaking openly, literally, spelling out explicitly exactly what he is saying, appears to be attempting to communicate outside of that traditional social context.

Though this method of persuasion at first appears very western in style (though more 'Anglo-American' than 'Continental'), the Mohists do not have the push toward sceptical critique, and dialectical refinement, that is so typical of the west. Their logic is still first and foremost pragmatic. Even critique of fundamental notions remains within the context of the practical. It does not occur to them to question every possible contingency, to demand a response to every possible counter-example. The world of social praxis is taken for granted as the context within which all philosophical discussion and dispute should take place. In this respect their methodology still remains thoroughly situated within the sensibility of the Chinese tradition.

The Ideals of Unity and Conformity

> Mozi said, 'In ancient times, when the people were first born and before there were laws (penalties) and government, it is said that people had different values. One person had one value, two people had two values, ten people had ten values—the more there were people, the more the values. Moreover, people approved their own values, and condemned what was valued by others. Thus they all condemned one another. Within the family, fathers and sons, older and younger brothers became resentful and hateful. They separated and dispersed, unable to live in harmony. Throughout the world, people resorted to water, fire, and poison to undercut and harm one another.'

In this passage, Mozi expresses his profound distaste for any sort of pluralism, and his opposition to anarchism. He views contrasting values as necessarily conflicting values. Without unity of value, harmony is not possible. Pluralism is chaos. Just as Hobbes, in the modern west, was to presuppose that the natural, pre-cultivated, human state is one of individualistic self-preservation, so does Mozi assume that the pre cultivated human state is one of a narrow-minded partiality that fears the aggression of others, and is intolerant of difference. Pluralism is the same as individualism, and individualism is lack of mutuality, *wuxiang* 無相. Thus, according to Mozi, mutuality, *xiang* 相, and harmony, *he* 和, require a unity, *yi* 一, that has no room for difference, *yi* 異. If there are any rebellious elements, this unity must be imposed on them for the sake of the harmony of the whole.

A natural harmony, even a dissonant harmony, among a plurality of differing voices is inconceivable to Mozi. Diversity leads only to disagreement, and disagreement leads to conflict. The Mohist conception of social 'harmony' requires unity, sameness of value, identity, exact similarity; it requires a rejection of disunity, plurality, difference of value, non-identity, and any divergence from exact similarity. Thus it is really in the interest of *conformity* that all diversity is to be avoided. This belief that difference leads to conflict depends on a presupposition of a universal tendency to totalization: that each individual will attempt to impose its values on all others, and preserve itself by resisting the imposition of the values of others. If this is the meaning of difference, then certainly pluralism and discord are indistinguishable. This view of difference sees what is Other as wholly alien and dangerous. There is no possibility of communication and no possibility of stability and equilibrium. What is Other, *bi* 彼, is radically and irreparably to be shunned, *fei* 非.

The Mohists see each individual, *ti* 體, as a member that has its place in a whole, *jian* 兼. The whole itself is not just an aggregation of individuals, but is a collection that is hierarchically structured. This hierarchical structuring is the source of the unity and integrity of the whole, and so must be maintained at all costs if the whole is to survive. The wholeness of the whole is contained and preserved by distinguishing it radically from everything that opposes its wholeness, from what threatens to destroy its unity and integration. But, as we have just seen, the units have a tendency to want to disconnect from the whole: their particularity is self-centered, an anti-social source of disunity. In disconnecting, each unit seeks not only independence, but to set up its own opposing unity, one that must impose its difference on the others if it is to avoid being imposed on by the others. Thus, the stability of the whole requires a structure that is in rigid control of the individuals.

Chapter 11, 'Conforming with Superiors,' shows how the Mohist vision of social conformity requires a very specific kind of unified structure—a single thread running through and unifying the whole. If this thread is missing then there is nothing to keep the whole from falling apart, and in the political realm a state of chaos ensues. This unity should be top-down, imposed from above and followed from below. A single 'ruler' is required for the functioning of a group. Order requires an enforced unification of standards of judgment, *shifei*, through systems of reward and punishment. 'In ancient times the sage kings devised the five punishments so as to bring order to the people. These were like the main thread binding a skein of silk or the main cord controlling a net, by which the sage kings bound and hauled in those among the people of the world who failed to conform with their superiors.'[3]

---

3   *Shang tong*, 'Conforming with Superiors,' in *Hsün Tzu, Basic Writings*. I have modified Watson's translation.

The unification of the multitude is possible only by imposition, and this imposition is to be effected by enforcing strict laws (the five punishments). In this way, the Mohists anticipate the Legalist conception of unity through enforced punishments and rewards. Thus, unity is externally imposed, maintained only by force. Hence, the only way that one can attain a state of unity, and thus of harmony, is to impose a single set of standards from above. This unity is then distributed throughout the society as a whole by means of a very specific kind of hierarchical structure. Each member of the whole must take its place on an appropriate level within this hierarchical system. Those at the higher levels are in charge of those at lower levels. The standard of right and wrong to be followed is imposed by the higher levels on those below. At the top of the hierarchical social structure is the emperor, but the emperor is not the author of the standards. The source of the standards by which we are to live our lives, and thus the ultimate source of unity, is *tian*. The Mohists discern its standards by reasoning about the universality of the concern of *tian*, and deriving this from its 'impartiality.'

From the elaborations in chapter 12, a second version of 'Conforming with Superiors,' probably from one of the three factions into which the Mohists split, we can see that the mechanism of conforming to one's superior is that of conforming to the mandates of those above. This is enforced by an extensive system of social surveillance in which the members of the community themselves stand guard against each other. At each level, and throughout the realm, the subjects cooperate in reporting for praise those who conform to the values of those above, and in reporting for punishment those who reject the values of those at the level above. In this way, the natural recalcitrance of each individual is to be reined in with standards rigidly and iteratively maintained from the upper levels to each successive level below, through rewards and punishments. Any individual that attempts to assert its difference must be treated as insubordinate, and since such an assertion of difference constitutes a danger to the whole, it is to be punished.

Thus, difference and partiality are also equated. To be different is to be subversive, to maintain one's loyalties not to the whole but to a *subgroup* whose aim is to overthrow the hegemony of the ruling system. Those whose loyalties are divided in this way are not to be trusted. Only those who remain equally loyal to every member of the whole are trustworthy. Thus, maintaining and enforcing a clear and unbreachable divide between what is within the group, This, *shi* 是, and what is without, Other, *bi* 彼, and therefore antagonistic to the group, is essential to the health and wholeness, and indeed survival, of the group. What lies within is to be approved; what lies without is to be rejected. There are thus two incompatible evaluative attitudes: approval, *shi* 是, and rejection, *fei* 非. What is approved is incompatible with what is rejected, because what is rejected, if given any leeway, will work only to undermine the stability of the system. The Mohists expend a lot of energy cataloging everything they consider to be injurious to the harmony of the social system. In particular they have great misgivings about the values of the Ruists, whom they consider to be extremely dangerous to the health of the state. In the judgment of the Mohists, the Ruists are not only profligate and wasteful, they are elitist and, with their conception of 'graded love,' encourage a partiality that can only be injurious to the whole.

Models and Paradigms

How do we distinguish what is to be affirmed from what is to be rejected? If the people are to be able to report behavior for praise or blame, they need to be able to recognize praiseworthy and blame-worthy behavior. In chapter 35, 'Rejecting Destiny,' *Ming* 命 'mandate; calling; life; that with which we have no choice but to deal', we find the statement:

> 必立儀，言而無儀必由運均之上而立朝夕也。是非利害之辯，不可
> 得而明知。

> It is necessary to establish a model; preaching a doctrine without a model is like marking the hours of night and day on a turning potter's wheel. The distinction between right and wrong, benefit and harm, cannot be attained and clearly understood.[4]

Without clear cases, models, and paradigms that exemplify the values being taught, there can be no clear application of value judgments. Now, a model is a particular instance that demonstrates the ideal qualities by which other cases are to be judged; a paradigm is not, as is sometimes thought, a general style of thinking, but a *particular* example that is typical of its kind. They have a particular usefulness for practical action since they rely on natural processes of recognition and do not require unwieldy attempts at clarification and verbalization. What the Mohist empha-sizes is the necessity of paradigms for successful practice of a

---

4   Chapter four, *Hsün Tzu: Basic Writings.*

doctrine. Without clear exemplars one cannot be sure about what to do, or how to behave, what to praise or what to blame, what to reward or what to punish, what to approve or what to reject.

'Master Mo said, "All those who conduct their affairs cannot do so without models and standards. There have been no cases of those who have been able to be successful in their tasks without models and standards. Even accomplished officials about to take up a high ministerial position all have models. Even the most accomplished workers performing their tasks have models. A worker uses a square edge to make a square, uses compasses to make a circle, makes vertical with a plumbline, and straightens with a filament." ' Notice how Mozi juxtaposes the accomplishment of the manual worker with the accomplishment of an official in a high ministerial position. Whether this is deliberate or unconscious, it indicates the social strata that are closest to Mozi's concerns.

Now, it is not obedience to a *rule* that the Mohist says is necessary, but emulating a standard, imitating a model, an example given as a paradigmatic instance. A rule is an instruction attempting to describe literally, preferably without resort to imagery or metaphor, what ought to be done in what circumstances. The aim is to be as explicit as possible, ideally leaving as little room as possible for interpretation. The success of the applicability of the rule depends on the degree to which the description is exhaustive and precise. In the interest of clarity, these conditions are specified as literally and clearly as possible in order to minimize the possibility of vagueness and overinterpretation. A paradigm is not a description, but an actual example. The example is supposed to be self-explanatory. Although there are many qualities instantiated by the example, the context is supposed to be sufficient to allow it to function as an exemplary model by which to judge other instances. The success of the applicability of the paradigm depends on the degree to which the relevant desirable qualities are immediately recognizable. Ideally, a well crafted rule, and a well chosen paradigm will be easily applicable for most situations: there should be relatively few problematic cases. However, problem cases cannot be ruled out entirely for either rules or paradigms. When applying a rule, one needs to recognize whether it is appropriate for a particular case, whether it is *similar enough* to what is specified in the rule. When applying a paradigm, one also has to judge the degree to which the case in question is *sufficiently like* the paradigm. There will inevitably be times when the case in question cannot be easily classified. In these cases, there is room for judgment. Paradigms provide explicit instances, and rules provide explicit descriptions, but interpretation is necessary in both cases.

One always has to judge *to what extent* the test case is like the paradigm, or to what extent the situation in question matches the description, and so neither rule nor paradigm necessarily succeeds in determining all instances. This is something that will prove problematic for the Mohists, and of interest to the Daoists.

Now, the paradigm cases of paradigms given by Mozi are utterly precise! Square edges, compasses, and plumb lines do not admit of much leeway in their application at all. These are the kinds of models that the Mohists were used to using on a daily basis, as craftsmen and artisans. If one does get creative in one's application of the edge, there is little that one can do that will not be immediately *recognizable* as 'deviant.' Given that the Mohists think of paradigms in these terms, they do not anticipate the limitations that can arise with other kinds of paradigms. In particular, they are unaware of how imprecise concepts of human significance can be. They believe that good and bad behaviour can be modeled as simply and precisely as with the tools of carpentry.

The later Mohist *Canon*

The later Mohist *Canon* is another ancient Chinese text that is exceptionally difficult text to decipher. After the demise of the Mohists, there was little active interest in the *Canon* beyond keeping it preserved for posterity. The philosophy behind it was lost more than two thousand years ago. In the last hundred years or so there has been a resurgence of interest, and scholars have attempted to reconstruct its ideas. But this text, despite its explicit concern with clarity, *ming* 明, and distinction, *bian* 辨, remains dense and pithy almost to the point of impenetrability. Valiant attempts have been made to restore the philosophical significance of the *Canon*. But we must not be misled by the preciseness of the reconstructed doctrines into assuming an equal precision in their abduction. Despite the explicit demand for clarity, the sentences are highly enigmatic, and often far from easily intelligible. They often require considerable emendation (itself a highly suspect practice, despite its indispensability). For these reasons the most elaborately structured of reconstructions are often highly tentative.

Though the Mohists aimed for precision, they used a language whose openness resists such precision. Their sentences aim to defy the openness of the classical written language; but, of course, that very openness of the language creates a formidable obstacle to the process of its own refinement. They attempted to sharpen the edges of a soft, fluid language—but could do so only with the soft, fluid tools of that very language itself.[5] The very project of using indeterminate tools to increase the determinacy of those very tools themselves is a laborious process that is hampered by an infuriating and paradoxical circularity, but it is not impossible. Our way in (and perhaps even theirs) to a clear understanding of their newly defined, newly refined terminological system, is not evident. The best we can do is to construct possible systems that are compatible with what we have left of their 'definitions.' Of course, the Mohists would not have been able to close off meanings with any finality. As we shall see in later chapters, one's success in warding off intruders must always be finite, as indeed is one's success in recognizing what counts as intrusive, and distinguishing it from what is intrinsic. But this does not mean that one cannot increase the *degree* of precision, or decrease the degree of indeterminacy relative to some context or purpose. Indeed, that this is possible is established quite straightforwardly by the fact that it is actually the case! Scientists, lexicographers, and philosophers spend large amounts of time increasing the precision of their definitions, just as technologists make more precise equipment with less precise tools. But, if the Mohists opened up a space for the dialectical refinement of the medium of language, the process of refinement and closure seems to have come to a halt with the demise of the Mohists themselves.

Clarity 明 and Knowing

A3–A6

知,材也。	知也者:所以知也而必知。	(若明。)
慮,求也。	慮也者:以其知有求也,而不必得之。	(若睨。)
知,接也。	知也者:以其知過物而能貌之。	(若見。)
{智},明也。	*{智}也者:以其知論物而其知之也著。	(若明。)

Understanding is a capacity. As for understanding, it is the means by which one knows, and thus surely knows. It is like clarity.

Deliberating is seeking. As for deliberating, using the understanding one also seeks but does not necessarily obtain. It is like glancing.

Knowing is connecting. As for knowing, using understanding one experiences a thing and is thus able to recognize (describe) it. It is like seeing.

---

5   On the fluidity of the classical Chinese written language, see Marcel Granet, 1934. *La Pensée Chinoise.*

> Wisdom is clarity. As for wisdom, using understanding one discusses a thing and one's understanding is manifest. It is like clarity.

The metaphors used to gloss these 'epistemic' terms include *cai* 材, timber (raw material, talent, capacity, stuff), *qiu* 求 seeking, *jie* 接 connecting (touching, making contact). 'Making contact' characterizes 'knowing' as an achievement word: while deliberating seeks but does not necessarily obtain, knowing also succeeds in making contact.[6] But most significantly for our concerns, knowledge and understanding are explicated by the Mohists in terms of similes of light, vision, and clarity: 睨 *ni*, to glance; 明 *ming*, to be clear; 見 *jian*, to see, to appear; 著 *zhuo*, to be bright, evident. Clarity, as we shall see, will be associated with distinction making: distinctions and judgments should be made simple and clear, so that they can be easily understood and followed. The Mohists construe *ming* as a form of evidentness, what appears clearly to be so. It is so clear that what one knows is certainly known; thus, *zhi* 知, is the capacity to see clearly what is manifest: to see what is so, and to distinguish it clearly from what is not so. Zhuangzi will also use the term *ming* but the sense he will give it contrasts dramatically with the straightforward usage of the Mohists.

The Mohists are also concerned about making clear the distinction between knowing and not knowing, a distinction that the Daoists are keen to undermine. None of us has complete knowledge: we have knowledge and lack knowledge; we have understanding and lack understanding. The Mohists resolve this by distinguishing clearly between knowing or understanding, and what is known or understood, and by distinguishing clearly between what is known and what is not known:

B48
知其所不知,說在以名取。雜所智與所不智而問之,則必曰,"是所智也,是所不智也。" 取去俱能之,是兩智之也。

One knows what one doesn't know. The explanation lies in choosing according to its name. If one is confused about what one

---

6   The term *qiu* seeking is taken up by Gongsun Longzi in the *Bai Ma Fei Ma* dialogue, in which we see the beginnings of an intuition of 'intentionality' being worked out. A4 tells us that what we seek we do not necessarily obtain. Gongsun Longzi shows us that whether we obtain what we seek depends on how we describe it.

knows and does not know, one must inquire into the matter. Then one must say, 'This is what I know, and this is what I do not know.' When one is capable of both choosing and discarding, this is knowing them both.

B37

於一有知焉,有不知焉,說在存。石一也,堅白二也而在石。故有智焉,有不智焉,可。

With regard to one thing, one has knowledge about it, and one has ignorance about it. The explanation lies in what is there. A stone is one thing; but hard and white are two and are in the stone. Thus it is possible for one to know (something) about it, and to not know (something) about it.

That is, one may know the stone and not know the stone insofar as one knows that it is white but does not know that it is hard. One may see that it is white and assume that it is made of chalk and therefore soft, whereas in fact it is a piece of coral and so is hard. What one knows and does not know of something are a matter of distinguishing what makes it up, *cun* 存.

A81 聞,(博)*傳,親。或告之,傳也。身觀焉,親也。

Becoming aware: passing on; personal. Someone reports it: this is passing on. One observes it in person: this is personal.

This section distinguishes two modes of becoming aware, one direct, the other indirect. What one observes in person is knowledge that one can trust. But we can also become aware of something without having direct experience of it. We can be informed about things by other people. Bertrand Russell makes a similar distinction between knowledge by acquaintance and knowledge by description. When one hears a description one first of all knows what it is that is said, but one also thereby knows something about the object of description. My nephew, Paris, lives three thousand miles away, and I have never met him, but I know that he has just learned to crawl, because my brother told me so. Indeed, if I were to trust only what I had personally experienced, there is very little that it would be possible for me to know. The vast majority of what I claim to know is what I have learned from others. In chapter 16, 'Impartial Concern,' Mozi justifies his doctrine of impartial concern ('universal love') by showing that it was practiced by the sage kings. But it is clear that he could not have personally observed the practices of the ancient sages. 'I am not a contemporary of theirs, did not hear their sounds, or see their forms. I know it from what was written on bamboo and silk, inscribed on metal and stone, engraved on ceremonial vessels, and passed on to the descendants of later generations.' Again, universal concern implies being concerned about people I do not know, people I have never met, and never will meet. But surely one can be concerned only about what one knows about. The Mohist replies that I can indeed know about people I am not personally acquainted with by hearing about them through report. And I can know about them by learning that they are just *like* the people I do know.

B70   聞所不知若所知,則兩知之。說在告。

One hears that something one does not know is *like* something one does know, and thus one knows them both. This is explained by *reporting.*

In this way one is able to expand one's knowledge. All one needs to know is that something one does not know is like something one does know, and that suffices to know it. Thus am I able to know about those I do not know: all I have to learn is that they are like those I do know and so have concern for them, and I can learn this by report, whether written or spoken. This expansive move, enlarging one's horizons from what one knows to what one does not know, is something we shall find echoed in Zhuangzi's philosophy only with a very different significance.

Language

Chinese philosophy from its very beginnings has been concerned with language and meaning. The senses of language that engage Chinese philosophers are several: 言 *yan*, the teaching of doctrines, passing on of ways *dao* 道, of doing things and ways of understanding the world; 名 *ming*, 命 *ming*, the naming of things and stations, declarations of ministerial edicts; 書 *shu*, the writings that pass down the histories and traditions; the meanings of specific words expressing value; and even the general relations of these to the worlds they describe and evoke. The Confucian *Analects* can even be understood as a sustained series of meditations on the meaning and significance of the value terms of Confucian philosophy.

The students of Confucius would often ask him 'What is *ren*?' Confucius would respond with a very personalized and specific characterization. The kind of responses Confucius gave indicates the nature of the discourse within which such questions were formulated. It is easy for a western philosopher to confuse this question with a demand for a clarification of an essence: that is the typical philosophical context in which such a Socratic sounding question would occur. But to transfer such a context of discourse to Zhou dynasty China results only in confusion. By examining Confucius' style of answering we can recover something of the presuppositions of Confucian discourse. Confucius' students asked about *ren* because they wanted to understand what *ren* is. But understanding what *ren* is in the context of their discourse is not a matter of knowing its essence, through articulating its single, correct definition. One might rephrase their questions more literally as, 'What about *ren*?' and gloss this as, 'What do *you* say about *ren*?' Confucius' students wanted to know how to recognize *ren* when they came across it; and they wanted to be able to put it into practice. But they wanted to be given *examples* and *admonitions*, not fixed and final 'definitions.' Most importantly, they wanted to know how *Confucius* thought about it. They wanted to know what Confucius specifically had to say, what kinds of people and behavior Confucius would value. They wanted to know how to cultivate themselves in a manner of which Confucius would approve. It is significant that they continued to ask after the same terms, and each time Confucius responded with a very different kind of reply. They did not imagine for an instant that any one of his sayings could exhaust his understanding. Their conception of the meaning and significance of these terms was one that allowed their understanding to deepen and grow, sometimes with new possibilities and on occasion in surprising directions.

Confucius would always respond with a pithy phrase encapsulating one aspect of his attitude, an aspect that was appropriate for that particular questioner on that particular occasion. The purpose of his utterance was not to begin an argument over whether or not he was *right*, whether or not he understood *ren* correctly. It would be entirely inappropriate for his interlocutors to respond by thinking of a counter-example! The accounts that Confucius gave were not intended as foolproof definitions. He was not engaged in a dialectical search for the Form of *ren*ness. Thus, the function of a Confucian dialogue contrasts starkly with that of a Platonic dialogue. The purpose of discussing virtue with Plato was most definitely *not* to find out what Plato thought about virtue, or to be given examples of virtuous behavior and virtuous people, but to engage with him in an argument, composed of tentative definitions, followed by counter-examples, and rejections or refinements of those definitions: hoping always to approach closer and closer to *the* correct understanding of the pure essence of virtue itself.

A definition *defines*. It *delimits*, strives to reduce openness, and to achieve closure, finality.[7] It aims to bring to clarity and distinctness what was previously 'only' intuitively understood. To strive to define a term, in this sense, is to strive to close off explicitly any uncertainty about its meaning, to respond to all possibility of sceptical critique, to achieve a *final* statement about *what it is*. There can be little doubt that this is not the purpose of dialogue in the Chinese philosophical tradition. For this reason I hesitate to apply the term 'definition' to the concern with meanings typical of most early Chinese philosophical texts. The explanations of terms are certainly pithy, and as such are intended to 'distill the essence' of the term, as it were. But the kind of 'essence' they attempted to encapsulate was not considered to be final and definitive: it was not a matter of getting right the necessary and sufficient conditions for the application of the term.

It is no exaggeration to say that the question of Being, the issue of '*what it is* to be' and of '*what it is* to be so' have negligible significance in early Chinese philosophy. Part of the reason for this is that there is no counterpart to the western concept of Being, and the reason for this is that *there is no single word in classical Chinese that performs the multifarious functions of the verb 'to be.'* The western concept of 'being' is an amalgamation of its three basic functions: existence, identity, predication. These three are, from a logical point of view, quite distinct functions: they cannot be reduced to one another. The word can be used by itself to indicate that something exists. Indeed, the word is often thought of as simply synonymous with 'existence.' But, this is quite strange, since its most common functions are to express identity and predication, and is very rarely used to point out that something exists. It is more commonly used to make an identity statement: 'The Morning Star is the planet Venus,' 'Neo is the One.' Two things that one might believe to be distinct are asserted to be one and the same. Most commonly, the verb functions predicatively as a copula. Most subject-predicate languages require that the predicate of a sentence either be a verb, or contain a verb. If the predicate is adjectival, then a verb is required to 'couple' the subject to the predicate in order to complete the sentence. Any verb that functions in this way

---

7   There are, of course, other senses of 'definition' but I am using the term in a quite specific sense: the sense in which a definition picks out necessary and sufficient conditions for the application of a term.

is a copula. Three of the most basic copulae in western languages are: 'to be,' 'to seem,' and 'to become.' Thus 'Being,' 'Seeming,' and 'Becoming' become three of the most basic western philosophical concepts. When the verb 'to be' is used emphatically— 'What *is* a human?'—it seems to reach deep into the object of inquiry, past the superficial and accidental, and into its very core, its very essence. Thus, this concept of Being, at least as understood in Greek ('*einai*'), German ('*Sein*'), and English, is a complex fusion of existence, essence, and identity.

Now, in classical Chinese, these three functions are performed separately. Existence is usually indicated with the word '*you*' 有, occasionally with '*cun*' 存 or '*zai*' 在; identity with the final particle '*ye*' 也, or more emphatically with the word '*nai*' 乃. The equivalent of predication is performed by *juxtaposition* of the term that expresses the topic with the term or phrase that constitutes a comment on the topic. The sentence may or may not end with the particle '*ye*' 也, for clarity or for emphasis. Though there are words that are able to perform a copulative function in Chinese (the most notable being *wei* 為) none of these is necessary, and none of them carries any connotation either of essence or of existence. It is important to realize that there is no temptation to conflate these words or functions in the classical Chinese language into a single concept. The use of the word '*you*' 有 as a straightforward translation of 'Being' is thus highly misleading.

Early Chinese texts do however often contain passages in which the significance of a term for a particular thinker is spelled out in terms of *clusters of associations*. The typical form of these glosses is X為Y也 'X *wei* Y *ye*.' The word that functions as a copula here, *wei*, has several meanings. Its primary sense is 'to make' or 'to do'; it also means 'to deem,' 'to be deemed,' 'to call,' 'to be called,' 'to take as,' or simply 'as'; and it can sometimes be conveniently, if incompletely, rendered in English simply as 'to be.' It can be approximated with the phrase 'to act as.' But it is important to keep in mind that it is not grammatically necessary, and when it is used the senses of 'acting,' 'making' and 'calling' are definitely operative. Now, whether it is the first or the second term that is being explicated depends on the context. And most often the explication consists of a single word or a set of words that are by no means synonymous with the term in question. Such clusters of associations provided by philosophers in their explications of key terms emphatically do not spell out necessary and sufficient conditions for the application of the term, or for being what is deemed.

Each philosopher gives his account, tells his own story, about how the most important words and ideas connect together. A為B也. A *wei* B *ye*; or, A也者謂之B. *A ye zhe, wei zhi B,* 'As for A call it B.' This is a stipulation about how evaluative terms are to be associated. Let us take things of this sort to be admirable; let us take things of that sort to be admonishable. Thus, such texts are not so much dictionaries as *manifestos*. Each amplification on a term is an exhortation. In the *Analects*, each exhortation is a response to request for elucidation, and is appropriate to the circumstances at hand. In one context, the question has one significance: it arose in response to particular issues, and the answer will be tinged accordingly. In other circumstances, or in talking to a different inquirer, different aspects will surface as relevant. By collecting these sayings, one builds up an under-standing of how the speaker values things, how they recommend that we live our lives. By cogitating on the connections between the terms, and between the sayings, one further develops one's linguistic web of understanding. But the web remains open; and different cogitators will continue to weave the fabric in different ways. In this way, as the webs begin to diverge, followers develop into different schools, or scholars develop rival interpretations.

The later Mohist *Canon* continues this concern for explicative commentary on a term. They also wanted to understand the significances of terms, to become clear about their terminology. But for them it was a matter of compiling a glossary or a lexicon: a text in which one could look up a fixed characterization of the term in question. The Mohists thus attempt to be more systematic than Confucius. While they are still not interested in discovering the essence of some particular virtue, the definition of a term, they nevertheless do desire to simplify its usage, by giving a *single* account that will *always* remain appropriate regardless of context. Thus they sought to provide an understanding of the term that would be applicable in all contexts. They did not continually ask after the same term, giving different characterizations each time, as did Confucius. Nor did they strive to provide complex definitions with the aim of articulating refinements that reach closer and closer to the truth. Rather, they gave only one clarification, though sometimes in the form of a couplet, once and for all. Now, applicability to *all* contexts is not really possible, even as an ideal, without a sustained dialectical refinement of one's understanding. But, the Mohists did not take seriously the unlikely possibilities that might be dreamt up by a sceptic, and instead confined their clarifications within pragmatic constraints.

Meaning, reference, and time

Despite the Mohist concern with finality in their accounts of terms, their understanding of how terms gain application to things takes place within a thoroughly *processive* world view. The unstated presupposition is that things are always changing. The Mohists are interested in how words relate to things, and how they fail to relate, and they explain this in temporal terms: relating and failing to relate are thought of, not as abstract forms, but as processes in time. They focus specifically on how a term may fail to relate. The Mohists identify two ways in which a term can fail, '*guo*' 過, to apply, '*zhǐ*' 止. It may simply fail to match the object at any time, and it may fail to match the object for some period of time. The matching of a term to a thing is called 'pausing,' '*zhǐ*' 止. The metaphor is revealing: it implies a refraining from movement, a stability of placement that is only temporary. The word can stop with the thing, but only for a while.

> A50
> 止,以久也。無久之不止,當牛非馬。(若*矢過楹。)有久之不止,當馬
> 非馬。(若人過梁。)
>
> Applying: because it endures. The not applying on account of lack of enduring: as in 'A cow is not a horse.' It is like an arrow having missed 過 its target. The not applying on account of some enduring: as in 'A horse is not a horse.' It is like a person's having crossed 過 a bridge.

The Mohists are aware, then, that terms are applicable *zhi* 止, 'pause,' only so long as the thing, or perhaps the characteristics of a thing, endures *jiu* 久. After the duration of the thing, or its characteristics, the term is no longer applicable. There are then, two kinds of not applying, *buzhi* 不止. The first is where the characteristics do not endure *at all* in the object, *wujiu* 無久, and the second is where there is some enduring, *youjiu* 有久. These are each illustrated in terms of two senses of *guo* 過, crossing; going past, that exemplify two ways of being mistaken. *Wujiu zhi buzhi* refers to the term's not being appropriate because the characteristics do not endure at all in the object. The example given can be taken as indicating that the word 'cow' does not apply to a horse, and *vice versa*. The explanation is that a cow (or rather its characteristics) does not endure at all in a horse, and *vice versa*. This is failing to hit the mark at all: in the way that an arrow misses, *guo* 過, the post altogether. The second type of non-application *youjiu zhi buzhi* refers to the term's not being appropriate when there has been a period in which the relevant characteristics did endure in the object. That is, the term did apply for a while, but now that the thing has changed it is no longer applicable: as when the word 'horse' is no longer appropriate as a descriptor of what was once a horse (referring to its remains after its death for example). This is like a person's having crossed, *guo* 過, a bridge. This last example will prove to be of great interest to Zhuangzi, and as we shall see, in my reading he will use it to undermine the system being set up by the Mohists.

The Mohists also recognize the possibility that some characteristics may continue to last indefinitely.

A51

必,不已也。謂*{商}熟者也。(若弟兄。)一然者,一不然者,(必)*止不必
也,是非必也。

Necessarily: unendingly....Like elder and younger brother. If one case is so, and another case not so, then necessarily it is not necessary: this is the non necessary.[8]

Some terms always apply; there is no ending *buyi* 不已 to their enduring, like the relation between elder and younger brothers: the younger can never catch up or take over! They are always elder and younger, and so the Mohist says that they are necessarily so, *bi* 必. However, if once it may be so, and then it may not be so, that is, if the circumstances can differ, then the application of the term to the object is surely not necessary. Now, *yi* 一 may mean 'in one case,' but it can also have the sense of 'once' or 'at one time,' and since the initial gloss makes a reference to the temporal notion of ending, it seems appropriate to take it in the temporal sense. Thus, necessity and contingency are understood in terms of change and lack of change. If it is always so, we may say

---

8   Graham has suggested emending the first *bi* in the last sentence to *zhi*, so that it reads 'If one case is so, and another case is not so, then the application is not necessary.' Since the sentence is intelligible as is stands, I prefer to keep it without emendation. The second sentence, on the other hand, I do not find intelligible, and have simply inserted an ellipsis into my translation.

that it is sure (necessary/certain); if it is sometimes so, and sometimes not so, then it is unsure (uncertain/not necessary). It is noteworthy that the explicit definition of necessity is in terms of actual endurance and change, not possible endurance and change. The Mohist conception of necessity is thus not a concept of strict necessity, but of strict universality. In the example given of the relation between elder and younger brother, it is not just that this relation does not change, but that it *cannot* change. But the Mohist definition does not make reference to this impossibility! Now, in classical Chinese there is no tradition of emphasis on strict universality, or strict necessity. I have found no other texts that explicitly insist that *bi* allow for no counter-examples, and none that insist that there be no possible counter-examples. Nor have I found any that in practice attempt to refute a *bi* claim with counter-examples (actual or possible). Here, however, we seem to have the insistence that if at any *time* it is not so, then we cannot call it 'necessary.' This appears to be the first time that a characterization of a term explicitly requires strict universality, though again we must keep in mind that this does not amount to strict necessity. Of course, my acquaintance with the long and monumental tradition of classical Chinese texts cannot but be minuscule, and may not constitute a fair sampling, but I would not be surprised if this concern with necessity, or strict universality, began and ended with the later Mohists.

The *Canon* explicitly takes up the theme of the changing of characteristics, in its account of the term *hua* 化 'transformation.'

A 45 化,徵易也。〔若{蛙}為鶉。〕

> Transformation: the characteristics change. It is like a frog turning into a quail.

Transformation is glossed as the change of signs, marks, characteristics. Graham notes that the change of signs is associated with transformation also in the *Xunzi* and in the *Lüshi Qunqiu*. The example given, of a frog turning into a quail, seems peculiar: frogs do not turn into quails. Both animals, however, do call to mind typical processes of transformation, indeed of metamorphosis: from tadpole to frog, and from egg to bird, and one would expect either of these to be given as an example. I hesitate to suggest appropriate emendations to the text, but in this case it would be unproblematic so long as independent graphic evidence could be culled to support it.

Now, it is this understanding of change that will, in Zhuangzi's hands, lead to the unraveling of the Mohist system. However, the Mohists do not appreciate the significance of this acknowledgment of transformation for the kind of clear distinction making that they praise. They are indeed so aware of change that they define their linguistic jargon in terms of change and enduring. But they do not seem to notice the gradual and graduated nature of such change. Or, if they see it, they are oblivious to the significance it has for their ideals of clarity and distinctness. They see that when things endure a term will apply; when they change the term will no longer apply. But there is no mention of the interim, no appreciation of the significance of the process of transformation itself.

Paradigms and Models

The *Canon* again takes up the early Mohist theme of paradigms and models, and expands on their significance at length. Paradigms are related to criteria, being so, similarity, and exactitude.

> A70　法,所若而然也。意規員三也,俱可以為法。

> Paradigm: what it is similar to in order to be so. The idea, compasses, a circle: these three may all be taken as paradigms (of a circle).

Here, as with the early Mohists, we have a recognition of the role of standard exemplars for the making of judgments. And again, as with the earlier Mohists, the paradigm cases of paradigms are exact, leaving barely any room for openness of application. The paradigm case of knowledge for the Mohist craftsmen involves the use of compasses and squares to reproduce circles, angles, verticals, and straight edges. And when one is making tools for efficiency of use, general approximation and imaginative re-interpretation are more likely to be a hindrance than of much help! Hence, as technicians the Mohists valued exactitude, and their ideal paradigms exemplified this value. We see this characteristic of such technical models and standards stated quite explicitly in the following:

> B65
> 一法者之相與也盡,若方之相(召)*合也。說在方。方貌盡,俱有法而異
> ,或木或石,不害其方之相(台)*合也。盡貌 (若方也),物俱然。

As for the correspondence (with its objects) of a single paradigm, it is exhaustive. It is like the mutual matching of squares. The explanation lies in the square-edge. The limning of squares is complete: they all follow the paradigm, though they may be different, some wooden, some stone, yet this does not diminish their mutual matching. They are all like the square-edge, and so all the things are so.

Here the exactness of match is expressed in terms of 'exhaustiveness' *jin* 盡 of 'correspondence' *xiangyu* 相與. The fit is exhaustive. All squares are alike in terms of their shape: they all match one another by tracing completely the guidelines formed by the shape of the paradigm, the carpenter's square. All squares are isomorphic with the paradigm of a square.

A71　(侔)*因,所然也。然也者,*{貌}若法也。

The criterion: is where it is so. As for being so, it is because the characteristics are like the paradigm.

The criterion, *yin* 因, is the characteristic in virtue of which an ascription is made, in virtue of which something is deemed to be 'so' *ran* 然. Thus being white in color might be the characteristic in virtue of which something is deemed 'white':

B70　是若其色也,若白者必白。

This is similar in color: being similar to the white, it is surely white.

Again, having a mane and pulling a chariot may be characteristics in virtue of which something is deemed to be a horse:

A85　命之馬,類也。若實也者,必以是名也。

Naming it 'horse' is categorizing: being like the object, we must surely use this name.

Dichotomous Values

Opposites have been categorized into two kinds by Aristotle: contraries and contradictories. Contradictories are dichotomous opposites: they cannot both be present, nor can they both be absent. The presence of either necessitates the absence of the other.

Contraries are mutually exclusive, but they are not dichotomous opposites: the presence of one displaces the presence of another, but the absence of one does not necessitate the presence of other. 'Red' and 'not red' are contradictories; 'red' and 'green' are contraries. Contraries and contradictories are defined in terms of logical properties. I would like to suggest a type of opposite defined pragmatically: contrasts are opposites that show up in our dealings with the world, they are differences of which we are intuitively aware because of our natural capacities, and our pragmatic needs and functions. Contrasts can show up in pairs, but they can also show up in larger sets. All sets of subcategories into which we intuitively classify things constitute contrasts. The significance of contrasts will reappear in the next chapter, in our consideration of Daoism.

Evaluative contrasts—merit and fault, benefit and harm, praise and blame, reward and punishment, affirmation and rejection—are central to almost all Chinese philosophical thinking. As we have seen, with the early Mohists, these opposites must form a clearly constructed system of mutually exclusive values, and thus approach the status of contradictories, otherwise one will be paralyzed in action. Praise and blame will not be clearly merited; and reward and punishment will be meted out inappropriately. Without the clarity of stark contrasts between distinct opposites, there can be no standards, no reliable modes of behavior. If one does not know that virtue will be appreciated, if one cannot be sure that virtuous behavior will not be punished, then one cannot act confidently, and may not act acceptably.

In the *Xiao Qu* 'Minor Selection' chapter of the later Mohist *Canon*, sections 6A/9 to 6B/1, we come across the following gloss on the term for disputation, *bian* 辯:

夫辯者,將以明是非之分,審治亂之紀,明同異之處,察名實之理。

As for disputation 辯, we use it in order to clarify *ming* 明 the distinction *fen* 分 between right and wrong *shifei* 是非, to examine the rules of order and disorder, to clarify the points of sameness and difference, and to inspect the patterns of names and objects (claims and achievements).

Thus, disputation is intimately bound up with making clear the boundaries between opposites. Indeed, the term for disputation, *bian* 辯, is almost interchangeable with its cognate, *bian* 辨, 'distinction,' and we can think of it as disputation about the distinction between alternatives. Now, the motivation for disputation over distinctions is intimately bound up with the purpose of taking control of social order and testing merits of entitlement. The purpose of disputation is to bring to light the distinction between opposites so that they can then be known, and edicts understood and acted upon.

A29-30 譽,明美也。誹,明惡也。

To praise: is to make clear the admirable (beautiful). To blame: is to make clear the detestable (ugly).

Note the function of *ming* 明 here. It means to make plain, to make evident. To praise is to bring into the light what is admirable, *mei* 美; to blame is to bring into the light what is contemptible, *e* 惡. To praise is to make clear that someone is admirable; to blame is to make clear that someone is contemptible. While there is no direct claim of mutual incompatibility, such an emphasis on the clarity of the distinction between the two does not leave much room for an appreciation of their compatibility. Indeed, we have already seen in B48 that the Mohists insist on the possibility of distinguishing aspects when distinguishing what is known from what is not known. In this case they would be likely to make a similar demand: if something is both admirable and contemptible, then one must be able to distinguish where it is admirable and where it is contemptible: '*This* is what is admirable; *that* is what is contemptible.'

Benefit and harm are characterized in terms of likes and dislikes, *xi wu* 喜惡.

A26-27:

利,所得而喜也。得是而喜,則是利也。其害也非是也。
害,所得而惡也。得是而惡,則是害也。其利也非是也。

Benefit: is what you gain and take delight in. If you gain *this* and take delight in it, then this is a benefit. If there should be any harm, it is not *this*.

Harm: is what you gain and detest. If you gain *this* and detest it, then this is a harm. If there should be any benefit, it is not *this*.

Notice that these characterizations turn harm and benefit into *mutually exclusive opposites*: if there is something that is harmful, then it is not what is pleasing, and so is not beneficial; if there is something that is beneficial, then it is not what one detests, and so is not harmful. The Mohists refuse to accept the possibility that something might be both beneficial and harmful. They feel the need to be clear about such distinctions, especially about benefit and harm, praiseworthy and blameworthy behavior, because they see this as essential to the health and welfare, and indeed survival, of the whole. The dichotomous system of evaluation to which they are prone gives them little alternative.[9]

Dichotomies and Disputation

Now we come to a more abstract discussion of opposites. The Mohists discuss this under the title 'Same and Different' *tongyi* 同異 and thus makes explicit their recognition of the role of similarity and difference in the making of judgments. Things are judged to be of a kind and requiring the same name, that are *alike*. As we saw in A85 above, 'Naming it "horse" is categorizing: being like the object, we must surely use this name.' And again in B70 'This is similar in color: being similar to the white, it is surely white.'

    When grouping together things that are paired as same and different, we arrange things into opposites. The *Canon* distinguishes two kinds of opposites:

    A88
    同異。

---

9   The shaman, as healer, is perhaps more likely than an artisan to be aware of the ambivalence of his/her potency *de* 德. The skill of healing, for example, depends on an understanding of how natural substances can be both beneficial and harmful. A drug is both a medicine and a poison. There are times when a drug may be beneficial, and times when it may be harmful. But more significantly, there are times when it is both beneficial and harmful. Chemotherapy is both beneficial and harmful—indeed, beneficial because it is harmful. By flooding the body with a powerful poison one hopes to kill off the greater harm. Indeed, in many, if not most, difficult decisions, we compromise: we choose something that may not be ideally beneficial, but that is harmful to a minimal acceptable degree. For the reasons we have discussed, the Mohists are reluctant to countenance such possibilities: because of the dichotomous system that the *Canon* sets up, it is impossible for them to see how to deal with such situations. Note that an acknowledgment of the ambivalence of some situations, does not entail the ambivalence of all, and thus does not undermine the distinction between benefit and harm. It undermines only the *dichotomousness* of the distinction.

交得放:　　　　有無, <多少, 去就, 堅柔, 死生, 長少

兩絕勝:　　　　是非, 成未, 俱適, 存亡, 姓故, 貴賤>

Same and different:
Interdependent and complementary: something and nothing; more and less; away and towards; harder and softer; dying and living; older and younger.
Antagonistic dichotomies: **affirming and rejecting** *shifei*; completed/not yet; proceeding together (?); present/absent; (??); noble/base.

Differences fall into two kinds: those that are interdependent and complementary, and those that are dualistic and antagonistic. From the examples given, we can infer that interdependent and complementary opposites are relative opposites and a matter of degree: having and lacking, more and less—these, according to the Mohists, make sense only as comparisons. Interestingly enough, even 'living and dying,' 'older and younger' are not taken to be absolute opposites. These are unlike the first four examples in that the change goes only one way: from living to dying, and from youth to age. But they are like the former insofar as they are relative to each other and a matter of degree.

Evaluative judgment between alternatives, *shifei* judgment, falls into the second category, 'alternatives, separate and vanquishing, *liang jue sheng* 兩絕勝,' or 'antagonistic dichotomies.' Affirmation and rejection are neither relative nor by degrees; they are two separate and opposing attitudes, one side of which must win, as we shall see below. It is here that we reach the heart of the dispute, as I construe it, between Zhuangzi and the Mohists. Zhuangzi maintains that what may appear to be antagonistic dichotomies are really interdependent and complementary— especially the opposites of affirmation and rejection.

B35: 辯也者, 或謂之是, 或謂之非, 當者勝也。

As for disputation: one calls something affirmatively, another calls it negatively. The one that matches wins.

Disputation gets another gloss in B35, and it is here characterized in terms of *shifei* judgment. It is contending over the alternatives of affirmation and negation, which as we have just seen are antagonistic dichotomies.

A74

辯,爭(攸)*{反}也。辯勝,當也。或謂之牛,或謂之非牛,是爭(彼)*{反}也。是不俱當。不俱當,必或不當。(不若當犬。)

> Disputation is contending over alternatives. Victory in disputation is to be correct/match. One says it is an ox, the other that it is not: this is contending over alternatives. These do not both match. *If both do not match then one must not match....*

Here we have the statement that such alternatives 'do not both match.' It is explicitly stated only in the assertoric mood and not as a necessity. However, the sense of the claim in context suggests again that the Mohist would agree also with the claim that they cannot both match. This would also explain the categorization of *shifei* judgment as mutually exclusive alternatives. It cannot be that something is the case and that it is not the case. This is as close as we get to a statement of a principle of contradiction. The last sentence asserts that in any disputation one of the disputants must be wrong. This does not yet tell us that one of them must be right. But it appears that this does follow from the following:

A73 (攸)*{反},不可兩不可也。凡牛,樞非牛,兩也。無以非也。

> Opposites: it is *not acceptable to have both alternatives unacceptable*. All oxen partitioned off from non-oxen are the two alternatives. There is no way to reject [both].

My justification for interpolating the word 'both' in the second sentence comes from the first sentence, which explicitly states that it is not acceptable to have both alternatives unacceptable. At most one alternative may be unacceptable, which means that at least one must be acceptable. If it is possible for both sides to be unacceptable, then they are not alternatives that the Mohist would describe as mutually exclusive opposites. Thus, since contraries *can* both be false at the same time, argument over contraries would not count as disputation. Note that Mohist logic takes acceptability *ke* 可 and unacceptability *buke* 不可 as basic, where we talk of 'truth' and 'falsehood.' These evaluative terms are quite explicitly normative: one's claims are judged according to their acceptability.

Disputation sets up distinctions, or antagonistic dichotomies, between mutually exclusive opposites: acceptable 可 and unacceptable 不可, correct 當 and incorrect 不當. The boundary between these opposites is fixed and clear, and this clarity is necessary to enforce conformity with the values imposed from above, which in turn is necessary to ensure the proper functioning and well being of the social system.

     Zhuangzi's political intuitions are very different. His mode of thinking arises out of the Daoist appreciation for the cycles of natural change. As we have seen, the Mohists are aware of transformation, and indeed their philosophy presupposes a world that is changing. But paradoxically, the sharpness of the Mohist ideal arises because they have too crude a vision. They see only black and white, acceptable and unacceptable. They fail not only to appreciate the significance of the transition between the two, but they fail to notice these border regions altogether. We shall now pick up our philosophical backpack and journey back south to the state of Chu. Here we shall try and awaken our peripheral awareness, and draw our attention to the field of vagueness in which Laozi's words are embedded.

CHAPTER SIX

Vagueness and the *Laozi*[1]

The writings of the early Daoists are permeated with the unmistakable flavor of vagueness. The highly metaphorical, laconic, and imagistic text of the *Laozi* seems, for better or worse, to have all the determinacy of a Rorschach blot. The text communicates with suggestive and paradoxical language that may at times encourage the interpreter to blur just a little *too* quickly the boundary between reading into and reading out of the text. But vagueness is not just a stylistic quirk of Daoist writing, it is also important as a philosophical theme. It is on occasion taken up explicitly, but it is not expounded on at any great length. So the question arises, 'What clues are there to uncovering the significance of vagueness in the *Laozi*?' The purpose of this chapter is to bring to light, or perhaps 'reconstrue,' one manner in which vagueness informs, as a kind of inchoate presupposition, the process oriented world view expressed in the *Laozi*. By 'inchoate' I do not mean to suggest that this understanding is undeveloped or lacking in sophistication, only that it remains unfocused, throwing a diffused light from the periphery.

The concept of vagueness in western philosophy and linguistics

Vagueness in general

Vagueness is itself a notoriously vague concept! It may have any or all of several meanings: the term is often used loosely to refer to linguistic phenomena such as ambiguity, polysemy and metaphor, and even just plain uncertainty and confusion. It has important similarities with the concepts of family resemblance and open texture, which will be explored in the next chapter. An expression is ambiguous if it embraces several quite distinct meanings, such that the context in which it is embedded will not isolate which of them is the correct meaning. Thus, in the sentence 'I shall go to the bank by

---

[1]   A version of this chapter appears in *Philosophy East and West*, Vol. 54 No 4, 2002.

the river' the word 'bank' is ambiguous: the context is not sufficient to determine whether the speaker is going to the riverbank or to a financial institution. Polysemy is the deliberate use of such multiplicity of meaning for whole sentences, paragraphs, and even complete texts, with the intention of expressing all these meaning possibilities simultaneously.[2] Poetic, mythical, and religious texts especially work in this way: one may, for example, identify the literal meaning, the historical reference, and the spiritual signifi-cance of a genesis poem.[3] Metaphorical language involves the non-standard usage of a term according to peripheral meanings set by analogy, or culturally defined similarities that guide the meaning, while still leaving open the particular unfolding of the meaning of the metaphorical expression.[4]

All these strategies and devices can be found in both Western and Chinese philosophy—but in Chinese philosophy they have generally functioned as an integral and *necessary* part of philosophical writing, while in Western philosophy they have all too often been identified, either as rhetorical flourishes with no cognitive value, or as seductive and deceptive evils. As we have seen, this self-conscious distrust of open language and elaborate literary tropes seems to have been almost entirely absent from Chinese philosophical writing, with a few notable exceptions, such as the *Xunzi* and the later Mohist *Canon*.[5]

Vagueness proper

The term 'vagueness' as it is used in the philosophical and linguistic literature, refers not to confused and uncertain language, nor to all forms of indeterminacy in general, but to one particular kind of indeterminacy of meaning, and it is this concept that will provide the key for our exploration of the two major Daoist texts. It was the Stoics who first emphasized and problematized the phenomenon of vagueness, and they did this primarily by noticing

---

[2]   Umberto Eco has contributed much that is insightful to the interpretation of polysemic texts through his discussion of 'isotopies.' See, for example, his book, *The Role of the Reader, Explorations in the Semiotics of Texts.*

[3]   The alchemical texts of the Renaissance period seemed on the surface to tell strange stories, but to those with the keys to decoding them they gave explicit instructions for concocting elixirs and potions, and also contained secrets about the metaphysical structure of the universe.

[4]   See Eco, *The Limits of Interpretation*, and also, *Semiotics and the Philosophy of Language.*

[5]   See, for example, Granet's *La Pensée Chinoise.*

the logical paradoxes to which it gives rise. Their example was that of the 'heap,' *soros*, for which they constructed '*sorites*' paradoxes, which we shall examine below. Such paradoxes can be constructed from any vague concept, typical examples of which include 'bald,' 'tall,' 'thin,' and 'red.' A vague concept has traditionally been characterized as one for which there exists a class of borderline objects—that is, objects of which the concept could meaningfully be predicated, but about which there is no definite answer to the question 'Is this object correctly so described or isn't it?' Thus, a shade between red and orange, or a person who has lost quite a lot of hair may furnish borderline instances of the concepts 'red' and 'bald.' Mark Sainsbury has challenged this traditional understanding (that the presence of a class of—actual or possible—borderline cases is definitive of vagueness), and shows how the mere phenomenon of such a class need not result in genuine vagueness.[6] As Sainsbury points out, a class of borderline objects may *itself* have sharp boundaries and thus need not exemplify the most characteristic logical properties of vagueness, which we shall recount in the section below. His preferred formulation defines a vague concept as one that lacks sharp boundaries. A sharp boundary exists when every possible individual in the vicinity of the boundary falls determinately on one side or the other of the boundary.

With vague terms there is no clearly marked boundary demarcating what falls within the territory of the term, and distinguishing it from what is alien. Applicability of a vague term becomes a matter of degree: as one moves further and further away from standard cases, it becomes gradually less and less clear whether or not the term may still be applied. At some stage it definitely has no applicability, and here we have reached the territory of the standard non-cases, but the transition to this stage does not occur across a sharply defined boundary. Instead, there is a *continuum of gradual differentiation* from one extreme to the other. Such a series of differentiated objects may be modeled heuristically by envisioning a single object undergoing a continuous transformation.

Imagine a freshly sprouted sapling, for example, which will eventually become a fully grown tree. Now, the word 'tree' is itself ambiguous: in one sense a sapling already is a tree, insofar as it is a plant of a certain kind. But in another sense it has not yet become a tree, insofar as the word is used to refer to a fully grown specimen. At which precise moment will it become a tree? At the

---

6   See Sainsbury, 'Concepts without boundaries,' in *Vagueness: a Reader*.

moment it reaches ten feet in height? At eight feet perhaps? Or if becoming a tree is a matter of maturation, at what precise moment of maturity does the change take place? Of course, such a question is absurd—there is no such precise moment. Growth is a long process, and the sapling that starts out as not yet a tree will eventually mature into a fully grown tree, but there is no single moment at which a sudden and miraculous change takes place—there is no sharp boundary separating its being a tree from its not being a tree. In this way, the concept 'tree' may be said to be vague. If one is not fully persuaded about the ambiguity of the word 'tree,' then think about the sapling. At what precise point does it cease to be a sapling? Is there a precise height, or a precise moment of maturity? At what precise moment does a child become an adolescent, or an adolescent become an adult? At what precise moment do we stop being young, and start being old?

These transitions do not occur in an instant—there is a period, an extended period of slow, relentless, and barely discriminable transformation from one to the other. The immediate logical consequence of this seemingly trivial (and deliberately laboured!) point is startling. If there is a period between being a tree and not being a tree, then there is a period when it is not true that the object is a tree, and it is not true that it is not a tree. Now, it is important to stop and think about this carefully. It is a simple logical consequence, but it is one that cuts deep into one of our most basic intuitions, and the psychological resistance to accepting it can be overwhelming. Now, according to the Principle of Bivalence, which many people take to be an axiom derived from plain common sense, any sentence can have, and must have, only one of two truth-values: either it is true or it is false.[7] Truth and Falsehood are mutually exclusive opposites defined by their opposition and by the sharpness and unbreachability of the distinction between them: if something is false it cannot be true, and if it is true it cannot be false. Moreover, if it is not true then it must be false, and if it is not false then it must be true. Now this is a fundamental and highly intuitive principle, but as our equally

---

[7]   The principle of bivalence may be expressed formally, quantifying over propositions, as follows:

$$\forall P \, (|P| = T \lor |P| = F)$$

A stronger version implying exclusivity of truth and falsehood would be:

$$\forall P \, [\, (|P| = T \lor |P| = F) \, \& \, (|P| = T \iff \sim |P| = F) \,]$$

intuitive musings on the concept 'tree' have shown, this common sense 'law' is broken by a very ordinary common sense concept. For such an intuitive law of logic to be violated by such an ordinary concept under such mundane circumstances, is no trivial matter. If even our most exemplary concepts wreak logical mischief, then there is a serious conflict between our ordinary everyday concepts, which tend in this way to be vague, and our logic as most intuitively formalized—our simplest and most basic intuitions are inconsistent.

But our problems do not end with the flouting of a single logical principle. The Law of Excluded Middle, and what has been considered the most sacrosanct and inviolable of all laws, the Law of Contradiction, may also be violated by vague concepts. The Law of Excluded Middle tells us of the content of any proposition that either it *is* so or it *is not* so, or of any object and any appropriate descriptive term, either the object *is* correctly described by the term or it *is not*.[8] There is and can be no middle ground, nothing between 'is' and 'is not.' To use the terminology of western ontology, 'Being' and 'Non-being' are mutually exclusive alternatives, and there are no cracks, no fissures for anything to slip in between. With all due respect to Descartes and his medieval predecessors, the Law of Excluded Middle entails that it makes no sense whatsoever to talk of 'degrees of Being.' There is no middle ground, no in-between, no penumbra between the light and its shadow. This is another obvious and intuitive principle. Yet as we have just seen in the case of our plant that is no longer a sapling, and yet has still not become a tree, with vague concepts it is not only not simple or obvious, the

---

[8]   The law of Excluded Middle can perhaps be thought of as the first order counterpart of the second order Principle of Bivalence. The latter is a metalogical principle determining the number of possible truth values. Thus it is possible to construct logics that reject the Principle of Bivalence: multivalent logics, for example, that allow more than two truth values, some that even allow an infinite number of truth values.

In symbolic terms, the law of excluded middle may be given form, quantifying over propositions, as:

$$\forall P \ (P \lor \sim P)$$

or in terms of second order predicate calculus:

$$\forall \phi \forall x (\phi x \lor \sim \phi x)$$

law simply does not hold.[9] That is to say, there is a period of *becoming*, between being so and not being so, in which neither is definitely the case.

Finally, and startlingly to our most treasured logical intuitions, we may even in some circumstances be tempted to classify the penumbral object as *both* falling under and not falling under the concept. The penumbral status of the object makes us reluctant to issue a judgment one way or the other. But a persistent questioner may not be satisfied with our hesitation. Some people are made very uncomfortable by the presence of indeterminacy, and their discomfort is not altogether without justification. If we are pushed to respond, we sometimes feel that the most appropriate and least misleading response is not 'yes,' 'no,' or 'neither'—but 'both'! The 'yes and no' response is not that uncommon. Sometimes the 'yes and no' answer is appropriate because the question is ambiguous: in one sense 'yes,' but in the other sense 'no.' But sometimes it is appropriate because the key term in question is vague, and the object or circumstance that it describes does not determinately fall on one side or the other. It is a tree *and* it is not a tree—not just in different senses of the word, but in the same sense, at the same time, and in the same respect. In this way, the logical principle that we hold with the deepest conviction, the Principle of Contradiction, is also violated.[10] It may be objected that

---

9   Let 'a' be the name 'Alice' and 'Tx' be the predicate 'x is tall.' Then in the penumbral region, the following will be true: 'It is not the case that Alice is tall and it is not the case that Alice is not tall.'

$\sim Ta$ & $\sim\sim Ta$.

From this, we get, by De Morgan's equivalence:

$\sim(Ta \vee \sim Ta)$.

Performing first and second order existential generalizations yields:

$\exists\phi\,\exists x\sim(\phi x \vee \sim\phi x)$,

which can be shown through quantifier equivalences to yield:

$\sim\forall\phi\,\forall x(\phi x \vee \sim\phi x)$,

which itself is a direct denial of the Law of Excluded Middle as formulated in note 11.

10   The principle of contradiction may be formalized as follows:

admitting contradictions destroys the possibility of logical reasoning, since anything follows from a contradiction. But that anything follows from a contradiction is not a fact, but a theorem of standard bivalent, truth-functional logics. However, non-standard logics have been developed that reject this principle, and the rule of inference that depends upon it, *reductio ad absurdum*.[11] It would thus seem that it is some such non-standard formalization of logic that maps more closely our natural modes of reasoning. Note, again, that this contradiction is neither meaningless nor an obstacle to communication. On the contrary, if you wish to know whether or not a particular sapling I planted has become a tree, and I reply 'Well, at present I suppose I should say that it is and it isn't,' you would in all likelihood know exactly what it is that I am trying to say! Rather than inferring that I must have lost my sense of Reason, or my capacity to communicate in English, you would probably infer that the plant must lie somewhere in the penumbral stages of growth, between being a mere sapling and being a fully grown tree. Note also that this violation, which entails that the sentence is *both* true *and* false, is inconsistent with the violation of the Law of Excluded Middle, which entails that the sentence is *neither* true *nor* false! Thus, the penumbra of vague concepts is a shadowland of paradox. Vague concepts violate apparently inviolable laws, and they do so inconsistently.

It is quite common for philosophers and logicians to dismiss such concepts as anomalies—exceptions to an otherwise well-defined and logically well-behaved language. However, when we stop to make an inventory of exactly which concepts are vague, and at exactly how and why they are vague, we find that the list of offenders expands and multiplies until the pressing question becomes not 'Which concepts are vague?' but 'Are there any concepts that are not vague?' Bertrand Russell, in his infamous

---

$\forall P \sim (P \mathbin{\&} \sim P)$

or in terms of second order predicate calculus:

$\forall \phi \forall x \sim (\phi x \mathbin{\&} \sim \phi x)$.

[11] See for example, Rescher and Brandom, *The Logic of Inconsistency: A Study in Non-Standard Possible-World Semantics and Ontology*, and Graham Priest's, *In Contradiction: A Study of the Transconsistent*, and Susan Haack's, *Deviant Logic: Some Philosophical Issues*. Some of these alternative logics attempt to preserve the principle of contradiction, but can only do so by adopting a non-standard semantics or ontology.

1923 paper[12] that revived the problem of vagueness for twentieth century philosophy, commenting on the law of excluded middle, says:

> Baldness is a vague conception; some men are certainly bald, some are certainly not bald, while between them there are men of whom it is not true to say they must either be bald or not bald. The law of excluded middle is true when precise symbols are employed, but it is not true when symbols are vague *as, in fact, all symbols are.* (emphasis added)

Indeed, the purpose of Russell's paper was to demonstrate that *all* concepts, including logical ones, are vague. If indeed all or even most concepts fail to obey the laws of logic, this is a matter for serious concern. This is not the place to scrutinize Russell's arguments, but I believe that he is right that the majority of our everyday concepts—observational concepts that are empirically acquired, and concepts of ethical and social relevance, pragmatically acquired concepts in general, have the property, not only of vagueness, but of several other forms of indeterminacy as well.

In Galen's *On Medical Experience*,[13] we read of the consequences of *sorites* reasoning on any concept that involves a degree of magnitude:

> According to what is demanded by the analogy, there must not be such a thing in the world as a heap of grain, a mass or satiety, neither a mountain nor strong love, nor a row, nor strong wind, nor city, nor anything else which is known from its name and idea to have a measure of extent or multitude, such as the wave, the open sea, a flock of sheep and herd of cattle, the nation and the crowd. And the doubt and confusion introduced by the analogy leads to contradiction of fact in the transition of man from one stage of his life to another, and in the changes of time, and the changes of seasons.

According to Galen, concepts that admit of degree are susceptible to *sorites* paradoxes and are thus vague. Any term which we may qualify with such hedges as 'quite,' 'very,' or 'extremely' will then be vague. Concepts that have exemplars that admit of degree, that have better and worse examples, will thus also seem to qualify.[14] Now, while it is true that vague concepts admit of degree, I am not

---

12   Bertrand Russell, 'Vagueness,' in *Vagueness: a Reader.*
13   Galen, 'On the *sorites*,' in *Vagueness: a Reader.*
14   Lakoff and Johnson explore this phenomenon, which has sometimes been confused with vagueness, in *Women, Fire and Dangerous Things.*

sure that it is true that all concepts that admit of degree, or that have better and worse examples, are necessarily vague. The fact that some shades of blue are 'bluer' than others does not *by itself* entail that blue is a vague concept, or the fact that penguins are much less 'bird-like' than sparrows, and whales much less 'mammal-like' than cats, does not *by itself* entail that these concepts are vague. Nevertheless, there is a close connection between degrees of exemplification and lack of sharp boundaries, that means that in practice such concepts are indeed as a matter of fact vague. And this, I believe, is the value of Galen's point.

I believe that the phenomenon of vagueness is intimately tied to our natural recognitional capacities, since our natural recognitional capacities always have their parameters of limitation. There are limits to our capacities to make immediate intuitive discriminations. Suppose that there were a precise wavelength at which colors change from red to orange, a last shade of red, and an exact instant at which an adolescent turned into an adult. This sharp dividing point would be perceptually inaccessible to us, and so the manner in which we use these terms would still exhibit vagueness. Moreover, since our worlds are constructed by our concepts, and are not less real for that, and since our pragmatic concepts are vague, I take it that vagueness is as much a characteristic of the world as it is of our epistemic access to it, or indeed of our language.

Now, if vague concepts wreak such logical havoc, how do we as a matter of fact make judgments in the borderline regions? My question is not about what enables us to make such judgments, though this is an important question, but simply about the manner do we actually do so. It is my contention that in such regions, which have come to be known in the literature by Russell's evocative metaphor as the 'penumbra' of the concept, our attitudes and intuitions are variable, they are shifting and unsettled. We may, for example, in some circumstances and under some conditions consider objects in the penumbra as falling into *neither* the positive nor the negative extension of the concept, that is, as neither correctly nor incorrectly described by the term in question. This, indeed, is the manner in which we dealt with the concept 'tree' in the example as it was described above. To decide that the plant is neither a tree nor not a tree, however, is perplexing, since we see clearly that the penumbral case is one to which the concept is, and ought to be, applicable. We may, alternatively, be fickle in our application of the term. That is, we may be inclined at different times to take the penumbral case as falling under the concept or under its contradictory, even without any clearly relevant contextual differences. Now, although in making any such specific decision, we make a determinate choice with regard to any particular instance of a borderline object, the logical problems referred to above do not thereby disappear. On the contrary the logical problems still remain, since the characteristics of vagueness typical of *the penumbral region as a whole* will not be affected by a single, arbitrarily made decision.

It may be thought that the reason for this sort of indeterminacy is that a final decision cannot be made by a single individual, and that the corroboration of a community of language users is required for arbitration. This view however runs into the difficulty that in the penumbral regions different equally competent users of the language will often have different intuitions, responses and judgments, and that these responses will themselves typically be different at different times.[15] In fact, one might insist that it is precisely because of the indeterminacy of community usage that such terms are used *incorrectly* if they are used precisely! In every one of these cases, despite the difference of decision (or lack of decision), the language has been used correctly—complete understanding of such pragmatic concepts of natural language *requires* the uncertainty and indeterminacy of borderline cases.

Now it is important at this point to make several clarifications. The first, *pace* Williamson, is that our inability to make a decisive judgment on one side or the other in the penumbral regions is not a matter of having insufficient information. We may know the exact height of a person and still be at a loss how to answer the question. We may see the exact colour of an object, even know its precise wavelength, and still be unable to classify it as a case of orange. We may know exactly what mood we are in, and still be unable to decide whether or not it counts as being happy. A person with powerful realist intuitions might reply that the reason we cannot make a decision is that we still do not know everything relevant: we still do not know where the objective boundary lies. From my anti-realist position, I would raise a rhetorical question: does it really make sense to talk of objective boundaries to socially constructed pragmatic concepts?

The second clarification is that while it may be possible to replace the vague concept causing the uncertainty with a less vague one ('of medium height,' for example), this does nothing to resolve the logical problems that follow as a consequence of *the vague concept itself*—it is merely an evasion of the issue. In a similar way,

---

15 See Max Black, 'Vagueness: an exercise in logical analysis,' in *Vagueness: a Reader.*

distinguishing senses of words by adding restrictive or qualifying clauses may produce an acceptable description of the penumbral object, but it does not and cannot remove the vagueness (and therefore any ensuing logical problems) of the *original* expression.

One final clarification must be made, and it is one that is especially important to issues concerning interpretation of the *Zhuangzi*. It is important to distinguish the indeterminacy that is due to vagueness from the sort of indeterminacy that arises for relational concepts—a favourite notion of interpreters of Zhuangzi. Words like 'short' and 'tall' are not only vague, their application is *also* always relative to some context. From the point of view of a Watutsi or a Scandinavian, a person who is 5'10 is short, while from the point of view of a Pygmy the same person is tall. This perhaps can be considered a kind of indeterminacy, insofar as there are always many such contexts from which different acceptable judgments may be made. This kind of indeterminacy results simply from *failing to specify the context* relative to which the judgment is to be made. It is not the same as the indeterminacy due to vagueness. Once the specification has been made ('Is 5'2 tall *for a Pygmy?*'), the indeterminacy that is due to context-dependence, or relationality, vanishes. The indeterminacy that is due to vagueness, on the other hand, still remains, for it is a phenomenon that is completely context independent. The answer to the question, 'Is 5'2 tall (for a Pygmy)?' remains stubbornly entrenched in the penumbral region.

There is another way in which vagueness gives rise to contradiction and paradox, and that is through the infamous *sorites* paradox of the Stoics. The word '*sorites*' is derived from the Greek word for heap, *soros*, the paradigmatic example of vague concepts since the Stoics first drew attention to them in the West. In the following, I present an intensified version of the *sorites* paradox, replacing macroscopic grains with microscopic specks of dust, a version that makes the truth of the premises, and thus the soundness of the argument, more obvious and persuasive. Now, it will readily be admitted that one speck of dust does not constitute a heap of dust. Moreover, the addition of only one more speck of dust to a dusty spot will not be sufficient to transform the dusty spot suddenly into a heap of dust—one single speck of dust can never make that much difference by itself. These two truths are so trivial as hardly to need stating, yet their consequence, their deductively valid logical consequence,[16] I hasten to add, is that no amount of

---

[16] Some writers describe this phenomenon as the 'fallacy' of the heap, with reference to its use in slippery slope arguments. Strictly speaking this

dust could ever constitute a heap! At each addition of a speck of dust we are forced to concede that that speck cannot turn the 'non-heap' into a heap of dust! Thus, since we are forced to concede this at every addition, the spot can never become a heap. But if no spot can become a heap, then no dusty spot has ever become, nor ever will become a heap. Thus, there are no heaps of dust, nor will there ever be, not just as a matter of fact, but as a matter of logical necessity![17] What is perhaps even more disturbing is that the *sorites* paradox runs both ways. It is clear that one cannot destroy a heap of dust merely by removing one single speck of dust. But from this we can logically conclude that everything is a heap, since eventually even zero specks of dust will constitute a heap. Similar paradoxes can be generated for any vague term, and therefore, with almost every empirical observational term, and with terms that are of human, social, or ethical relevance—any 'pragmatic concept'— simply by considering the gradual temporal process of transformation from what is not so to what is so, and *vice versa*. Indeed, the very possibility of generating such a *sorites* continuum may be taken as a touchstone of vagueness, as this image of a smooth

---

is incorrect. The argument form is a deductively valid one, at least according to traditional logics. In fact, the natural intuition on which it depends can be modeled and formalized as a mathematical induction, defined over a *sorites* series $\{0, n, ...n_m\}$ the first member of which has a property, P, and the last member of which lacks P. Then:

1. $P(0)$
2. $\forall n[P(n) \Rightarrow P(n')]$
3. $\forall nP(n)$

from which in turn it follows that $P(n_m)$, where n' is the successor of n, and the successor function is defined such that the unit of succession involves no significant difference between n and n' (or for maximum plausibility no discernable difference).

17   Note that, despite the superficial resemblance, these paradoxes of transformation do not have the same function as the Eleatic paradoxes of change, which are supposed to show that something cannot become what it is not. The *sorites* paradoxes are not designed to prove, and neither do they imply, the impossibility of change. On the contrary, it is taken for granted that change is possible, that something can indeed become what it is not. The problem raised by the Stoics may rather be expressed as a dilemma relating negligible and significant changes: for vague concepts the accumulation of negligible changes logically can be shown never to add up to a significant change; but we also know from experience that the accumulation of negligible changes does indeed add up to a significant change.

transition encapsulates the intuition that a vague concept cannot have sharp boundaries.[18]

Traces of Vagueness

Reflecting on these processes of transformation we may focus our attention on several distinctive factors. Firstly, there is a pair of complementary *opposites*: one finds a term and its contradictory, or in terms of the extensions of the concept, an object that instantiates a quality and an object that lacks that quality. Next there is *transformation* from one of these to the other. That is, one may typically imagine an object that has a property or quality changing into one that lacks it. What is not tall, for example, becomes tall, what is red becomes not red; one who is happy becomes unhappy, and so on. Incidentally, there are two points to be noticed about this 'process' of transformation. The first is that one does not require an *actual* process of transformation between opposites, but only the *possibility* of transformation. If a concept is vague, then all that is required is that one be able to conceive of possible processes of transformation from objects that instantiate the concept to those that instantiate its contradictory.[19] The actual temporal transformation is not strictly necessary, nor is the actual existence of objects exemplifying intermediate, or penumbral, stages of the process. The second is that the possibility of transformation is not by itself a sufficient condition for vagueness. What is required—the next characteristic that is relevant for our concerns—is a *continuum* of transformation from one to the other. The *sorites* process, or series, must form a smooth continuum of transformation such that any two adjacent stages in the process, or objects in the series, must be observationally indistinguishable (with regard to the applicability of the term in question). Any discretely observable change between the property and its opposite—any sharp borderline—will render empty

---

[18] Suppose we run through the argument again, replacing imperceptible specks of dust with beans or pebbles. Then we might say for a certain size and shape of pebble, that four pebbles appropriately placed does indeed constitute a heap, or even, for another size and shape of pebble, that three pebbles appropriately placed constitutes a heap. Does this show that 'heap' is not a vague concept? Clearly not. The fact that a concept is vague does not mean that it has no clear instances of application. All that is required for the concept to be vague is for there to be instances of application that are not clear.

[19] We may distinguish the *sorites* process—the gradual process of transformation between opposites—from the *sorites* series—a static series of objects, derived by reifying selected stages of the *sorites* process.

the penumbral region of borderline objects. The connection between process and vagueness is thus manifested when process is conceived of as the temporalization of such a continuum.

Thus, boundarilessness, penumbral objects, contradictoriness, the possibility of *sorites* paradoxes, as well as the presence of opposites, of transformation, and continuity, are all distinctive characteristics of vagueness, and as such will give us very strong textual clues to the relevance of vagueness as an implicit theme. We are now ready to begin our task of locating these textual traces of vagueness in the text of the *Laozi*. As we proceed, the poetic, suggestive, and metaphorical nature of Chinese philosophical method will be readily noticed, and the need for our switch from an analytic to a semiotic methodology in reading these texts will become evident.

Vagueness in the *Laozi*

The *Laozi* is, together with the *Zhuangzi*, the earliest of the texts that express the nature oriented philosophy that appears to have originated in the southern state of Chu—the school that has come to be known as 'Daoism.' The idea that has taken central place in Daoist philosophy, and after which it has been named, is that of 'the way, *dao* 道.' For the early Confucian tradition of the central plains '*dao*' referred primarily to the ways passed on by tradition: the human ways of social interaction encoded, with greater or lesser flexibility, by the cultural canon, and inculcated through social praxis. For the Daoists *dao* was associated more directly with the intricate, spontaneous and chaotic regularities of nature than with what they conceived to be the artificial regularities of culture. One must, however, resist the temptation to see these two as mutually exclusive. Indeed, the Confucian *dao* was flexible and highly sensitive to the intricacies and complexities, and unpredictability, of human interaction. While the Daoists observed the patterns of nature to provide a model for human life and social interaction, and even for the governing of a state.

The world as it is depicted in the *Laozi* is one that undergoes constant change, alternating with complex interacting cycles of growth and decline: expanding and contracting, tightening and loosening, sharpening and wearing down, swelling and subsiding. The direction of movement that the *Laozi* emphasizes, in what A. C.

Graham characterizes as a 'deconstructive' move,[20] is what we might portray as the phase of 'decline.' Indeed this is one of the distinctive traits of Daoist thought—this preference for the weak, the soft, the dark, the retreating the counterpart (though by no means the equivalent) in the Chinese tradition of the western *via negativa*. The Daoists observed that the phase of decline is the process of returning to the root, the 'origin,' the source of energy that enables the processes of growth and maturation to take place. This 'origin' is not an absolute 'nothingness' out of which things are once and for all 'created,' but more like the source of a river, a wellspring which itself needs to be replenished if it is to be inexhaustibly productive. It is conceived of as a womb in which energies may be rejuvenated, before giving birth once again to light, heat, sharpness, and strength. It is, according to the *Laozi*, this constant returning to the origins that is the source of the longevity and inexhaustibility of the world of nature. In this way, the text describes poetically, metaphorically,[21] in the most general of terms, how the changes of the world take place, and urges us to adopt these modes of change in our own interactions with the world. When we exemplify this *dao* in our lives, we are then able to engage with the world more efficiently, successfully, and productively.

Thus, there are many themes at work giving the text its recognizably Daoist flavor: returning to the source, naturalness and simplicity, the emphasis on the feminine, the dark, the retreating, the mutual dependence and transformation of opposites. I shall now proceed by scouring the text for traces of vagueness, which I shall classify under the following headings: a) vagueness and the penumbral, b) opposites and transformation, c) growth and decline d) *sorites* paradox and contradiction, and e) boundarilessness and continuity. We shall find reference to vagueness, and much discussion of growth, decline, and the transformation of opposites. However, we shall also find that the connections between these characteristics are not explicitly treated in the text. Although, with this highly condensed and poetic text it is only to be expected that explicit connections should be few and far between. If the vagueness referred to is a result of *sorites* processes, for example,

---

[20] One that 'transvalues' a traditional ordering of values. See Graham, *Disputers of the Tao: Philosophical Argument in Ancient China*.
[21] This is a clear instance of how different Chinese philosophical methodology is from the dominant methodology of the west. Generality of description is achieved by explicit and deliberate metaphor, rather than by an attempt at refining a literal set of necessary and sufficient conditions to capture what is universal.

this is not unequivocally stated. There are also frequent references to paradoxes and things penumbral, but again, the text is not explicit about the extent to which the paradoxicality arises from the penumbral stages of transformation. Whether and to what extent this reticence weakens the plausibility of the abduction I leave to the reader to decide.

The footnotes to each heading cite chapter numbers in which these characteristics are discussed with greater or lesser explicitness. In order to be as persuasive as possible, I try to limit my citations to passages that do not require controversial interpretation.

Vagueness and the penumbral[22]

> The way as a thing, is confused, obscure, *hu xi huang xi* 忽兮恍兮
> confused! obscure! inside there are images
> obscure! confused! inside there are things
> hidden! darkly! inside there is something seminal
>   *Laozi,* chapter 21

The *Laozi* is, in many ways, an elegy to vagueness. The intimations of vagueness are both explicit and implicit. To the extent that this concern is explicit, however, the significance of this vagueness does not have an immediate and obvious affinity with the significance of linguistic vagueness as it has been conceptualized in the western tradition. This ought not to surprise us. If the *cultural significance* of concepts is a function of their historical development, then it would be astonishing if we were to find direct parallels of concern and of methodology between these two cultural traditions. Only those who believe that philosophical thinking reveals concepts of *a priori,* universal significance, would expect this to be the case. But one may even concede the presence of concepts of universal concern without being committed to their having universal cultural significance. Broadly speaking, a Chinese philosophical generalization has a different function from a generalization of a modern western philosopher. For the latter the aim is usually to arrive at a formal or structural analysis. The questions guiding the process of philosophical analysis might be 'What are the universal characteristics determined by the concept? What are the necessary characteristics?' In the Chinese tradition, on the other hand, the context of discussion tends to be pragmatic: How ought one to

---

[22]   Chapters 1, 9, 14, 15, 21, 25, 35, 36.

understand and cope with the world,[23] with natural disaster, with misfortune, with those in power, with the vicissitudes of life, and with the prospect of death? Thus, one ought to expect that when vagueness is explicitly discussed, its significance will be circum scribed by such pragmatic concerns. The vagueness that is praised in the *Laozi* is not then a *purely* linguistic or logical phenomenon arising from certain formal properties of concepts, but is rather something that shows up in our 'concernful' relation to the world. It is indeed the vagueness of *dao*, the way of nature—its subtlety, mysteriousness, and imperceptibility—that can be observed in the natural processes that surround and envelop us, and that we ourselves embody. The significance of this vagueness in the *Laozi* is its pragmatic role in enabling us to observe, imitate, and follow, rather than work against, the natural processes in which we are organically embedded.[24]

Now, such vagueness may be thought of as arising both out of the fullness and richness of nature that escapes the crudity of our categorizations, and also out of the subtlety, *xi* 希, minuteness, *wei* 微, and indescribability, *miao* 妙, *xuan* 玄 of its processes of transformation. Its subtlety is so refined as to verge on the imperceptible. Approach, the *Laozi* tells us, and it recedes. No matter how closely we focus we can never diminish the horizon of indeterminacy. Every attempt to increase clarity will simultaneously result in a corresponding loss of determinacy.[25] The processes of nature have

---

[23]   I am using the words 'cope' and 'world' in a Heideggerian sense. Thus 'coping' refers not just to dealing with difficult circumstances, but in a more general sense expresses absorbed dealings in a human world. Again, 'world' refers not to an objective, external set of objects which we come up against, but to that with which we have an engaged involvement, and with which we are intricately interconnected. Thus, there can be no 'world' independent of human praxis, and *vice versa.*

[24]   The question arises, 'How is it possible to work against nature? Is it indeed possible for anything to be unnatural? Is the concept of that which goes against nature even meaningful?' This is an important question to which the Daoist can, I suspect, give a satisfactory response with the notion of the artificial, *wei* 偽. The question also arises, 'How does vagueness enable us to realign with natural process?' The details of the answers to both of these questions lie well beyond the scope of this paper.

[25]   This phenomenological interpretation parts company with the Laozi insofar as the description of the horizon of indeterminacy is explicitly transcendental—that is, it is explicitly taken to be a necessary condition of the very possibility of conscious awareness (or, rather, of Dasein). I take it as obvious that only the most outrageous (and implausible) of abductions would find this concept of the transcendental at work in the Laozi! Another

their limits of discernability—not all differentiation is immediately detectable by natural organs of perception. At some point the fruit on the tree will have become ripe, but no amount of close observation (with unaided perceptual organs) will be able to detect the subtleties of the continuous process of ripening—any more than one can discern with the naked eye the movement of the stars across the sky. On a still summer's day the shape of a cloud transforms dramatically, while the most careful scrutiny reveals its outline to be entirely motionless!

Opposites and Transformation[26]

> Something and nothing engender each other
> Difficult and easy produce each other
> Long and short vie with each other
> High and low overthrow each other
> Sound and voice harmonize with each other
> Front and back follow after each other

One of the most familiar themes of the *Laozi* is the interdependence and mutual transformation of opposites, as exemplified in the notions of *yin* and *yang*.[27] '*Yin*' and '*yang*,' as we have said, do not really refer to *properties* of things, but are fundamental metaphors that shape our understanding of the phases in the processes of development of things. They are interpretive models which we may freely apply to deepen our understanding of the pragmatic significance of changes and of contrasts. Moreover, how we understand the phases of things depends in large part on our own circumstances, on our purposes, and on the context in which the changes are to be understood. One and the same thing, phase, or process may be modeled by *yin* in one context, and by *yang* in another. Thus, the rising of the moon at night may be *yin* in comparison with the rising of the sun, but is *yang* when compared with the surrounding darkness. Now, one may identify *yin* and *yang* phases in the processes of things, but the absolutes of pure *yin* or *yang* can never really be instantiated—somewhat as shades of orange may be

---

possible heuristic for understanding the Laozi's claim is Heisenberg's uncertainty principle, according to which some indeterminacies can be diminished only at the cost of increasing other indeterminacies.

26   Chapters 2, 20, 22, 26, 29, 36, 41, 43, 45,77, 78.

27   The terms '*yin*' and '*yang*' do not hold a central place in the Laozi text; in fact, they occur only once, in chapter 42. However, the significance of opposites in the Daoist tradition has come to be understood and expressed through these metaphors.

more yellow or more red but can never be completely red or completely yellow. These opposites alternate with cycles of ascendancy. There are times when the *yin* phase is dominant and times when *yang* is dominant, but the two always swirl and tumble around a constantly shifting center of balance.

It is instructive to understand this cyclical process of transformation by using as a model the processes of growth and decline. There is, however, no straightforward correlation—growth and decline do not correspond in a simplistic way with *yin* and *yang*. *Yang* may be understood as the process of growth as it dissolves into the process of maturity and aging—returning to the source. *Yin* is both the winding down of the process, and at the same time the nourishing and recuperative power on which the phase of growth depends. *Yin* and *yang* may thus be used to model all kinds of differentiations: the lightening and darkening of day and night, the warming and cooling of the seasons, the drying and moistening of the atmosphere, and by extension, the active, progressive, energizing, and the passive, retreating, nourishing aspects of human beings and of nature.[28] It will be noticed that the kinds of opposites that are emphasized in the *Laozi* are not simple contradictories but what I have termed pragmatic 'contrasts'— culturally defined, or naturally arising, pairs of contraries that have an intuitively recognizable relation that gives them a pragmatically useful function. What is significant here is that, whether contrasts or contradictories, these opposites depend on and, through gradual processes, transform into one another.

Transformation as growth and decline[29]

Growth[30] In chapter sixty four we read, 'A tree one fathom around grows from a flimsy sapling.' Here we see emphasized the natural process that leads from the minutest of increments to the greatest of transformations between opposites, what we referred to earlier as a '*sorites* process.' As undetectable changes accumulate, larger changes slowly become discernable, and eventually the result is a

---

28   These aspects were culturally associated with the male and the female respectively. Note, however, that these are not identified with the biological categories of male and female, but refer to degrees of maleness and femaleness that may be instantiated in any thing or process, and without implying any distinction between 'animate' and 'inanimate.'

29   Chapters 2, 4, 5, 22, 23, 29, 43, 45, 56, 58, 64, 76, 77, 78.

30   Chapters that deal with the process of growth: 42, 51, 63, 64.

radical transformation. What we find first described in the world of nature we next find immediately extended to human achievements:

> A terrace of nine layers arises from accumulating dirt,
> A journey of thousands of leagues begins with a footfall.

Here the *Laozi* emphasizes that just as grand spectacles of nature grow from the smallest beginnings, so too in human affairs, the large depends on and grows from the small. Note that these are quite explicitly *sorites* transformations, although no paradox is drawn from them. The significance of the *sorites* transformations here is entirely confined to the relation between the vast and the minuscule, and to the function of the process of accumulation, or iteration. Thus by concentrating solely on the task at hand, no matter how trivial it may seem, the final goal will take care of itself, no matter how distant and unattainable it may appear. In time what lies beyond the limits of attainability will eventually be encompassed without any boundary ever having been crossed.

Decline and return[31] We also find in the *Laozi* a description of a reversal, or returning movement, a wearing down of *yang* back to *yin*. This is the reversal of the accumulation, the gradual dissipation of the minuscule that dissolves the vast into nothing. This reversal of the *sorites* process is still another *sorites* process: the iterative relation between the minuscule and the vast remains the same. The *Laozi*'s emphasis on the relative priority of this reversal or return, *fan* 反, is reminiscent of the second law of thermodynamics of modern physics, according to which the overall trend of processes is towards a decrease of structure, and a dissipation of energy. However, unlike the second law of thermodynamics the *Laozi* does not envision a final outcome of absolute exhaustion. The *Laozi* describes the observable patterns of the world of nature in which we are embedded, and these are not one-sided, but cyclical. In the *Laozi*'s words:

> the myriads of things arouse one another
> we thereupon observe their return
> things teeming and swarming
> each returns again to its root (16)
>
> it grinds down the sharp

---

[31]   Chapters that deal with return to the source: 14, 16, 25, 26, 28, 34, 40.

> loosens the knots
> eases the glare
> blends into dust (4)

All sharpness will lose its edge with the passage of time. *Yang* on its way up inevitably falls. Definition of structure, individualization of 'things,' and localization around centers of organization, all eventually relax. Delimitation of 'unities' by circumscribing their boundaries, organic individualization of enduring 'entities'—these are merely beginning phases along a path of development that leads back to their evanescence. As we have already noted, in the Daoist tradition, the darker, more elusive *yin* phase is acknowledged as drawing closer to the source. Indeed, the Daoist world view can be seen as a sustained meditation on the rejuvenating potency of this return to the source. In this way, what we ordinarily think of as decline, degeneration, and decay are looked on, not as harmful and threatening, but on the contrary as necessary for nourishing life. It is this cyclical return that allows what is limited to continue without exhaustion, as though it were unlimited, inexhaustible. It is thus the importance of the dark, the retreating, and the feminine for cycles of nature, and especially for rejuvenation of natural processes that is put forward as worthy of emulation.

Paradox and Contradiction[32]

Perhaps the most distinctive characteristic of the *Laozi* is its air of paradox and contradiction. The text is replete with identifications of opposites, or rather with assimilations of opposites. Things ordinarily considered to be incompatible, on opposing sides of a boundary, are brought closer together, their similarities made more significant than their dissimilarities, in a move that dissolves the boundary, exposes its insurmountability as illusory:

> Great completeness seems lacking
>   - its use is indefatigable
> great fullness seems empty
>   - its use is inexhaustible
> great straightness seems crooked
> great skill seems awkward (45)
>
> agreement and censure—how much *do* they reject one another?
> beautiful and ugly, how far apart *are* they? (20).

---

[32] Chapters 5, 10, 14, 20, 41, 45 (4, 14, 16).

> The bright way seems dark
> the way forward seems to retreat
> ...
> high virtue seems [low] as a valley
> great whiteness seems sullied (41)

Attention is drawn here to the manner in which opposites, in particular the kind of opposites that I have termed 'contrasts,' are similar to one another, rather than the extent to which they are different. We are not given blatant contradictions, but are told that fullness *is like* emptiness, and that straightness *is like* crookedness. Such a process of assimilation works by blending opposition and softening differences. Thus the function of paradox here is to blur the boundaries between apparently irreconcilable opposites, which is made possible because of their mutual dependence and continuity. More often than not, these paradoxes are a direct result of the Daoist concern with the potency of retreat, of holding back: rejuvenation is cyclical, and the cyclical process is a continuum in which opposites are mutually connected through gradual becoming. Moreover, by being aware of how opposites transform into one another, and by paying close attention to the tendencies and momenta of the penumbra, we are able to take advantage of the processes of transformation, directing and redirecting the cycles of development.

Boundarilessness and Continuity[33]

It is with these final characteristics that our abduction runs into some difficulty. It is not that these characteristics cannot be found in the *Laozi*, but that their significance is not immediately and obviously connected to the other characteristics in the way that we have noticed in our discussions of vagueness. To the extent that boundarilessness and continuity are discussed, they are not specifically connected to transformation between *opposites*. Boundarilessness in the *Laozi* is rather a matter of setting no *outer* limits, so that boundaries, *jiao* 徼, are not delimiting barriers that create a closed system, but frontiers that open it out and render it always incomplete. Continuity, *yi* 一, is what enables the world processes to proceed without respite, and without interruption, as though they were inexhaustible. Any connection with the transformation of opposites, and thus with the boundaries that separate opposites (rather than the boundaries as outer reaches), is

---

[33]   Chapters 1, 14, 16, 22, 25, 34, 39.

not stated explicitly. Nevertheless, there is no inconsistency between these two significances of boundarilessness. On the contrary, the two significances blend well together, merging unproblematically in the notion of 'continuity.' Thus, although our abduction may not be 'watertight,' its strength and plausibility, I suggest, are not significantly diminished.[34]

In summary, what we have found is ample evidence of concern with opposites, transformation, subtlety, and imperceptibility, and with the processes of growth and decay. There is even direct and explicit concern with vagueness, insofar as this shows itself in the subtlety and imperceptability of natural processes. It is with boundarilessness and continuity that we ran into some difficulty. For the strongest abduction they would be discernable in the text, and explicitly connected with the other characteristics of vagueness in an appropriate manner. Now, I have been able to identify the characteristics of boundarilessness and continuity, but with a slightly different significance from what we would expect in connection with vagueness. This does not by itself suffice to make the abduction of vagueness implausible. What is interesting is that once attention has been drawn to the phenomenon, when one looks askance at the text, its aura becomes unmistakable. But when one tries to pinpoint its presence, it slips away from one's grasp. Not only does the *Laozi* extol the virtues of vagueness, and itself exemplify those very virtues, it exemplifies them in the very manner in which it extols them! Thus, the *Laozi* hints at vagueness, dropping clues and leaving traces, and we perceive the vagueness not directly, but in the shadows, always on the verge of appearing, but never fully manifest.[35]

---

[34] Indeed, 'watertightness' is not appropriate here anyway, since we are not attempting to establish the 'truth' of the real meaning of the Laozi's words. Instead, we are aiming to construct a plausible (given textual evidence, social, cultural, historical information and so on) and workable (coherent, sustainable, applicable) interpretation—the more plausible and workable the better.

[35] For a rich, beautiful and extensive exploration of the rhetorical strategies of indirection in the Chinese tradition, see François Jullien, *Detour and Access: Strategies of Meaning in China and Greece.*

CHAPTER SEVEN

Vastness, Imagination and Penumbral Cases

Essence and Definition

One of the most central and fundamental concepts at the heart of western philosophy has been the concept of essence. The essence of a thing is *what it is*: not just what it happens to be, but what it has to be in order to be the thing it is, or the kind of thing it is. This idea has its origin in the awareness that there are limits to how much something can change and still be the same thing, or the same kind of thing. The essence of a thing (or kind) is what cannot change without the thing turning into something else: it is what is necessary for it to be what it is. One way of specifying the essence of a thing is to list the conditions (or properties) that individually are necessary, and that together are sufficient, for the thing to be what it is. Since we are dealing with what a thing *is*, with what it is in its innermost *being*, as it were, the concept of essence tends to be a realist one: essences are thought of as existing independently of our perceptions, our language, and our understanding. They are a part of reality that we must discover. In medieval Scholastic terminology, the realist claims that essences are *de re*, 'of the thing' itself.

However, not all philosophers have been realists about essences. Some have been very sceptical about these mysterious inner necessities. The nominalists, for example, proposed that they arise conventionally, from how we categorize the world: they follow from our terminology, our definitions, our linguistic stipulations. Essences are not *de re* but *de dicto*, 'of what is said.' The essence of a thing is a matter of how we describe it. We can describe it so that any thing we wish would be included in its definition, so long as we do not choose contradictory things. Thus, according to the nominalist, we could define human beings either as rational animals or as featherless bipeds. According to the first definition, being rational would be part of the essence of being human; according to the second definition it would not. The necessities arise solely by stipulation, and as the logical consequence of such stipulation. This is a thoroughly conventionalist understanding of necessities.

There is a weaker version of a conventionalist claim, and this is that necessities follow from how we describe something, but not solely as a result of stipulation and its logical consequences. They follow in such a manner that once we set our vocabulary, some necessities that follow from that description must still be discovered by experiment. Thus, there are tendencies in things that we may describe differently depending on how we define our terms, but that we must describe consistently once we have a set vocabulary, and that we must discover despite the fact that they depend on how we define our terms. That is, once we have a set vocabulary, some things will follow, but not as a matter of logical necessity! They will follow because of what is out there regardless of our hopes, desires, and demands. This second understanding, while it recognizes the role of language and convention in the formation of essences, is not a nominalist understanding. Now, whether one is a realist or a nominalist about essences, they are taken to be fixed, precise, and determinate: they can be specified completely and accurately. Moreover, the things that have those essences must remain self-identical, self-contained. This basic intuition about the 'identity' of things is hard to make any more intelligible, but it might be glossed with the assertion that there can be no *unclarity* as to what things are, except insofar as we may be ignorant about them.

The concept of essence is also closely related to that of *meaning*. If essence is a matter of ontology, then meaning is a matter of semantics. Meaning and essence have been considered two sides of the same coin, insofar as definition is the single result of giving either of them a linguistic expression. A definition is the explicit description of a set of conditions, characteristics or properties that individually are necessary, and taken together constitute a sufficient condition, either for the attribution of a *term*, in which case the definition expresses the meaning of the term, or for some *thing's* belonging to a certain category, in which case it expresses the essence of the thing. Insofar as a definition describes an essence it constitutes a necessary, and analytic, truth. It thus expresses the distinctive characteristics that are already found within the content of the concept to be defined.

But how do we gain knowledge of these supposed essences? The early twentieth century phenomenologist, Edmund Husserl, attempted to give a description of how we are able to gain epistemic access to such essences. The function of the imagination was central to his account. To find the connections between meanings or senses that constitute knowledge of an essence we simply 'observe' a sense, *Sinn*, as it 'appears' to us in its evidentness, *Evidenz*—in less contentious language, we reflect on our understanding of it, and explicate the contents of the sense. This practice he referred to as 'eidetic reflection' or 'eidetic variation in *imagination*,' and theorized as reflection on *eide*, forms; the faculty that he posited, by which we are able to gain such epistemic access to these essences, he called 'eidetic intuition.' One isolates a particular region of Being (the physical, the biological, the mathematical, the pragmatic and so on), and focuses on some particular concept or sense ('physical object,' 'living thing,' 'proof,' 'utensil'). Then one begins the process of eidetic variation in imagination: one imagines an instance of something constituted through that sense, and then varies in imagination particular properties, one after another, altering and transforming the imagined instance. With some of the variations what one imagines will no longer be constituted by the original sense, it will have become an instance of something different. With other variations the thing imagined remains constituted by the sense despite the changes. The properties that cannot be changed without change of sense are properties that are essential. Those that can be varied without any dramatic transformation of sense are not.

This kind of epistemology is not uncommon, especially among practitioners of analytical philosophy, although without the ontological extravagance. To the extent that such 'level headed' thinkers reject this view, it is the ontological *extravagance*, and not the epistemology that they reject. According to this epistemology, we are able to reflect on and describe the contents of concepts—what we mean by what we say. We are able to gain *a priori* access to conceptual contents and conceptual necessities, to describe all that is contained in any particular concept or meaning as a necessary part of its content, and that is sufficient to clarify and distinguish its 'boundaries.' In this way the use of a term, and its applicability in all cases, is determined in advance—we simply ask ourselves of any imagined variation, 'Is the term applicable or not?' To the extent that we know what the term means, we simply know the correct answer to that question. We are to be able to anticipate all possibilities in advance so as to determine precisely the content of our concepts. This intuition lies at the heart of one of the most notorious of analytical methods: that of thought experiments that have no grounding in reality, and that are more implausible than our wildest science fiction fantasies! ('Would I still be the same person if I sprouted two heads and turned into an alligator?')

Historical sketch

Plato and Socrates developed a method for gaining epistemic access to essences, *qua* Ideas: the dialectical method. This method was instrumental in shaping the nature and direction of western philosophy for centuries to come. It involved striving toward an ideal realm of perfect essences that stands apart from the impermanences and imperfections of worldly existence. The Being of Parmenides and the celestial realm of Ideas of Plato might be depicted as a pure, crystalline, mathematical structure, in the philosophical tradition of thought tracing back to the number mysticism of Pythagoras. Now, the human soul, though it is entrapped in the mire of the physical, is nevertheless able to achieve a vision of this perfection since it is itself a spark of the sublime. And the method of attaining this vision, which is at the same time both an intellectual and a religious practice, is that of the purification of the soul, or in practical terms the purification of the understanding, the removal of the obstacles that lie in the way of a clear vision of the essences of Beauty, Truth, Goodness, and Being. However, this intellectual method is only a propaedeutic, a preparation for the ultimate revelation, for as long as the soul is tied down by the body, the vision of perfection can never be complete. It is only with death that the ultimate ecstatic vision becomes possible.[1]

The philosopher starts with a question: 'What *is* justice?'; 'What *is* virtue?' Their aim is to seek to understand the Ideal as it is in itself, as it would be if it were possible for it to be exemplified in the world of becoming. However, this kind of perfect knowledge is in real terms unattainable. The Ideal can never be exemplified in the actual world as it is in itself. The vision of the Ideal is something that we can only prepare for—perfection cannot be attained so long as we are limited beings. But the path is paved through the *dialectical* method. The aim is to develop an understanding that will account for all instances and only instances of Justice, Virtue, Beauty, or whatever Idea it is the *being* of which is to be understood. The method begins with a suggestion for a possible characterization of whatever idea, or Ideal, is in question. But one does not rest satisfied with that characterization: one will then want to know if that characterization is correct, if it specifies everything

---

[1]   A similar shamanistic/mystical otherworldly contact will be seen to be operative in the fundamental ideas of Daoist thinking also, although, as we shall see, its aim and significance are entirely at odds with the Platonic vision.

that is essential, and thus allows for all acceptable variations. If one can imagine something that satisfies the proposed definition but is clearly not an instance of what was to be defined, then there is something wrong with the proposed definition (it does not yield *only* instances of what was to be defined). Conversely, if one can imagine an example that does not satisfy the characterization, then again the characterization is inadequate (it does not yield *all* instances of what was to be defined). Both kinds of instances function as 'counter-examples' for each proposed definition, and from the counter-examples *reductio* arguments can be constructed refuting the proposed definition. The counter-examples constitute grounds for rejecting the definition in one of two ways. One may reject the proposed definition altogether, or one may suggest a modification. One must be vigilant when proposing a modification to ensure that it is not *ad hoc*.[2] Ideally, if one's proposal has any merit one will take the second route, and one will continue in the same way, accumulating refinements to the resulting refined definitions drawing all the while closer to an absolute and perfect understanding of the being (essence, form) of things.

Through this dialectical method one is able to find what it is that allows many particulars—despite their variety, multiplicity and difference—to be of the same kind. One is able to explain, through the dialectical refinements, how this bewildering variety of individuals can still be *the same* despite their apparently inexhaustible differences. The dialectical method is thus able to explain how unity, sameness, stability, and reliability could be possible, even in a world of difference and flux, such as that embraced by Heraclitus and by the Sophists. Both Socrates and Plato had little patience with mere examples, or lists, of particular things that exemplified the kind in answer to their philosophical inquiries. Their avowed concern was to explain the unity, the *sameness*, of those multifarious things—to isolate exactly what it is that they all have *in common* despite their apparent differences. As the laborious dialectical procedure shows, what explains their sameness—despite our familiarity with the things in question—is far from obvious. This feeling of certainty that there must be *a* what it is, *an* essence that accounts for its kind, has become what is perhaps the single most important historical condition of western philosophizing. Whether or not there is a natural tendency to search in this way for unities as some philosophers think, this

---

2   An *ad hoc* refinement simply includes the counter-example in the definition, listing it as an exception, without any clear account of why it is an exception.

historical grounding for the development of our cultural predilection is quite evident.

Aristotle's views on definition and essence although markedly different in content from Plato's have what is, from the point of view of a broader comparative context, an interesting similarity. With Aristotle too we find a preoccupation with *to ti ein einai* 'the what it is to be' of things, the 'being' or 'essence'[3] of things. The concern is threefold.[4] We want to understand what *makes* things what they are, how they are *constituted*, and how they are *classified* into natural kinds. Each of these yields a kind of definition. The first is appropriate for events, and is a matter of understanding the *cause* of the event, insofar as it is considered as an effect. The second is especially appropriate for artifacts, and articulates the *form* that shapes the matter into the kind of thing it is. The third is explicitly a method for understanding the 'what it is to be' of things, the *essence* of natural kinds. It is the third kind of definition that is of interest here. One seeks for what it is that all instances of a distinct natural group have in common—this characteristic will isolate a *genus*. One then looks for distinctive subgroups, and examines each subgroup carefully to identify what *all and only* the members of the subgroup have in common. Notice the presupposition, here, that there is such a common something. Each of these subgroups will constitute a *species* of the genus. One continues in this way until one reaches the smallest naturally distinctive subgroup, the *infima species*. The characteristic of this subgroup will then be its defining characteristic, its *differentia*. Now, since all the members of the *infima species* will have the characteristics of the higher genera to which it belongs, these characteristics will be necessary for the species. And since the *differentiae* will be characteristic of only the *infima species*, the *differentiae* will be sufficient for the species. Note that I do not say that they are necessary and sufficient for the application of the species-term. It would be incorrect to represent this as merely a

---

3   There are other Aristotelian terms that have been associated with, and even translated with the same word, essence. These include *ousia*, and *physis*. Aristotle explicitly connects *ousia* and *to ti ein einai* and so there is some ground for considering these together. However, he makes no explicit connection between *physis* and *to ti ein einai*. For this reason, the concept of *physis* falls outside the scope of consideration of this chapter, though whether there is such a connection and what it might be would make an interesting topic of inquiry.

4   See Barnes, Schofield, and Sorabji, *Articles on Aristotle*, Vol. 3, *Metaphysics*, and Vol. 1, *Science*. More generally, see Jonathan Lear, *Aristotle: the desire to understand*.

linguistic matter. For Aristotle it would be more appropriate to characterize these as necessary and sufficient conditions for *being* a member of the species.

In *Ideas*,[5] Husserl has a concern with essence that he explicitly traces back to Aristotle. Husserl's phenomenology posits a transcendental realm of *Evidenz*, a self-evident realm that he calls 'absolute consciousness,' a consciousness which has been 'purified' of its connections to the psychological. We gain access to this absolute realm of apodictic knowledge through the reflection of consciousness on itself, since, in its purity and transparency, consciousness as transcendental ought to be able to reflect on its own conditions of possibility. It is this eidetic insight, intuition of *eide*, 'forms,' that also gives us direct reflective access to the senses, *Sinne*, that inform and constitute our understanding of our world, and it is a close and careful description of those senses as they reveal themselves to the reflective gaze of consciousness that yields necessities of both formal and material varieties. Formal necessities are yielded by reflection on the logical structure of consciousness, that is, of all knowledge in its most absolute and encompassing generality, while material necessities are obtained by reflection on the more localized structures of the various regions of Being. Phenomenological analysis yields *a priori* knowledge through such 'explication of senses,' a mode of analysis which, as we have already noted, is not unlike the analytical philosopher's analysis of concepts. The necessities that are thus isolated are, according to Husserl, the *a priori* structures that define the particular ontologies for each particular region of Being.

This quest for determining precisely what things are is manifested not only in the Continental brands of Rationalism, but also has a counterpart in the reductionist analyses of the Empiricist tradition of Anglo-American philosophy, and of the Vienna Circle. Bertrand Russell's phenomenalist analyses attempt to *reduce* all objective knowledge to knowledge of sense-data, and Carnap's positivistic reductions were to provide similar analyses of material object statements into observation statements. The purpose of these reductive analyses was to uncover the necessary and sufficient conditions for the application of individual words or of complete sentences, and so can clearly be interpreted as a concern with definition in our sense.

---

5   Husserl, *Ideas*.

Anomalies and Irregularities

The problem since the time of Socrates has always been the actual production and acquisition of these perfect foolproof understandings. The knowledge that is supposedly packed neatly within the concepts themselves has from the beginning proved extremely and curiously elusive. This elusiveness should be taken very seriously. That the final goal in the quest for essences and definitions is unattainable was acknowledged by Plato from the very beginning. The reason that such Ideal essences are not attainable by us is that we are creatures of becoming in a world of becoming. We are finite temporal beings with finite temporal capacities. Things are always changing, understandings are always developing; the ultimate perfection in its infinitude cannot be revealed through the finite. The case of mathematical knowledge seems to provide an instance of essences that somehow are attainable. Indeed, it is the knowledge of the 'magical' proportions of geometrical figures that lies at the heart of the number mysticism of the Platonic and Pythagorean tradition. However, the development of alternative geometries with axioms that run contrary to our natural intuitions might lead one to suspect the veracity of those intuitions. And, Wittgenstein's reflections on rule following make room for an extremely sceptical glance at the kinds of intuitions that lie at the base of such *a priori* reasonings. Post-Quinean naturalistic epistemology is also more open to the suggestion that even our most fundamental intuitions may be open to doubt. But the unattainability of essences might have a more radical significance than the uncontainability of the finite in the infinite. It is the role of the counter-example, the anomaly, the irregularity, or unanticipated case, that is at issue. Does the counter-example merely indicate the necessity of refinement? Or might it be that the ineliminability of the possibility of counter-examples shows us something more significant?

When following the dialectical method, any attempt to produce a definition will result either in a challenge from a counter-example, or may be taken as a challenge to imagine such a counter-example. In some cases these counter-examples will be clear instances of things that meet the conditions described by the *definiens*, and yet do not fall under the *definiendum*. In these cases we simply acknowledge that the proposed definition has been falsified. We then have a choice whether to simply modify the definition, or reject it altogether. The epistemological doctrine of *fallibilism* emphasizes the ever present possibility of such counter-examples: for all we know, something might show us to be mistaken. Fallibilism is sometimes confused with scepticism, but the fallibilist does not challenge our claim to know things, as does the sceptic. The fallibilist merely challenges our claim to know things with finality and certainty. Fallibilism is the epistemology of the pragmatist, not of the sceptic. The more interesting cases, however, are those in which the counter-examples, actual or imagined, real or possible, do not clearly falsify the definition. That is, the counter-examples are *not clearly not* instances of the *definiendum*. They are indeterminate, penumbral cases. As we shall see, it is these cases that, by their indeterminacy, call into question the very possibility of definition, and therefore the very notion of an essence.

From the beginning of the twentieth century, there have been stirrings of discontent with the Greek metaphor—of self-contained, well defined and self-transparent essences—that has moulded so much of western philosophical thinking about language, meaning, and metaphysics. In a more general sense, discontent with this picture began to surface long before the analytic logicians began to notice that something was awry. Friedrich Nietzsche injected a heavy dose of anti-essentialism into the Continental tradition. The Freudian conception of the unconscious opened up a gaping wound in the Cartesian *Ego*, a self that is supposed to be transparent to itself, whose contents and intentions are capable of revealing themselves completely when bathed in the reflective light of reason. More recently still, Derrida has taken such 'contaminating' forces, together with Heidegger's deconstruction of the western tradition of thinking Being as presence, and worked them into the structuralist linguistics of Saussure, and the transcendental phenomenology of Husserl, with profoundly challenging and productive results.

Even within the boundaries of the analytic tradition there have been dissident voices, of which the earliest and most sustained meditations appear to have begun with Wittgenstein. Wittgenstein and Waismann were to realize the impossibility of the ideal of the reduction and containment of meaning, and Quine recorded his rejection of this account of meaningfulness in his celebrated paper 'Two Dogmas of Empiricism,' in particular in his rejection of what he called the dogma of reductionism.[6] Even Carnap, in his response to Quine's rejection of analyticity,[7] acknowledges the ubiquity of what he calls *intensional vagueness* in natural language. I quote the passage in full since it deals with

---

6   W. V. Quine, *From a Logical Point of View*. Quine himself attributes this insight to the philosophy of science of Pierre Duhém, and a precursor to Quine's naturalism can be found in Dewey's pragmatism.

7   Carnap, 'Meaning and Synonymy in Natural Languages.'

many of the issues with which we are concerned. We determine the meaning of any term starting with an enumeration of clear instances:

> The essential task is then to find out what variations of a given specimen in various respects (e.g., size, shape, color) are admitted within the range of the predicate.... In this investigation of intension, the linguist finds a new kind of vagueness, which may be called *intensional vagueness*. As mentioned above, the extensional vagueness [*author's note*: the set of actually existing 'penumbral' cases] of the word 'Mensch' is very small, at least in the accessible region. First, the intermediate zone among animals now living on earth is practically empty. Second, if the ancestors of man are considered, it is probably found that Karl cannot easily draw a line; thus there is an intermediate zone, but it is relatively small.

Note that the issue of vagueness here has to do with the admissibility of variations within the range of the predicate: there will be clear cases of admissibility, and clear cases of inadmissibility. But in the process of investigation we will in all probability come across problem cases, intermediate cases, or as we have called them, penumbral cases. Carnap makes the comment that the number of *actual* penumbral humans is very small. He suggests, quite oddly, that there are very few living instances of intermediate species between human and non-human, but he does not tell us what he considers to be such an intermediate species, or where these exist! He also acknowledges that there is an evolutionary penumbra of 'humans,' but, again oddly, decides that it must be relatively small, without telling us why he thinks so.

> However, when the linguist proceeds to the determination of the *intension* of the word 'Mensch,' the situation is quite different. He has to test Karl's responses to descriptions of strange kinds of animals, say intermediate between man and dog, man and lion, man and hawk, etc. It may be that the linguist and Karl know that these kinds of animals have never lived on earth; they do not know whether or not these kinds will ever occur on earth or on any other planet in any galaxy. At any rate, this knowledge or ignorance is irrelevant for the determination of intension. But Karl's ignorance has the psychological effect that he has seldom if ever thought of these kinds (unless he happens to be a student of mythology or a science fiction fan) and therefore never felt an urge to make up his mind as to which of them to apply the predicate 'Mensch.' Consequently, the linguist finds in Karl's responses a large intermediate zone for this predicate, in other words, a high intensional vagueness.

The point here is that once we leave the realm of actuality and consider the possibilities that are opened up by our imaginative or descriptive creativity we can start to construct all kinds of intermediate cases. That these cases may bear increasingly little resemblance to actual cases does not matter to the linguist. The point is to explore the possibilities of meaning, to discover what is admitted, what is not admitted, and *what remains in the middle*. This middle range, because of the unlimited creative possibilities, becomes vast, perhaps even vaster than the clear ranges of admissibility and inadmissibility put together—though Carnap does not explicitly make this suggestion.

> The fact that Karl has not made such decisions means that the intension of the word 'Mensch' for him is not quite clear even to himself, that he does not completely understand his own word. This lack of clarity does not bother him much because it holds only for aspects which have very little practical importance for him.

Note that Karl's lack of understanding of his own word is not a matter of ignorance; it arises because he has 'never felt an urge to make up his mind.' It is not that he does not know whether a hawk-person really *is* a person or not; it is rather that he has not decided. Now, 'Karl' here is not really intended to name an individual person, but to stand for *any* person. The point being made is thus a general one about the meaning of such terms for the entire group of language users. It is thus the community of language users that has not decided how to apply such terms in the intermediate zones, and so the linguistic community as a whole does not have a complete understanding of the language it uses!

> In my view, it follows from the previous discussion that rules of intension are required, because otherwise intensional vagueness would remain, and this would prevent clear mutual understanding and effective communication.

We note that although Carnap recognized the presence of such forms of vagueness, his aim was to eradicate them from our language altogether. His justification is that the presence of intensional vagueness would prevent clear mutual understanding and effective communication. But he has already conceded that these outlandish cases barely make a dent in our everyday communications because 'they have very little practical importance.' That is to say, these outlandish cases do not generally show up in our everyday experience. What he is really after, then, is not *effective* communication as he says, but an ideal clarity that would, through explicit rules, authorize a single correct decision for each and every outlandish and fantastic possibility. Friedrich Waismann, his fellow Vienna Circle positivist, even before Quine's publication of his ideas, and perhaps as a direct result of his many conversations with Wittgenstein regarding the latter's new ideas, recognized at least some of the more radical implications of such extraordinary or borderline cases. We shall soon see how he used such cases to develop his concept of 'porousness' or 'open texture.'

J. L. Austin, in *The Meaning of a Word*,[8] discusses the limitations of ordinary language. Ordinary language works well in ordinary, familiar circumstances, but when circumstances become strange or unusual we are at a loss to know how to proceed. As Austin puts it, 'Ordinary language breaks down in extraordinary cases.' The problem arises because of the nature of the circumstances—they are so unusual that words in their familiar signification simply fail us. We either invent new words for every new strange possibility, or we make arbitrary decisions, or we simply refrain from making any familiar classification at all. We just describe the odd cases in all their oddness. 'The difficulty is just that: there is *no* short description which is not misleading: the only thing to do, and that can easily be done, is to set out the description of the facts at length....there are no limiting rules about what we might or might not say *in extraordinary cases*....Ordinary language *blinkers* the already feeble imagination.' The rules of ordinary language are limited by their lack of imagination: extraordinary circumstances are simply not anticipated. The rules that we do have are not sufficient to tell us how to respond. It is these cases that bring to our attention the openness of ordinary language, and its limitedness. The tools of ordinary language were developed and crafted through use in everyday situations, for dealing with and communicating about common cases. When something out of the ordinary occurs—something unanticipated— we may be at a loss as to what to do, what to say.

But we, in our post-modern condition, are no longer in a position to distinguish so clearly between the familiar and the unfamiliar. Encounters between cultures with vastly different customs and values, sub-cultures that create new social structures, are becoming more widespread. The rapidly accelerating development of modern technologies—of medicine, communication, computing, internet, travel, robotics, genetics, destruction—brings the unanticipated and the outlandish eerily and unnervingly close

---

8   Included in Harris and Severens, *Analyticity*.

to home. We are becoming increasingly unable to anticipate what will be achievable, and increasingly unsure how to deal with it.

These unanticipated anomalies indicate what Friedrich Waismann, the Vienna Circle positivist, termed '*porosität*,' porousness, which he rendered in English as 'open texture.'[9] These cases blur the boundaries of meaning, and thus the distinction between the inside of a concept and its outside, between what is 'contained' in the concept and what is not. They are, to extend the terminology of vagueness developed in the last chapter, penumbral cases, and as penumbral cases they demonstrate the continuity of what is so with what is not. As Waismann puts it, our concepts may be well defined in some directions, but they are not, and cannot be, closed off in every direction. We cannot anticipate all possible relevant cases and determine in advance whether they are to be included or excluded. To put it more vividly, novelty finds a way to slip through any attempted barrier wherever we are left offguard.

I have suggested that most concepts may exhibit properties of indeterminacy and vagueness to some extent, but it is not immediately obvious exactly how, for any given concept, it could admit of anomalies in this way. While it is clear how simple observational concepts ('red,' 'sweet,' 'clear,' 'smooth') that are instantiated in degrees, and that have limits of recognizability (because of the intransitivity of indiscernability), will have penumbral regions, it is not clear how this could be true of more complex concepts, especially those that seem susceptible of definition. A particular stumbling block might be concepts of natural kinds, things that have been thought of as having natural essences. It is not obvious how the natural kind concepts such as 'dog' and 'horse' can admit of degrees. Something either is a dog or it isn't, it either belongs to the species or it doesn't, it either instantiates the essence of *dogginess* or it doesn't. It does not seem to make much sense to say that there are degrees of dogness, and even less sense to suggest that a dog is a vague object, or that it has limits of recognizability. *Dog* is a natural kind, and as such has a natural essence: necessary and sufficient conditions, naturally determined, for belonging to the category. The concept 'horse,' likewise, is one that would ordinarily be taken as an example of a concept that is not vague—as a natural kind concept it does not, like redness or tallness, come in degrees.

Just as in the case of vagueness, however, the examples of open texture that Waismann describes are startlingly simple.

9   See Waissman, 'Verifiability' in *Proceedings of the Aristotelian Society*, *Supp. 19, 1945.*

Indeed, the example he uses is paradigmatic case of a natural kind, the concept 'cat' (*felix catus*). How big, he asks, does a cat have to be in order to be a cat? The question is strange because our concept of a cat is not determined 'in that direction.' We have never in practice encountered the need to decide cathood purely on the basis of size. But let us imagine now a *sorites* series formed by a cat in the process of growing larger and larger, until it reaches monstrous, gargantuan proportions. After a while we lose our confidence that we know what this creature is. Cats don't grow this big, but this creature does. Is there a point at which we can say confidently that it is no longer correctly to be called a cat, though we may still think of it as a catlike monster? There is a series of stages during which the creature is indeterminate, and these identify the regions of indeterminacy of the concept.[10] Again, our concept of being a cat is not determined in respect of linguistic capacity. So we may imagine another *sorites* series produced by a cat in the process of developing a more and more complex system of mewing (appropriate mews in appropriate circumstances), the sounds and apparent meanings becoming more and more like the English sentences that we would expect from human speakers of English. This creature delights us, but its capacity for speech makes us uncomfortable. We do not know how to classify it. The region in which this decision is problematic exemplifies yet another aspect of the open texture of the concept. And of course we may introduce many such *sorites* series for all kinds of odd characteristics. Moreover, we can combine and overlap these *sorites* series in strange permutations, producing ever stranger progressions of penumbral creatures.[11] It does no good insisting that because we have a instance of *felix catus*, or because it shares the genetic makeup distinctive of cats, it must therefore be classified as a cat—because this is precisely what Waismann is calling into question.

Now scientific definitions, since they have been honed for scientific purposes, are ordinarily thought to be immune from such possibilities. But Waismann insists that they too are riddled through and through with open texture. The concept of gold, for example, might be defined as the element with atomic number 79: that is, the element whose atom has 79 protons in its nucleus. This

---

[10]   The cat itself does not have to be literally fuzzy or blurry in order to be indeterminate. It suffices for it to be indeterminate whether or not it is a cat, for it to be indeterminate with regard to cathood.

[11]   Note that the creatures are quite definitely catlike, as are ordinary cats. What is in question, what is indeterminate is whether they count as *cats* proper.

seems like a clear enough definition, but it cannot account *clearly* for something that in all respects satisfies this criterion but that, say, emits a strange wavelength, one never seen before, and one that we have no (current) means of accounting for. Our current concept of gold has not been determined in that direction. If we should ever come across such an experience we should be required to make a decision. It is not determined in advance what that decision would be. We simply do not know what to say of such a substance. Our concept of gold does not tell us whether or not this instance is an instance of gold. This does not mean that the decision would have to be an arbitrary one—we can still hope to give reasons for any decision. We may *decide*, for example, that the similarities to clear cases of gold are great enough that the new substance be treated simply as gold, or as a new type of gold— luminiferous gold, perhaps. But we may also decide otherwise: our purposes, or lack thereof, might render other criteria more significant.

Thus, for any proposed definition of any concept, we imagine a variation, or indeed a process of change, with regard to some characteristic which has not previously been specified as relevant to the concept. We may begin with minute and undetectable variations, which at first seem to cause no significant problems, and slowly continue until the characteristic of the new variant looms large enough to overwhelm and outweigh the motive for the original classification. Whether or not any such characteristics turn out to be of central importance in the determination of the kind in question is something that, *ex hypothesi*, we cannot rule in advance. Here again we see the close relation, and the distance, between fallibilism and indeterminacy. If the new variant is one that varies in terms of a characteristic that is included in the definition, then it would require a correction of that definition, and so our previous scientific definition will have proven its fallibility. If the new variant satisfies the previous definition, and yet the variation inclines us to feel a pressure to revoke the categorization, then this leaves everything still undecided, and we have a genuine case of open texture.

Now, according to Waismann, we may remove the vagueness of an ordinary vague predicate by an arbitrary decision, and thus turn it into a sharp one. For example, we may decide for civic purposes that spring will end and summer begin at midnight on the 27th of May. But such a procedure, he says, is not available for open texture. The reason he gives is that we can never anticipate every possible direction of openness of the concept. More precisely, we can never be sure that we have anticipated every possible direction of relevant openness, since not every new possibility will turn out to have a bearing on whether the proposed instances count as instances. Now while this is true, it is not the whole truth. For it covers up the extent to which the scientific refinement of ordinary concepts is always possible. A scientific refinement of a concept would make a stipulation, creating by *fiat* a dividing line between positive and negative cases. Thus, according to any possible division of instances that precisely determines the extraordinary cases, one that determines which belong and which do not belong, as a result of a ruling as to necessary and sufficient conditions in the cases of open texture, we end up with a particular proposed definition, and accordingly a particular specified essence.[12] This yields a particular 'precisification' of the concept, to use Kit Fine's (rather awkward) terminology in his analytic discussions of vagueness. However, although such precisifications are always possible—indeed the history of western science is in large part the history of such precisifications of ordinary concepts—their actual success in eliminating all traces of open texture will depend on the degree of preciseness of the terms into which the concept has been defined. Thus unless we are able to start with a set of absolutely precise concepts in terms of which all other concepts must be definable, there can be no hope of eliminating all traces of open texture. Secondly, even if we succeed in precisifying as much of natural language as possible, the language that results, though it may be of great productive value for the precise sciences, will be of little or no value for the everyday language that we need in order to communicate with our fellow beings on the everyday level, or for the embodied knowledge with which we engage our world. It will be too precise to have intuitive conditions of application.

In the *Philosophical Investigations*, Wittgenstein suggests that our Platonic yearning for essences, our *a priori* sense that there must be *a something that is the same* despite difference and despite change, is a mere prejudice. Rather than insist that there be must such an essence no matter what, we ought to observe how a term is actually used in all its variety of cases. 'Don't say: 'There *must* be something in common'—but *look and see* whether there is anything common to all.' We examine each case in its individuality and try to understand how and why we think of it as the same as the others, and how we think of it as different. Then what we discover, rather

---

12   No reification of *possibilia* is intended by this terminology. And the proposed definition does not specify a precise essence insofar as not all directions of indeterminacy will have been closed off in any such precisification.

than a coherent well defined essence running through all the instances, is a complex network of characteristics intertwining like the fibers of a thread. The unity of the concept or meaning is like the unity of the thread, held together by 'crisscrossing and overlapping' fibers, but there is no single fiber continuing the whole length of the thread. Even if there were one, it would not be necessary for the strength and coherence of the thread—at least, if it were needed in some cases, it could well be superfluous in others. In suggesting that we be open to the possibility that there may be no set of common properties, Wittgenstein is urging us to resist the hypnotic power of the demand that there must be an essence.

This metaphor invites comparison with the Mohist metaphor of the thread that unifies, but Wittgenstein's metaphor is designed to show us how harmony and continuity do *not* require a singular thread running through the whole. Indeed, Wittgenstein's deeper exploration of the metaphor of the thread demonstrates the implausibility of the Mohist intuition: a skein of silk may require a binding thread, but a rope retains a formidable amount of strength despite its lack of a single binding thread. Neither external constraints nor internal unity are required to maintain coherence and integrity.

In our description of any given instance as an instance of a kind, some properties may well turn out to be necessary. But the properties that are necessary will not individually be sufficient to make the instance an instance of the kind in question. Now, if Wittgenstein is right, we cannot be sure, and certainly cannot presume that the joint set of all necessary properties will be sufficient to make the instance an instance of its kind. According to this disputed intuition, there is a clear boundary between what is essential and what is inessential, or accidental. Wittgenstein's metaphors of the thread and of family resemblance blur this distinction between the essential and the accidental. Instead of a sufficient set of necessary properties we now have a set of necessary but insufficient properties together with an *open* set of marks, features, characteristics, none of which can strictly be held to be necessary for instancehood, and no combination of which can strictly be said to be sufficient for instancehood, but which nevertheless constitute *strong reason* for regarding something as an instance of what is in question.[13] Inclusions and exclusions in particular cases may indeed be justified by reference to such marks or characteristic features, but reference to such marks in any

---

[13]   John Canfield, *The Philosophy of Wittgenstein*, Vol. 5: *Method and Essence*; also, Vol. 7: *Criteria*.

particular inclusion or exclusion will not necessarily be extensible to other similar instances—they may be included or excluded for yet other reasons, or for no reason, simply because that is how the word is used. The ultimate ground to which Wittgenstein appeals is not an exhaustive list of such features or characteristics, nor is it an exhaustive list of sets of disjunctions of such properties. The 'bedrock' to which we appeal to decide cases is simply to the contingencies of social practice: and there is no good reason to believe that our practice must be decided for all possible cases, if only because our actual practice is finite.

It might be thought that Wittgenstein's own notion of language games helps to resolve the indeterminacy, insofar as words can have different functions in different language games. But while it is true that different language games might sometimes distinguish different senses of a term, there is no reason why this should always be true. To insist on this is to fall into the trap of presuming that there must be a determinate 'what there is' in question, that the term has a determinate essence in each of different language games. It seems to me, however, that the metaphor of language games works quite distinctly from that of family resemblance: the two may overlap in some places, but they will come apart in others. I understand Wittgenstein's language games as more akin to Husserl's 'regions of Being'—purged of course of its essentialism! Thus, taking the word 'really' as an example, one might see fit to distinguish one set of usages in the physical sciences, another set of usages in the human sciences, and yet another set of usages in everyday life. But there is no reason why its usage in each of these language games may not still be characterized by family resemblance.

The construction of Wittgensteinian penumbral cases is significantly different from the vagueness cases. In these latter, a penumbral object is constructed along a continuum of opposites, and may itself be described by both the term and its contradictory in *one and the same sense* of the word under consideration. Things may be both warm and not warm, and not in two distinct senses of the word 'warm.' We may be thoughtful and at the same time thoughtless, happy and not happy, without distinguishing subtle differences in meaning between the first and second uses of the term. Wittgenstein's penumbral cases are constructed in virtue of a cluster of qualities that constitute characteristic features of the kind of thing in question. Thus penumbral cases may be constructed by finding an appropriate grouping of characteristics that includes sufficient important ones to make it hard to deny that the object is correctly described, and also lacks sufficient important ones to make it hard to affirm that it is indeed as described, or else that includes characteristics strongly felt to be incompatible with what would ordinarily be considered to be a thing of that kind. One is in this way pulled in both directions, and thus the problem of making an appropriate decision that we found in vague penumbral cases again surfaces, only for a different reason. Note that family resemblances do not strictly provide *criteria* for deciding cases, as is sometimes thought, but at most they provide compelling or highly persuasive reasons, and that in the end it is social practice that, in many unclear cases, will have to determine correct usage—where there is a correct usage. If even social practice does not settle the matter, the case remains penumbral. Just as with decision making in the vague penumbral cases, one may make different decisions at different times; different people may make different decisions; different groups of people may make different decisions (depending on the criteria they hold most important); and some may be pulled in both directions simultaneously and feel it necessary both to affirm and to deny the description.

Wittgenstein warns us against attempts to avoid such indeterminacy through appealing to different 'senses': it is, say, a game in one sense of the word, but not in another. By appealing to different senses, different criteria from the cluster of concepts may be taken in order to specify different possible analytic truths, different definitions—different precisifications of our ordinary concept. And these in turn will yield different judgments in penumbral cases—which cases could now be identified as things that satisfy one definition but not another. They may also yield different judgments in what used to be clear cases. Take the concept of fruit, for example. Our ordinary concept excludes tomatoes and aubergines and cucumbers, but the scientific definition makes these clear cases of fruits. Thus under our ordinary language definition a tomato is a clear case of a vegetable, while on our scientific definition it is a clear case of a non-vegetable. Moreover, there is no simple answer as to which is the right judgment and which is wrong. Since both definitions are possible, both judgments are acceptable. Through such precisification one can remove penumbral contradictions by appeal to distinct analyses of the term in question.

But this talk of senses, although it seems to offer a way out of the logical problems associated with indeterminacy, is unsatisfactory. It is implausible in many cases to think of different clusters as identifying different senses of the same word. Chess, football, solitaire, and peek-a-boo are all games. They share a family resemblance, but they are also very unlike one another. Do we say that they each are games in a different sense of the word 'game'? If we are tempted to do so, how many senses of the word are we willing to differentiate? Is there no limit to proliferation of senses? Talk of different senses separates different aspects of the term too radically. It turns them in effect into distinct meanings. Since sense may in this way be divided into an indefinite number of combinations of subsets of family resemblance characteristics, we would end up with an indefinitely large number of distinct, but remarkably similar, senses for each concept. On the contrary, the meaning of the word, rather than being composed of an infinite set of clearly defined, and not easily distinguishable, senses, is more simply conceived of as itself indeterminate. This is because our actual *use* is itself indeterminate. We do not, in practice, have well-defined sets of consistent usage of terms that correspond with such clearly distinguishable senses. Of course, for scientific purposes we may choose one such precisification and stipulate that as our definition, thus making all our other uses scientifically incorrect. But we must remember that our scientific term is now a *new* concept—or at least that it may have become a piece of technical jargon that is not clearly identifiable with the ordinary language term. Just as with the precisification of vague terms, the contradiction is not genuinely *resolved*—one has merely replaced the ordinary indeterminate concept with two quite distinct technical terms with distinct definitions, neither of which is equivalent to the original indeterminate term.[14]

In the penumbral regions all the incongruities that we identified earlier, the traces of vagueness, will be characteristic of the penumbral 'creatures.' Living things are quite obviously creatures of Becoming—things that come into being and go out of being over time—and borderline cases of dog and horse can be found at the beginning and end processes of their lives. Is a horse foetus a horse? Is a recently fertilized horse ovum a horse? Is a dead horse a horse? Is a horse skeleton a horse? There is no distinct and well-defined boundary separating the fully formed horse from the periods that precede it and follow after it. A horse

---

[14] I do not mean to suggest that all scientific refinement must be seen as exchanging an old concept for a new one. Nor am I denying that it is possible for one and the same concept to grow and develop: indeed, this essential openness of concept and meaning is part of what I am arguing for. All I am suggesting here is that one cannot remove any contradictoriness that might result from open texture by appealing to distinct senses. The point here is exactly parallel to the point I raised in connection with 'precisifying' vague concepts.

comes to be, and comes eventually no longer to be, and thus two series of stages—the penumbrae of 'horse'—from *non-horse* to *horse* and back again from *horse* to *non-horse* are constructed for us by nature itself. Moreover it is not only the ontogenesis of particular horses that construct such *sorites* series, but the phylogenesis of the species too has left its own legacy of *sorites* series. Thus natural evolution provides yet another veritable cornucopia of *sorites* transformations and penumbral objects. Cultivation of breeds, and genetic modifications, are ways in which humans are currently actively constructing artificial *sorites* series.

Through such exercises of the imagination we begin to open up the possibility of varieties of vagueness and indeterminacy. Indeed, as soon as the suggestion is made, one finds one's imagination racing ahead, tripping over itself, in the attempt to construct all kinds of continua! Once unleashed, our imaginations refuse to give up their freedom. We find our imaginations exhausting themselves trying to dream up ways to make possible the impossible. Thus we strain to invent monsters and phantoms that defy our ability to classify, that upset our ability to categorize neatly and to keep our world orderly and sensible. We start conjuring up chimeras and mutations in unheard of ways, opening up in all directions dimensions of transformation and metamorphosis. But this very activity of the imagination—its infiltration into our very ability to conceive has more serious consequences for our traditional philosophical understandings. We have seen how the vagueness involved in the process of transformation unsettles the distinctness of being and becoming, by blurring the boundaries between being and non-being. We have also explored the consequences of open texture and family resemblance: how clarity and distinctness, essence and definition, are infiltrated and 'contaminated' by the anomalies they strive in vain to outlaw.

Having struck the chords of open texture and anomaly, we are now prepared to return once again to the *Zhuangzi* and shall listen for where the text resonates in sympathy.

CHAPTER EIGHT

Qi Wu Lun:
Anomalies and the Grindstone

夫言非吹也, 言者有言。其所言者特未定也。果有言邪? 其未嘗有
言邪? 其以為異於鷇音, 亦有辯乎? 其無辯乎?

> Discourse[1] is not wind. A discourser has a discourse, but what is
> said is exceptionally unsettled (indeterminate). Is there really
> discourse? Or has there not yet ever been discourse? As for being
> different from the peeps of fledglings—are there indeed
> disputations over dichotomies, or are there none?

Zhuangzi tells us about what is said that it is 'exceptionally not yet
determined.' We have here a quite explicitly stated doctrine,
although one that is not easy to interpret—one that itself is
'exceptionally undetermined'! Though it is explicit, we are still left
with the ponderous task of interpreting it, of abducing and
developing the sense of the discourse: what is said is exceptionally
not yet determined. One way of understanding meaning is as 'what
one says.' So, saying that what one says is exceptionally unsettled
may be interpreted as saying that meaning is exceptionally
indeterminate. When one engages in discourse, one has something
to say, but what one says is, in some way, not quite fixed. But if
what one says is not fixed, not yet settled, indeed, 'exceptionally
undetermined,' has one really said anything? Is an indeterminate
discourse no discourse at all? Does one really have to be completely
clear in order to say something? Do distinctions really have to be
clearly determined dichotomies as the Mohists tell us, or can one
still say something even if one's distinctions are exceptionally
vague?

Zhuangzi appears thus to be drawing attention to, and
calling into question, the Mohist insistence on clarity, *ming* 明, of

---

[1]   *Yan* 言 can mean 'words,' 'speech,' and can especially in a
philosophical context refer to the doctrines of a thinker or philosophical
school.

distinctions, *bian* 辨, and disputation, *bian* 辯 about the correct application of dichotomous distinctions. Dichotomous distinctions do not make things any the clearer. '言惡乎隱而有是非?' 'How is discourse obscured so there is (the dichotomous judgment of) Yeah and Nay?' Contrary to the insistence of the Mohists, dichotomous evaluations actually succeed only in making discourse obscure. In fact, Zhuangzi goes on to tell us that to see things clearly is to see the possibility of overlap between affirmation and denial. To see clearly is to see the ever-present possibility of indeterminacy, of paradox and contradiction. Thus, Zhuangzi takes the Mohist metaphors of clarity and vision and gives them a radical reinterpretation. *Ming* 明 no longer connotes the sharpness of distinctions, but rather the illumination of indeterminacy and contradiction. When one sees clearly one *allows* the indeterminacy of vagueness to manifest itself. Illumination does not just crudely and forcefully banish the darkness, but allows the shaded to manifest its degrees of shade.[2] In Zhuangzi's words:

欲是其所非而非其所是，則莫若以明。

If you desire to affirm what is denied and deny what is affirmed, then nothing is as good as *ming* illumination.

As we have seen, the *shifei* of the Mohists aims for a determinacy that demands a clear boundary between things that are affirmed and those that are rejected. Zhuangzi asks us to take the *shifei* of the Ruists and Mohists, and then to affirm what they deny and to deny what they affirm. Now the traditional interpretation (and translation) of this passage has it that each affirms what the other denies. Now, while it may be true of the Ruists and Mohists that each affirms what the other denies, I do not find it satisfactory as a translation of the sentence. Even if one

---

2   Husserl's phenomenological method requires us to turn to the things themselves, to allow them to manifest as they are in themselves, clearly and distinctly. Heidegger shows us that such a return to the things themselves must always be hermeneutic—how things manifest themselves is always a matter of how we attend to them and interpret them. Derrida, I suggest, continues this deconstruction of the phenomenological project by pointing out that what appears as 'present' to our phenomenological reflections is in fact already infiltrated to its core with traces of its own absence. Thus a genuine phenomenological sensitivity to our own understanding immediately reveals that its own indeterminacy is out of our control.

presupposes that the point being made is a relativistic one, this interpretation still requires the grammar to be stretched just a little beyond comfort. The problem lies in the changing reference of the pronoun. The original reference, earlier in the passage, is to 'the Ruists *and* the Mohists'[3] and, according to the grammar of Zhou dynasty Chinese (as, surely, with the grammar of most languages), the pronouns ought ordinarily to be taken as continuing this reference, unless some indication is given otherwise. If the reference were to change so drastically that each time of its repetition it were given yet another referent, it would be extraordinary for this not to be indicated explicitly by the grammar of the sentence. In short, it is not impossible for the traditional reading to hold, but it is extremely unlikely from the point of view of grammatical simplicity.

Now that we have preserved the paradoxicality of the original, the question arises as to how to make sense of it. The interpretation I prefer gives prominence to the literal contradictoriness, or at least the literal recommendation of contradictoriness, of the text. Now, contradictions are ordinarily taken as beyond the pale of understandability. We know that we have made the most glaring of errors when we find ourselves tied up in contradictions. For this reason the deliberate assertion of contradictions is the hardest thing to interpret. Indeed, it is ordinarily a principle of interpretation that one's interpretation ought to be consistent, and that if it ends up contradictory we ought to reconsider the details. This is ordinarily a good principle to follow, but it has its limitations. In particular, one ought not to follow it when one is translating a clear and explicit contradiction. This is especially the case if there is a predilection for contradictions, and again if the text is pervaded with the aura of paradox. One may remove a single contradiction, or even several unrelated contradictions, if one has reason to believe that the writer had no tolerance for such things. But if the use of contradictions betrays a distinctive sensibility, then we must think again. Here, it is not the case that Zhuangzi ends up inconsistent, but that he is deliberately and explicitly contradicting himself. In such cases, even if we do not understand

---

3   It is surely significant that the reference to the Mohists occurs only in this binome '*Rumo*' 儒墨. It is not clear, however, exactly what the function of this binome is: whether it refers to both schools, to the arguments between them, or whether this combination actually signifies something else. While the Mohist writings are replete with *shìng* and *feìng*, the Ruist writings are not; and while the Mohists expend a great deal of effort *feìng* the Ruists and their doctrines quite explicitly, the Ruists waste little time returning the compliment.

the purpose or significance of the contradictions, we still ought simply to preserve the contradictions not only in our translation, but also in our interpretation. The problem for the interpreter of Zhuangzi is to understand the context and significance of this explicit recommendation of contradictoriness.

Zhuangzi implies that we *ought* to affirm what we deny and deny what we affirm. Now, I think it is significant that there is in this instruction no explicit reference to points of view, nor is there even any hint that we are to resolve the contradiction by relativizing to points of view. Indeed, the purpose seems to be to enable us to see beyond the apparent unacceptability of contradictions. But how do we do this? And, more importantly, Why? What is the virtue in contradicting ourselves? As we have seen, the canons of the later Mohists commit them to some form of a Principle of Contradiction, according to which it is unacceptable both to assert and deny the same thing. For any dispute over what to call something, either the suggested characterization matches, *dang* 當, or it does not, *budang* 不當. For example, I might consider whether the thing, *wu* 物, before me right now is a horse. According to the Mohists the answer must be either 'Yes' or 'No.' It cannot be both and it cannot be neither. In any dispute, one side, and only one, must match—one and only one of the disputants must win, *sheng* 勝. If one side matches, the other side does not. It is not possible for both sides or neither side to match. But we have seen that a sensitivity to vagueness and open texture remains open to the *possibility* of contradictoriness in the penumbral regions. The applicability of contradictory judgments draws attention to the fact that we are dealing with borderline objects of the penumbral region. Thus, it is not the contradictoriness itself that Zhuangzi is praising for it own sake, but rather the fact that contradictions might well indeed be applicable in the penumbral borderlands. Thus, *in the borderlands*, which might be more extensive than we generally think, getting clear involves abandoning presuppositions of mutual exclusivity that refuse to make room for contradiction. This is entirely at odds with the Mohist understanding of disputation over distinctions.

Disputation 辯

> 既使我與若辯矣，若勝我，我不若勝，若果是也？我果非也邪？我勝若，若不吾勝，我果是也？而果非也邪？其或是也？其或非也邪？其俱是也？其俱非也邪？

Suppose you and I are disputing. You beat me, and I do not beat you. Are you really right and I really wrong? If I beat you and you do not beat me, am I really right and you really wrong? Is one right and the other wrong? Or both right, or both wrong?

Zhuangzi takes up the theme of disputation as discussed by the Mohists, according to which one side or other of the disputants must win. He considers their intuitions of bivalence, or at least of dichotomousness, and wonders if there isn't perhaps some other possibility. He sees two other possibilities: we might both be right, or we might both be wrong! Now, the Mohist *Canon* has already explicitly ruled out the first possibility, and implicitly the second, simply by defining disputation as disputation over *alternatives*: if it is possible for both sides to be right, or to be wrong, then this is not properly to be called a disputation, 辯. If I say, 'This is a dog,' and you reply, 'No! It's a mutt!' it is possible for both of us to be right (if it is a mutt), or both to be wrong (if it turns out to be a fox). But this is not a genuine disputation over alternatives. The Mohist conception of alternatives requires that the two sides be incompatible. So, given Zhuangzi's concern with contradictions, he cannot be simply considering this simplistic possibility that the Mohist has already clearly allowed for and set aside. On the contrary, Zhuangzi is taking the Mohists' restricted sense of disputation *over alternatives*, and wondering if the two sides of such a disputation might not both be right, or both be wrong! He does not at this point explain how or why this could be possible.

> 我與若不能相知也。則人固受其黮闇，吾誰使正之？使同乎若者正
> 之？ 既與若同矣，惡能正之！ 使同乎我者正之？ 既同乎我矣，惡能
> 正之！ 使異乎我與若者正之？ 既異乎我與若矣，惡能正之！ 使同乎
> 我與若者正之？ 既同乎我與若矣，惡能正之！ 然則我與若與人俱不
> 能相知也，而待彼也邪？

If you and I cannot understand each other, then others will surely be left in the dark. Who shall we get to straighten things out? One who agrees with you? But if they agree with you how can they decide? One who agrees with me? Since they agree with me, how can they decide? One who differs from you and me? Since they differ from you and me how can they decide? One who agrees with me and you? Since they agree with us how can they decide? In this way if you and I and others are all unable to understand one another, are we to wait upon yet another?

Zhuangzi continues his considerations about disputation, and wonders about the possibility of arbitration. How would one settle such a dispute over alternatives? He raises a crude but clear version of the problem of the criterion. As he phrases the question, it is indeed insurmountable: if the only consideration about the arbitrator is who they agree with, then there can be no way to choose satisfactorily for both parties. In practice, however, who the arbitrator agrees with is not the relevant deciding issue. The settling of disputes is, in real terms, far more complex than who agrees with whom. There is an array of issues that we must take into account: each side may be open to the possibility of being mistaken; each side may even be open to persuasion by the other; each side may carefully reconsider reasons for their decision; one may consult an authority considered reliable and trusted by both parties: and this does not come close to exhausting the possibilities of fair and equitable arbitration. However, there is one type of argument for which Zhuangzi's suspicions are relevant. This is where one is arguing over fundamental values, and indeed over the very values that are relevant to deciding such fundamental disagreements themselves. That is, argument about the very criteria for settling arguments. Suppose that one side thinks that one must weigh and quantify accurately all the pros and cons and assess them according to some explicit theory, because intuitions without quantification and theoretization are dangerously lacking in logical rigor; while the other side thinks that it is better to imagine as fully as possible the relevant possibilities, and then to make a carefully considered intuitive judgment, because objective calculations without imagination and intuition are dangerously lacking in human feeling. Is it likely that they will even be willing to communicate with each other, let alone come to an agreement over these basic values? In this context we can see the relevance of Zhuangzi's concern over mutual understanding, *xiang zhi* 相知. When opposing sides have such fundamental differences, it is hard for them even to begin to understand one another, let alone have much respect for one another.

化聲之相待。若其不相待，和之以天倪，因之以曼衍，所以窮年也。

Changing voices waiting upon one another: if they do not wait, harmonize them with the grindstone of nature, make them accord with a graceful overflow—the means by which to last out your years.

Zhuangzi returns to the metaphor of music with his 'image' of argumentation as the alternation, or altercation, of voices. But opposing voices need not wait to have their turn! The simultaneity of disagreement need not result in cacophony, but may be productive of harmony: polytonality and dissonance provide new ways in which dissenting voices may sing together without shouting each other down.[4] This is not to say that all disagreements are mere dissonances that must, or even can, be made harmonious, but simply that not all disagreements need result in combat or conflict.

「何謂和之以天倪?」曰:「是不是, 然不然。是若果是也, 則是之異乎不是也亦無辯; 然若果然也, 則然之異乎不然也亦無辯。」

What do you mean by 'harmonize them with the grindstone of nature?' 'Affirm 是 what isn't, and attribute 然 what isn't so! If This 是 were really This, then there would be no disputing the difference between This and not This. If so 然 were really so, then there would be no disputing the difference between so and not so.'

Zhuangzi is asked to explain what he means by 'harmonize them with the grindstone of nature,' but his explanation is less than transparent. Nevertheless, we can see from his response that harmonizing with the grindstone of nature has to do with opposites, specifically the opposites of affirming and not affirming, and the opposites of being so and not being so. Again, these opposites are placed side by side in a manner that, if not contradictory, is at least paradoxical. The point might be one of the alternation of opposites, affirming and not affirming, attributing and not attributing, and this would certainly follow the image of circularity of the activity of the grindstone. But the sequel in which Zhuangzi suggests that This might not 'really' be This and that what is so might not be really what is so, hints at a deeper significance. It is not clear how to translate the word '*guo*' 果 here. It literally means 'fruit' and is often used in the metaphorical sense of what has indeed turned out to be the case, and so can be translated as 'really,' 'surely,' 'indeed.' The word, however, has no associations with any philosophical theory that distinguishes a hidden reality from an illusory appearance, and so we must be careful not to impose this sense inappropriately. The rhetorical force of the question seems to us at first somehow to lessen the certainty of affirmation and attribution,

---

4   Or perhaps, with polytonality and dissonance we rediscover more ancient possibilities of harmonization.

but it might also be the completeness, or maybe the 'absoluteness' of such judgments that is being called into question. Using the later Mohist *Canon* as my interpretive context, the question takes on the function of lessening the rigidity of dichotomous judgments. If affirmation and attribution were simple, complete, and dichotomous matters, with clear differences between This and not This, so and not so, then it is hard to see how any disputes could arise. Perhaps, then, the function of the grindstone is not simply to juxtapose opposites or exchange them in cycles, but somehow to blend them together, allowing them at intervals to manifest simultaneously.

This and Other

物無非彼，物無非是。自彼則不見，自知則知之。故曰：彼出於是，是亦因彼。彼是方生之說也。

Nothing is not *Other*; nothing is not *This*. Self-Othering they do not appear; self-affirming [reading 是 for 知, to preserve the parallel] one knows them. Thus it is said, 'the *Other* emerges from *This*, *This* also accords with its *Other*.' This is the explanation of the mutual engendering of *Other* and *This*.

'As for things, there are none that are not Other. As for things, there are none that are not This.' Put more colloquially: everything is Other; everything is This. Zhuangzi here takes up the theme of the Other of which the Mohist has demonstrated a morbid fear. The Mohist despises that which does not belong, and needs to eradicate it from his system for fear of corrupting the whole and planting the seed of disintegration. Zhuangzi responds by asserting the ubiquity of Otherness: nothing can escape its own otherness, because everything is already other. It is notable that there is no explicit reference to points of view here. But is it possible to make sense of this without reference to points of view? I think that the idea of the merging of opposites can be fruitfully juxtaposed with, or overlaid on, Zhuangzi's text here. When 'things' other themselves, recognize their own alterity, their kinship with what appears to be alien, they break down the barriers that ordinarily define them, and understand them-'selves' through a more expansive identification that refuses to acknowledge absolute boundaries between This and Other. Then they do not manifest as clearly identifiable things. They can be known as things when they confirm their identities through a self-affirmation that allows them to be separated clearly from their Others. In this way, This and Other are mutually dependent, and mutually arise. This does not mean simply that one is defined with reference to the other: it is not just that defining the boundaries of some thing, simultaneously defines an outside that it is not. Rather, there is a deeper significance, one that challenges the efficiency of the boundary itself: it implies an interdiffusion and interpenetration of these opposites. Moreover, the dichotomous opposites that the Mohist sets up take on a deeper significance for Zhuangzi: the existential significance of Life and Death, or rather of living and dying. This and Other, something and nothing, living and non-living, acceptable and unacceptable mutually give rise to each other. But by the same token, each is indeed also the potential source of dissolution of the other. There is no escaping this: living is dying; the acceptable and the unacceptable are not so easily separable as we would wish.

> 雖然，方生方死，方死方生；方可方不可，方不可方可；因是因非
> ，因非因是。是以聖人不由，而照之於天，亦因是也。

> However, when arising, then dying; when dying, then arising; when [an affirmation] is acceptable, it is not acceptable; when not acceptable, it is acceptable. An according affirmation accommodates what is denied; an according denial accommodates what is affirmed. Thus the sage does not follow, but illuminates it through *tian*, and indeed affirms accordingly.[5]

Now Zhuangzi takes the theme of the mutuality of opposites and iterates it, suggesting 'cycles' of interdiffusion and interdependence between This and Other, living and dying, acceptability and unacceptability, affirmation and denial. These are complex, interlocking, interweaving cycles and epicycles of interpenetration and interdiffusion, from which the sage has somehow to escape. It seems that the reason that the sage must escape is to maintain equanimity amidst the turmoil of circumstances and of our emotions, but it is not clear how it is possible for any thing or anyone to do so. Presumably the illuminating of the cycles, and of the interdiffusion, of opposites, allowing them to manifest plainly, either enables the sage to do so, or is a consequence of their being so

---

5   According to Graham's analysis, deeming affirmation *weishi* 為是 is a form of judgment that does not take into account the overlap and interplay of This and Other. According affirmation is an attitude that takes this into account as fully as possible: it tries to remain as open as possible to the complexity of the particular without forcing it into one of two dichotomous categories.

enabled. Yet, we are informed, with a paradox that strains intelligibility, that even this is an affirmation that accords—an affirmation of the sort that was just given a place *within* the interlocking cycles of things!

是亦彼也，彼亦是也。彼亦一是非，此亦一是非，果且有彼是乎哉
？果且無彼是乎哉?

This indeed is Other; Other indeed is This. The former indeed unifies affirmation and rejection; the latter also unifies affirmation and rejection. Are there really Other and This? Or is there really no Other and This?

Zhuangzi, in this passage, is playing here with three pairs of related opposites: *shi* 是 and *bi* 彼, 'This' and 'Other'; *shi* 是 and *fei* 非, 'affirmation' and 'rejection'; and *ci* 此 and *bi* 彼, 'this instance here' and 'the other one' (or, 'the latter' and 'the former'). *Shi* and *fei* are intimately related to the indexicals 'this' and 'that,' 'here' and 'there,' where this here is affirmed, and that there is rejected. But if we make these kinds of expansive identifications, then we create difficulties for our everyday indexical terms. How can we refer to things, distinguish things from other things, evaluate things? If we insist on shaking off such boundaries, then ordinary language begins to lose its grip. It is not obvious at this stage why we should consider this to be a good thing. Still, if we are persuaded by Zhuangzi's understanding of the mutual interpenetration and diffusion of opposites, then his application of this to our existential predicament will have a great significance. We see our lives, and our relation to other people, and our relation to our own deaths, in a new light: or rather, we do not just *see* these in a new light, but we actually *experience* them in a new way, one that has, perhaps, a greater chance of dissipating existential anxieties.

Using a horse that is not a horse

以指喻指之非指，不若以非指喻指之非指也；以馬喻馬之非馬，不
若以非馬喻馬 之非馬也。

To use an indication to illustrate how an indication may be a non-indication is not as good as using a non-indication to illustrate how an indication may be a non-indication. To use a horse to illustrate a horse's not being a horse is not as good as using a non-horse to illustrate a horse's not being a horse.

This is one of those mysterious passages that demand an interpretation and yet seem so paradoxical that finding a context and purpose for the statement is exceptionally difficult. The passage assumes that one would want to show that a horse is not a horse, and suggests a method for doing so. But no explanation of why one would want to do so is made clear. Nor is it obvious why, if the contradiction should hold, the negative method is better than the positive method. Moreover, the first sentence is made particularly hard to interpret because of the presence of the word *zhi* 指 which though it literally means 'finger' also has a more technical meaning, about which there has been some controversy.[6] The word has, by extension, the verbal sense of 'to point,' and thus also the nominal senses 'pointing' and perhaps 'what is pointed at,' or more abstractly, 'to indicate' or 'refer' and thus 'indicating' and 'what is indicated,' or 'referring' and 'what is referred to,' or even as some translators insist, 'concept.' In the work of Gongsun Longzi, at whom this passage appears to be throwing a wink, the term seems clearly to be functioning in some such abstract technical sense. The difficulty is over how best to translate this sense into English. The words 'concept' and 'meaning' might seem appropriate for this technical sense, but the problem is that these terms carry a host of epistemological and ontological associations derived from the peculiar histories of their usage in western philosophy. Since the history and consequent associations of the Chinese term could not but have been vastly different, choice of a more neutral term would be advisable. I have chosen the term 'indication,' not because it eases understanding, but because it reflects some of the awkwardness and difficulty of the original passage!

In this instruction, or suggestion, Zhuangzi leads us part of the way toward explaining how to use *ming*. He begins to hint at some kind of method for enabling us to *shi* what we *fei* and *fei* what we *shi*. If we want to see how something may be other to itself, we will not get far if we insist on looking at examples of things that are clear cases of reference ('indication'). Looking at clear cases of what is affirmed will only confirm our suspicions that affirmation and denial are mutually exclusive. In fact, this is a very common

---

6   We could take the two sentences as on a par, as two instances of paradox: the first giving the example of a finger, the second giving the example of a horse. The problem with this is that the term *zhi* has not been used in other texts as a standard example in the way that *ma*, horse, has. Indeed the connection with logic suggests that it is best interpreted in the way that Gongsun Longzi uses it, and this is in its more abstract sense of indicating.

reaction to discussions of vagueness, even among otherwise reflective people. Of course there is no vagueness, they insist, just look at all the things around us that clearly are what they are! The attempt to stretch the imagination with hypothetical counter-examples is usually met with an extraordinary resistance, a determination to decide firmly and decisively one way or the other, no matter how anomalous or unfamiliar the counter-example. Zhuangzi's suggestion, then, is that we approach the matter from the other direction: start with things that are not clear cases of reference. If we start with what is different, it might be easier to free up our imaginations, to be more open to the stranger possibilities. After reveling in the unfamiliar terrain, populated with mutants, monsters, and misfits, we slowly head back, only now aware of the continuity and affinities between the borderlands and our home.

Once one has become familiar with becoming unfamiliar, one will find it easier to make the explorations from home outwards. We might then start with a typical or paradigmatic case, but actively search for the seeds of its otherness. We take a prototypical case and make it less familiar, allow something here and there slowly to transform, to grow, to develop, so that the thing becomes increasingly peculiar. This, of course, is Wittgenstein's method in the *Philosophical Investigations*, and Waismann's method of exploring the openness and porousness of our concepts. Wittgenstein worries at the edges of familiarity, pushes us this way and that, trying to gain a sense for where the fabric starts to open, where it thins, how it thins, and its potential for being woven in new directions. When we enter the penumbra, the grip of language becomes less firm: *yes* and *no* become less clearly opposed. The deeper into the shade we go, the harder it becomes to make a persuasive decision. We are able to see the mutual interdiffusion of *This* and *Other*, but now that we have lost our grip, we are not sure how to cope, how to find our way, how to deal with penumbral things.

There is a tendency to overreact to this situation: if there are no sharp boundaries, then nothing can be differentiated from anything else, there is just a monotonous porridge of indifference. This reaction is not altogether without justification. Zhuangzi does, on occasion, have a tendency to draw such conclusions, especially when encouraging us to travel beyond the human point of view. The more vast and expansive Zhuangzi becomes, the more forgetful he becomes of things of human significance, the more dismissive he becomes of human values. There are times when he almost begins to identify pragmatic concern and human feeling with a pettiness that is not worthy of the vastness, the greatness of the sage. This, I think, is a dangerous tendency, because the ethical and the political remain solidly grounded in the human and the pragmatic. If, then, we take seriously the urge to expand utterly beyond the human, to lose all pragmatic concern, then we also thereby lose our ties to the ethical. For this reason, Zhuangzi's insight into the continuity of things that emerges as we leave behind the human should remain at the level of theoretical appreciation. As humans we are responsible to one another and for one another. A theoretical awareness of superhuman perspectives from which such responsibilities become insignificant does not free us from those responsibilities.

But, a recognition of the interdiffusion of self and other does *not* require us to abandon our humanity. The expansion of our identification of self and other does not require us to become altogether inhuman. On the contrary, it is a more thoroughgoing humanity that is able to acknowledge the fluidity and flexibility of its own boundaries, that is able to identify with and recognize the *value* of other 'individuals,' other peoples, other ways of life, other species, and with the natural world in which we are inextricably embedded.

Boundaries

古之人，其知有所至矣。惡乎至？有以為未始有物者，至矣，盡矣，不可以加矣！

The people of old, their understanding was far reaching! How far reaching? There was [the level at which] they thought that there have not yet begun to be things—Extensive! Exhaustive! Unsurpassable!

At the highest stage one does not discriminate things at all. This is the rarified stage of the view from nowhere, the stage that has gone utterly beyond all human concern, a stage that should remain at the level of theoretical appreciation: a limiting possibility, one extreme on the scale of human concern. Zhuangzi's response to the Mohist insistence on the need for dichotomous boundaries sometimes takes this startling and inhuman form: he sometimes insists that for the utmost and unsurpassable understanding there are no boundaries, no things, no judgments, no evaluations. He himself is very aware how distant and grotesque his ideas can sometimes be: 'vast and out of line, beyond human concern.' But he does not remain at this rarefied and horrifying point of view: he more often plummets to a perspective that is more recognizably and reassuringly human. After all, the majority of the stories in the *Zhuangzi* take place in the realm of human interaction, and most of his descriptions presuppose things, creatures, people—though things, creatures, and people that may be less than familiar, and that may develop in extraordinary ways.

其次以為有物矣，而未始有封也。其次以為有封焉，而未始有是非也。

> Next they took it that there are things, but that there have not yet begun to be bounded regions. Next they thought that there are bounded regions, but that there have not yet begun to be dichotomous judgments, *shifei.*

At the next stage, one allows for things that have no boundaries. These are the boundaries of the bounded regions, *feng* 封; the metaphor here is both political and geographical. The *feng* are the feudal regions in which 'things' are located and have their regional identities. In some way there is more now than undifferentiated mush, there is some kind of plurality of differentiable things, but these things are not grouped into bounded regions. The third stage allows for a plurality of differentiable things, and allows for them to be grouped into distinctive bounded regions, but still withholds the application of dichotomous judgment. Thus, even at these 'lower' levels, Zhuangzi still maintains that we will engage better with our world and with people if we at least diminish the sharpness of boundaries. On occasion, Zhuangzi takes a journey out beyond the bounded regions, from the real to the surreal, to the realm of the fantastic. But even then his aim is not to *demonstrate* the illusoriness of things, but to encourage us to be unafraid of the unfamiliar, and to urge us not to batter it down with our crude preconceptions. This is not, I hope, the absurd (and ultimately impossible) demand of the radical relativist that everything unfamiliar be tolerated, no matter how brutal and destructive it may be, but simply a plea for a greater openness to other possibilities.

Process

We notice that these stages of understanding that characterize the stages of the formation of things are described temporally. The highest stage of understanding takes it that there 'have *not yet* begin to be' things! It is not just that there are no things, but that things have not yet begun. There is an incipience that keeps this mode of understanding in anticipation. At the next stage, it is not that there are no boundaries, but that there have not yet begun to be boundaries. Things are not yet grouped off, regionalized. At the next stage, things are regionalized, but one does not (yet) allow them to judge or to be judged dichotomously.

The highest understanding of the people of old was their appreciation for the stage of no things. But one can also read this as claiming that they somehow lived permanently in this state! They related to the world as though nothing had yet come into being. Zhuangzi seems to be asserting this as the attitude toward which we ought to strive, and in doing so again appears to be advocating that we attempt to leave behind our human perspective. It is difficult to know how to understand these claims, or how to respond philosophically. If Zhuangzi is advising us to transcend the human altogether, then this is an altogether unhelpful philosophy. Those who have 'mystical' sensibilities will have more patience with these doctrines than I do, but they remain open to the criticism that such views roam dangerously far beyond the ethical. If Zhuangzi is describing a phenomenology of levels of awareness, this becomes extraordinarily interesting, though it does not escape the ethical criticism. Even if it were possible to remain in the utmost and unsurpassable phenomenological attitude, it is not clear (at least, from the admittedly human phenomenological standpoint) why we should do so. It would seem, at a naïve level of response, that, even if we were freed from our passions and anxieties, we would be unable to cope with the everyday world of things and people. At least, if we are still able to interact with 'things' there is no obvious explanation as to how this would be possible.

It is also possible that this is intended as a temporal description of the emergence of things, or perhaps as a *phenomenological* description of the 'temporal' emergence of things in our awareness. If this is so, then the highest level is not a level that Zhuangzi is necessarily recommending. It is simply the broadest, most fundamental, or 'original' level of description possible. At first there are not even things. It is not just that there are no things, but that there had not yet begun to be things. This is the time before the formation of things. All things come into being, and then disintegrate. For all things there is a time before which they can be identified completely and unequivocally. And there is a period during which the things begin to come to be: the process of their production, during which one cannot unequivocally say that the thing itself is there yet. This motif of 'not yet beginning to be there' is one that is picked up, developed, and indeed iterated in the following passage:

有始也者，有未始有始也者，有未始有夫未始有始也者。

There is a beginning.
There is not yet begun to be a beginning.
There is not yet begun to be not yet begun to be a beginning.

Zhuangzi is considering the incipience of things, the 'not yet begun to be.' This phrase *wei shi you*, though it is sometimes translated 'never,' I contend can have the connotation 'just about to become,' and if so, it draws our attention to the process of becoming. Through the iteration of this phrase, we find ourselves paying closer and closer attention to this process. But to the process of the becoming of what? He goes on to say:

有有也者，有無也者，有未始有無也者，有未始有夫未始有無也者。

There is something.
There is nothing.
There is not yet begun to be nothing.
There is not yet begun to be not yet begun to be nothing.

Thus he sets up the two poles of the spectrum: there being something, and there being nothing. He then considers the process during which something becomes nothing. Before there is nothing, there is the not quite nothing, and before that the not quite not quite nothing. The example Zhuangzi uses shows the level of generality that he is interested in: the processes of transformation between something and nothing. The iteration of the phrase '*wei shi you*,' incidentally, indicates that the meaning cannot be 'never,' unless we take the repetition to be merely emphatic. But if it refers to a period just before, then the iteration becomes meaningful.

俄而有無矣，而未知有無之果孰有孰無也。

Eventually, there is nothing, but we do not yet know of something and nothing which really is something and which is nothing.

At some point we suddenly realize that what was there has altogether vanished. But, because of the subtlety of the transformation, there is no clear dividing line between something and nothing. Zhuangzi seems to want to draw from this the conclusion that we cannot tell the difference between something and nothing. Now, Zhuangzi is right that there is a time when we cannot say clearly if we still have or no longer have the thing, there is a penumbral stage between its existence and its dissolution, but this is the case only in the penumbral region, the region of the 'not yet.' The instabilities of the penumbral region do not extend into the clear regions. It is entirely unpersuasive to be told that because there is no clear dividing line between being alive and being dead, we can *never* tell whether a person is alive or dead!

A recurring motif in the *Zhuangzi* is a bodily metaphor for these processes of becoming and unbecoming. At first there is nothing *wu*. Slowly, gradually, there begins an emergence: a slow development into something *you*. Then comes all the madness of living: the choruses and cacophonies of likes and dislikes, hopes and fears. Slowly the noise dies down and we are left with the shimmering silence that is the condition of the possibility of other things and creatures. Laozi's emptiness takes on several forms in Zhuangzi's hands: the holes and spaces of the pipes of nature; the breath that informs the ten thousand things; the emptiness at the center of the grindstone, and the axis around which it turns, *dao shu* 道樞.

The grindstone and the potter's wheel

萬物皆種也，以不同形相禪，始卒若環，莫得其倫，是謂天均。天均者，天倪也。

the ten thousand things disseminating
with different forms giving way to one another
beginning and ending like the rounds of a wheel
none attaining their match:
this is the potter's wheel of nature.
The potter's wheel of nature is the grindstone of nature.

The traditional reading of the metaphor of the grindstone of nature *tian ni* 天倪 has relied on the commentary of Guo Xiang, and in doing so has taken the activity of the grindstone to be an equalization and relativization of all things and viewpoints. But it is not entirely clear to me what exactly the analogy is: why a grindstone? And why nature? We have already seen above that Zhuangzi's gloss on the grindstone links it quite directly to the harmonization of opposites. Somehow the grindstone will blend together opposites that seem mutually antagonistic. Still, it is not immediately evident, what it is about the grindstone that facilitates this. I believe that situating Zhuangzi's philosophy in the cultural context of the significance of nature as embodied in the naturalistic tradition of the *Laozi* will enable us to provide a possible line of interpretation: an abduction of the function of the image of the grindstone in the Daoist cultural encyclopedia. This abduction also helps to make sense of the mysterious identification of the grindstone with the potter's wheel of nature.

The grindstone of nature is a vivid image evoking the slow and relentless revolutions of heaven and earth, and the softening, smoothing, pulverizing activity that is the result of the passing of time. There are several elements that are significant in this metaphor: the first is a cyclical regularity: things give way to their opposites in a regular exchange. The second is an unstoppable momentum: the cycles seem inexhaustible. The third is that function that the grindstone has of pulverizing, wearing down. We have already investigated the significance of the cyclical regularity as encapsulated in the understanding of *yin* and *yang*. This irrepressible movement wears down the artificially constructed barriers between apparently radically different things. Perhaps the most immediate manifestation of the revolutions of the grindstone in the Daoist 'lifeworld' is the the slow, heavy rotation of the earth itself: or, if this image is too anachronistic, the rotation of the circle of the heavens around the square clod of earth through an invisible axis whose pivot is marked by the Pole Star. The *yinyang* cycles, as day and night each transform into their partners, are iterated at other levels: the cycles of the moon, and the cycles of the seasons. These natural cycles are of both astronomical and agricultural significance, and so might well have been important factors in the understanding of a Daoist 'shaman.' Through the transformations of the seasons a natural displacement of opposites takes place: the heat of summer becomes the frozen winter; supple green plants come to fruition, and without ever losing their momentum find themselves withering back to their origin. In turn, supple green shoots emerge from its remains: the movement is a constant turning, a curvature that both moves always forwards and yet brings things around to the place from which they came. The transformation is dramatic: winter is not summer, but its polar opposite, just as cold is the absence of heat and life the absence of death—yet the process of change escapes detection at the closest level: its subtlety is below the threshold of perceivability.

故為是舉莛與楹，厲與西施，恢詭譎怪，道通為一。

Thus, artificial judgment picks out twigs and trunks, the ugly, and [the beautiful courtesan] Xishi: vast and anomalous, crafty and strange, the interdiffusion of the way makes them continuous.

The term I have translated here as 'artificial judgment,' '*wei shi*,' is a technical term that A. C. Graham has rendered as 'the that's it which deems' and that he argues is to be distinguished from *yinshi*, 'the that's it that goes by circumstance' (which I translate as 'judging accordingly').[7] The first of these is a mode of judgment that is final, and encoded in traditional dichotomous distinctions, while the second is the more flexible mode of judgment of the sage, one that accords with the transformations of things and their contexts. Here the opposites chosen are what I have termed contrasts: twigs and trunks, the ugly and the beautiful. But the opposition of these contrasts is far from absolute. Twigs and trunks differ in size, but over time one might become the other. A twig might in appropriate conditions sprout roots and slowly develop into a tree; conversely, a trunk might die on the outside, and slowly decay except for a single shoot. Things that are pleasing or displeasing in their looks do not necessarily remain that way, but are prone to change gradually and even dramatically. Situations can turn unpleasant in the blink of an eye. Environmental balances and bodily equilibria can follow winding and tortuous paths. Familiar things are connected by meandering paths of transformation to unfamiliar, peculiar mutations. The unity or continuity of things, then, is not a bland indistinguishability, but a holistic interconnectedness of developmental, organic pathways. Anything can theoretically become anything, but not by just any procedure: some processes have greater tendencies than others.

This process emphasizes the continuum that connects opposites across a no man's land without clear boundaries. We have found in the *Zhuangzi* the explicit thematization of boundarilessness, an insistent cautioning about imposing inflexible boundaries: boundaries that set limits, that make *artificial* constraints on what is possible and what is not, and also boundaries that serve to separate and delineate one thing from another. What something is and what it becomes is not marked by a sudden and radical displacement of identity, but a smooth, continuous evolution of that 'self-same' identity—what is so imperceptibly evolves into what it is not. *It* loses its identity while retaining its identity, when *it* no longer is what it was. A question is

---

7   See Graham's *Chuang Tzu The Inner Chapters: A Classic of Tao*, and also, *Disputers of the Tao: Philosophical Argument in Ancient China.*

raised here: what should be the attitude of the philosopher to such contradictions? The Daoist attitude seems happy to reconcile itself with the paradox; the analytic attitude demands a dissolution and a resolution of the inconsistency. The analytic attitude demands that we force the world into our perfect framework when it misbehaves; the Daoist attitude urges us to *understand* its paradoxical behavior.

Processes of birth, growth, development, and decay abound throughout nature, and they are not defined by sharp cut-off points. Things become what they are not, through an infinite series of imperceptible changes, resulting in dramatic transformations. Things come into and go out of being as mere stages of larger organic processes that do not respect the integrity of the demarcations and delineations of those constituent stages. What something is and what it becomes—a caterpillar, say, and a butterfly—is not marked by a sudden and radical displacement of identity, but takes place through a smooth, continuous evolution of something that remains itself, a metamorphosis—what is so, *ran*, imperceptibly evolves into what it is not, *buran*. 'Things' are processes that 'take place' along a continuum of transformation, and the temporal boundaries that delimit such pragmata are not points of separation but regions of connection. Presence and absence—we might even, from a western perspective, push the point and insist 'being' and 'non-being'—are not mutually exclusive opposites but lie along a continuum along which each transforms, imperceptibly and by degrees, into the other. In a world of process even Being becomes a matter of degrees!

But the grindstone of nature is also the potter's wheel of nature. What then is the significance of the potter's wheel? The potter's wheel is also huge and heavy, and relentless in its revolutions. But while the grindstone is slow and breaks things down, the potter's wheel is quick and builds things up. The grindstone is *yin*; the potter's wheel is *yang*. But they are also one and the same! The processes of transformation by which things develop and break down are the very same processes by which they develop and grow. Each reaches for its Other, as they pull each other up, and take each other down, in continuous, endless cycles of momentum. And never do they find a moment of completion.

Chapter six, 'The Great Ancestral Teacher' *Da Zong Shi* 大宗師 takes up the theme of living and dying that is raised in *Qi Wu Lun*, but it now becomes purged of the existential anxiety with which it was infused at its earlier introduction. The moral of *Qi Wu Lun* is now developed and internalized into a more thorough understanding of the interlocking cyclical processes by which things arise and disintegrate. The maker *zaozhe* 造者 places a great clod *dakuai* 大塊 on the potter's wheel of nature *tianjun* 天均, and utilizing the circular motion around the pivot introduces holes and spaces: making vessels and containers, forms and shapes of all kinds. Things form and shape one another, transform into one another. And as the potter's wheel turns the very same things that have been moulded are ground down into dust, thus forming the stuff for the moulding of other things. In this way the cyclical process can continue without exhaustion. Nothing is used up because everything is reused: a finite process becomes infinite by turning back on itself.

In chapter 25, *Ze Yang*, there is a curious definition of a technical term, *qiu li*, which Graham identifies with the Mohist *qu*, demarcation:[8]

> A ward or sector word . . . joins together the different and treats them as similar, disperses the similar and treats them as different. Now the fact that when you point out from each other the hundred parts of a horse you do not find the horse, yet there the horse is, tethered in front of you, is because you stand the hundred parts on another level to call them 'horse.' For the same reason, a hill or mountain accumulates the low to become the high, the Yangtse and the Yellow River join together the small to become the big....

We see here the gradual accumulation that transforms contraries into one another, what is this, *shi*, into its other, *bi*. The examples that the follower of Zhuangzi gives can be seen as belonging to two distinct types, the first involving the purely imaginary joining of parts to make the whole, and is not as it stands a *sorites* transformation. It can however with a slight modification be altered to produce a paradox of 'material constitution,' a kind of paradox that has close affinities with the *sorites* paradox.[9] The second set of examples, on the other hand contains clear instances of *sorites* transformations (again replacing contradictories with contraries): from low to high and from small to big. In chapter two Zhuangzi presents us with what now can be seen to lend itself to interpretation as the paradoxical outcome of *sorites* transformations: 夫天下莫大於秋豪之末，而大山為小 'Nothing in the world is bigger than the tip of an autumn hair, and Mount T'ai is small.'

---

8   For the connection between Zhuangzi's term and that of the later Mohists, see Graham's *Later Mohist Logic, Ethics and Science*, pp. 182-184.
9   For an interesting, if highly technical, collection of papers on paradoxes of material constitution, see Michael Rae, *Material Constitution, A Reader*.

What was previously a mysterious identification of opposites for no obvious reason is now given a context, that of a gradual transformation along a continuum. In the working of the natural grindstone then, the plains become mountains, the mountains become plains; what is lifeless comes alive, as what is alive gradually loses its life; what is small and dispersed accumulates to become great, or to become a single object, and what is one or great disintegrates into minuscule fragments. In all these processes, as in the process of growth, what is most general is that what is so, *ran*, imperceptibly and by degrees becomes what is not so, *buran*; what is present, *you*, likewise gradually dissolves away into absence, *wu*, and in the matter of judgment a-nd evaluation, *shifei*, what is affirmed and what is denied, *ran buran*, what is so and what is not so, will also, as we have seen in our earlier discussion of the logic of vague concepts, become interchangeable in the penumbral regions, the borderlands of indiscernability where even the most absolute of opposites meet and exchange identities.

CHAPTER NINE

Conclusion

Vast and out of line—Zhuangzi's imagination takes him far from human concerns. Giant sea creatures, creatures that live for thousands of years, spirit people able to live on the dew. Zhuangzi lets go of conventional limitations in order to explore beyond the boundaries. With the imagination he releases the transformations of things, lets them take new and unheard of courses. By following the transformations one is released from the anxiety of loss, and the fear of death. One identifies with the changes, with the penumbral stages, so that one does not fear them as a loss of identity. From a point of view that leaves human concerns behind, everything is lost and everything is retained in the torrent of flux. It is only conceiving of fixed identities that creates loss. Insight *ming* allows us to identify *with* the transformations—so that identity itself becomes fluid and penumbral. When identity is itself fluid and penumbral change can no longer be perceived as loss. But neither, of course, can it be perceived as permanence. Rather, one sees through the dichotomy of permanence and loss as artificial.

Human concerns seem to require fixity, simplicity, stability, in order to be understood. We know what kinds of things are useful, we understand our everyday categories. We know the right ways to behave and we know what is wrong; what is pleasant and what is painful; what is to be welcomed and what is to be feared. When we open up our imaginations, we open up the texture of these apparent certainties. We enter the shadows of our understanding where we ordinarily do not dwell. The further into the peripheries we go, the less familiar things become. Half way out things are still recognizable, but as we proceed they become stranger—till our familiar categories are no longer of any use. In the penumbral areas they are not altogether useless: they are to some degree applicable. But by the same token, they are to some degree not applicable. Thus, we are led to the possibility of contradictions. The contradictions, however, remain contained in the penumbral areas. In real terms, we do not have much tendency to stretch the contradictoriness into the clearing. This is because of the conditions of recognizability. In appropriate conditions some things appear clearly: water revives us when we are thirsty. Though there may be some conditions in which water may be both good for us and not good for us—if, say, we are dehydrated, but the only water source is stagnant and salty—this duplicity does not extend back to the everyday situations. In the same way, hard cases in contexts of legal reasoning do not invalidate the applicability of laws to clear cases.

But why should we emphasize the penumbral and the contradictory, why so much concern over the hard cases and the anomalies? Surely what is important is what is clear, what we can all agree upon. These cases enable us to function smoothly. The vague, the inconsistent, and the contradictory are hard to deal with, and can even be dangerous, since they allow us to slide all too easily across apparent boundaries, and if generalized seem to undermine values, and consistent behavior, altogether. The answer is simple: the world is penumbral. Life is penumbral. Even if there is for the most part clarity and simplicity. Human life and human interaction is riddled with complexity and uncertainty, with ambivalence and inconsistency. And we have no choice but to learn how to deal with these. It does no good insisting that because these things are difficult and dangerous, we must avoid them altogether. On the contrary it is precisely because they are difficult and potentially dangerous that it is imperative for us to learn how to deal with them. Burying our heads in the sand is not a solution, but an act of cowardice.

The world is always greater than our own experiences. No matter how vast our experience may appear to ourselves or to others, it always loses its immensity in relation to the vastness that surrounds it. The petty can never match up to the vast, but it can always ensure that there is room for growth! We can always leave the doors open, we can always take one more step, make one more unanticipated exploration. Always remain open. Being open does not mean being foolhardy. Openness is always sensitive to what is there, always responsive to the surroundings, always according with the environment and with the context. Thus it is held in check, but not by fixed categories, and fixed standards. The judgment is intuitive, based on previous experience, and on an innate capacity to recognize relevant similarities and importances, but how one fixes on what is relevant and what is important cannot always be stated clearly and unequivocally.

The petty is that which clings to its limitations, and judges all from within the confines of its capacities. The petty assumes that everything is like it. It cannot imagine anything different. Vastness is the overcoming of these limitations. It is a freedom from boundaries that cuff and restrain. But it is not an amorphous state of absolute freedom. Once one has shaken off the shackles, one must seek to understand where one is, and how to move in the new space that opens up. One cannot do just anything. One must explore the new possibilities, and make appropriate judgments—judgments that are sensitive to the new and unforeseen circumstances. The word judgment here seems out of place and final. Perhaps one ought to say discriminations, or better, discernments. With release into the imagination one tries out something new. The gourd that is too large to be useful for ordinary purposes can be used for extraordinary purposes. If it cannot make a drum, or cannot make a utensil, sit on it, make a sculpture, boil it, dry it in the sun, pour salt on it. One cannot say in advance how to use it, what will be the best method. One must manipulate it, examine it, and above all, *imagine* it in new arrangements and in new circumstances. And then unforeseen possibilities will reveal themselves. One must be sensitive to the qualities of that particular gourd to know the best ways of dealing with it. Sorites processes will transform the gourd in one's imagination from something familiar to something unfamiliar. But one must not be afraid merely on account of the changes or the unfamiliarity. One must respond to it in its own uniqueness, and within the uniqueness of each context in which it has its place, and always try to overcome the limitations of fixed and lacklustre categorizations. This, I suggest, is one way to interpret the significance of free and easy wandering.

I have explored the concept of vagueness as it has been understood by western philosophers and distinguished it from related terms. I have also shown how the dominant western world view remains, on the whole, intolerant of all such indeterminacies, while the dominant Chinese world view, in part as a direct result of Daoist influence, has been much more tolerant of vagueness even in its philosophical methodology. I then isolated characteristics of vagueness, paying special attention to those that arise from processes of transformation, and identified these as possible 'traces' of vagueness. My supposition is that themes in a text may be identified by the traces they leave—which is an especially important method for uncovering themes that are not developed explicitly. I then took up a reading of the Daoist texts in order to detect the extent to which traces of vagueness are evident. My finding is that such traces are widespread in the *Laozi*, though not conclusive. But I also found reasons for suspecting that the difference of *significance* of vagueness in the Daoist tradition from that of the western tradition may account for at least some of that difference. After a detailed reading of the significance of dichotomous judgment for the Mohists, and after an exploration of the role of imagination in opening up the texture of our concepts, I turned to the *Zhuangzi*.

In the *Zhuangzi*, I found much stronger evidence in favor of the presence of vagueness as an implicit theme, the key trace perhaps being that of permeability of boundaries, which I interpreted with the help of the metaphor of the grindstone of nature—the significance of which in turn I interpreted through my reading of the *Laozi*.

Using this model we are able to make sense of much of Zhuangzi's contradictory *shifei* talk, without having to interpolate reference to points of view. Instead, we are now able to see the paradoxes with which Zhuangzi plays as arising quite directly from the mutual interpenetration of opposites, blending them on a continuum despite their apparent irreconcilability. When Zhuangzi plays with contradictions formed from these opposites, if we take him as referring to the penumbral regions of concepts—where processes of transformation wear away the apparent barriers between opposites—there is no need to 'translate out' the contradictions by interpolating references to points of view. We can now understand fully the significance of these paradoxical phrases without resorting to imposing on Zhuangzi unstated doctrines of relativism or scepticism.

I conclude with one reservation. What we arrive at after our investigation of these two seminal Daoist texts is an understanding of how a world in process is permeated through and through with indeterminacy and vagueness, but an investigation of the logic of vagueness shows us how this leads to logical puzzles, paradox, and contradiction. Thus, the Daoist world view show us quite directly how a world considered from the standpoint of a process metaphysics, is a world that makes room for such vagueness and inconsistency. It is, however, then incumbent on those who adopt such a world view to show how such a world nevertheless remains plausible. Thus, the success and acceptability of such a world view depends on the extent to which such pragmatically oriented logics as those developed by Rescher and Priest, which allow for inconsistency and contradiction, can be plausibly defended. It is my belief that this is not altogether unlikely.

Bibliography

Allinson, Robert E. *Understanding the Chinese Mind: the Philosophical Roots.* Hong Kong: Oxford University Press, 1989.

Ames, Roger, ed. *Wandering at Ease in the* Zhuangzi. Albany: State University of New York Press, 1998.

Ames, Roger, and David Hall. *Thinking Through Confucius.* Albany: State University of New York Press, 1987.

— *Anticipating China: Thinking through the Narratives of Chinese and Western Culture.* Albany: State University of New York Press, 1995.

— *Thinking from the Han: Self, Truth, and Transcendence in Chinese and Western Culture.* Albany: State University of New York Press, 1998.

— *Daodejing: 'Making This Life Significant.'* New York: Ballantine Books, 2003.

Ames, Roger, and Henry Rosemont. *The Analects of Confucius: A Philosophical Translation.* New York: Ballantine Books, 1999.

Barnes, Jonathan, Malcolm Schofield, and Richard Sorabji, eds. *Articles on Aristotle.* Vol. 1. *Science.* London: Duckworth, 1975.

— *Articles on Aristotle.* Vol. 3. *Metaphysics.* London: Duckworth, 1979.

Braidotti, Rosi. *Nomadic Subjects: Embodiment and Sexual Difference in Contemporary Feminist Theory.* New York: Columbia University Press, 1994.

Buchler, Justus, ed. *Philosophical Writings of Peirce.* New York: Dover Publications, 1955.

Burns, Linda Claire. *Vagueness: An Investigation into natural Languages and the Sorites Paradox.* Vol. 4, *Reason and Argument.* Dordrecht: Kluwer Academic Publishers, 1991.

Canfield, John V. *The Philosophy of Wittgenstein.* 15 vols. Vol. 5: *Method and Essence, The Philosophy of Wittgenstein: A Fifteen Volume Collection.* New York: Garland Publishing, 1986

— *The Philosophy of Wittgenstein.* 15 vols. Vol. 7: *Criteria. The Philosophy of Wittgenstein: A Fifteen Volume Collection.* New York: Garland Publishing, 1986.

Cao, Shoukun 曹受坤. *Zhuangzi Zhexue* 莊子哲學. Taibei: Wenjing Chuban-she 臺北: 文京出版社, 1973.

Carnap, Rudolf. "Meaning and Synonymy in Natural Languages." *Philosophical Studies.* Volume 6, 1955.

Chan, Ping-leung. "*Ch'u Tz'u* and Shamanism in Ancient China." Ph. D. diss., The Ohio State University, 1972.

Ch'en, Ku-ying. *Lao Tzu: Text, Notes, and Comments.* Translated by Rhett Y. W. Young and Roger Ames. ROC: Chinese Materials Center, 1981.

Chen, Guying 陳古應. *Zhuangzi Jin Zhu Jin Yi* 莊子今註今譯. Taibei: Taiwan Shangwu 臺北: 臺灣商務, 1975.

Cheng, Chung-ying. "The Establishment of the Chinese Linguistic Tradition." in *History of the Language Sciences: An International Handbook on the Evolution of the Study of Language from the Beginnings to the Present.* Edited by Sylvain Auroux, E. F. K. Koerner, Hans-Josef Niederehe, and Kees Versteegh. Berlin: Walter de Gruyter, 2000.

Ching, Julia. *Chinese Religions.* New York: Orbis Books, 1993.

Chuang Tzu. *Basic Writings.* Translated by Burton Watson. New York: Columbia University Press, 1964.

— *Chuang-Tzu The Inner Chapters: A Classic of Tao.* Translated by A. C. Graham. London: Mandala, 1991.

Deleuze, Gilles. *A Thousand Plateaus: Capitalism and Schizophrenia.* Translated by Brian Massumi. Minneapolis: University of Minnesota Press, 1987.

Derrida, Jacques. *Limited, Inc.* Translated by Samuel Weber. Evanston, Illinois: Northwestern Unversity Press, 1988.

— *Of Grammatology.* Translated by Gayatri Chakravorty Spivak. Baltimore: The Johns Hopkins University Press, 1998.

Dummett, Michael. *Origins of Analytical Philosophy.* London: Duckworth, 1993.

Eco, Umberto. *The Role of the Reader: Explorations in the Semiotics of Texts.* Bloomington: Indiana University Press, 1979.

— *Semiotics and the Philosophy of Language.* Bloomington: Indiana University Press, 1984.

— *The Limits of Interpretation.* Bloomington: Indiana University Press, 1990. *Experiences in Translation.* Translated by Alastair McEwen. Toronto: University of Toronto Press, 2001.

Eco, Umberto, and Thomas Sebeok, ed. *The Sign of Three: Dupin, Holmes, Peirce.* Bloomington: Indiana University Press, 1983.

Eliade, Mircea. *Le Chamanisme, et les Techniques Archaïques de l'Extase.* Paris: Payot, 1951.

— *Shamanism: Archaic Techniques of Ecstasy.* Translated by Willard R. Trask. Vol. LXXVI, *Bollingen Series.* Princeton: Princeton University Press, 1964.

Endicott, Timothy. *Vagueness in Law.* Oxford: Oxford University Press, 2000.

Fann, K. T. *Peirce's Theory of Abduction.* The Hague: Martinus Nijhoff, 1970.

Fetzer, James H., ed. *Definitions and Definability: Philosophical Perspectives.* Vol. 216, Synthese Library: Studies in Epistemology, Logic, Methodology, and Philosophy of Science. Dordrecht: Kluwer Academic Publishers, 1991.

Fine, Kit. "Vagueness, Truth and Logic." *Synthese* 30, 1975.

Fung, Yu-Lan. *Chuang-Tzu: A New Selected Translation with an Exposition of the Philosophy of Kuo Hsiang.* 2nd ed. New York: Paragon Book Reprint Corporation, 1964.

— *Selected Philosophical Writings of Fung Yu-lan.* Beijing: Foreign Languages Press, 1991.

Gao, Poyuan 高柏園. *Zhuangzi Nei Qi Pian Sixiang Yanjiu* 莊子內七篇思想研究. Taibei, Wenjin Chubanshe 臺北: 文津出版社, 1992.

Ge, Rongjin 葛榮晉. *Zhongguo Zhexue Fanchou Tonglun* 中國哲學範疇通論. Beijing: Shoudu Shifan Daxue Chubanshe 北京:首都師範大學出版社, 2001.

Gernet, Jacques. *La Chine Ancienne: des Origines a l'Empire*. Paris: Presses Universitaires de France, 1964.

— *Ancient China: from the Beginnings to the Empire*. Translated by Raymond Rudorff. Berkeley: University of California Press, 1968.

Gibson, Roger F. *The Philosophy of W. V. Quine: An Expository Essay*. Tampa: University Presses of Florida, 1982.

Girardot, Norman J. *Myth and Meaning in Early Taoism: The Theme of Chaos (hun-tun)*. Berkeley: University of California Press, 1983.

Graham, Angus Charles. *Later Mohist Logic, Ethics and Science*. London: School of Oriental and African Studies, 1978.

— *Disputers of the Tao: Philosophical Argument in Ancient China*. La Salle: Open Court, 1989.

— *Studies in Chinese Philosophy and Philosophical Literature*. Albany: State University of New York Press, 1990.

— *Unreason Within Reason*. La Salle: Open Court, 1992.

Granet, Marcel. *La Pensée Chinoise*. Paris: La Renaissance du Livre, 1934.

— *The Religion of the Chinese People*. Translated by Maurice Freedman. New York: Harper & Row, 1975.

Guo, Qingfan 郭慶藩. *Zhuangzi Ji Shi* 莊子集釋. Taibei: Guan Ya Wenhua 臺北: 貫雅文化, 1991.

Haack, Susan. *Deviant Logic: Some Philosophical Issues*. Cambridge: Cambridge University Press, 1977.

Hansen, Chad. *A Daoist Theory of Chinese Thought: A Philosophical Interpretation*. New York, Oxford University Press, 1992.

Harris Jr., James F. and Richard H. Severens, ed. *Analyticity*. Chicago: Quadrangle Books, 1970.

Henricks, Robert G. *Lao Tzu's Tao Te Ching*. New York: Columbia University Press, 2000.

Hoy, David Couzens. *The Critical Circle: Literature, History, and Philosophical Hermeneutics*. Berkeley: University of California Press, 1978.

Hsün Tzu. *Basic Writings*. Translated by Burton Watson. New York: Columbia University Press, 1963.

Hu, Shih. *The Development of the Logical Method in Ancient China*. New York: Paragon Book Reprint Corporation, 1963.

Husserl, Edmund. *Ideas: General Introduction to Pure Phenomenology*. Translated by W. R. Boyce Gibson. London: Allen & Unwin, 1968.

Ivanhoe, P. J. & Paul Kjellberg, ed. *Essays on Skepticism, Relativism, and Ethics in the Zhuangzi*. Albany: State University of New York Press, 1996.

Jullien, François. *Eloge de la Fadeur: A Partir de la Pensée et de l'esthétique de la Chine*. Paris: Éditions Philippe Picquier, 1991.

— *The Propensity of Things: Toward a History of Efficacy in China.* Translated by Janet Lloyd. New York: Zone Books, 1995.
— *Detour and Access: Strategies of Meaning in China and Greece.* Translated by Janet Lloyd. New York: Zone Books, 2000.
Kaltenmark, Max. *Lao Tzu and Taoism.* Translated by Roger Greaves. Stanford: Stanford University Press, 1969.
Keefe, Rosanna, and Peter Smith. ed. *Vagueness: A Reader.* Cambridge: MIT Press, 1996.
Keightley, David. *The Origins of Chinese Civilization.* Vol. 1, Studies on China. Berkeley: University of California Press, 1983.
Kohák, Erazim. *Idea and Experience: Edmund Husserl's Project of Phenomenology in Ideas.* Chicago: University of Chicago Press, 1978.
LaFargue, Michael. *The Tao of the Tao Te Ching: a Translation and Commentary.* Albany: State University of New York Press, 1992.
Lakoff, George. *Women, Fire, and Dangerous Things: What Categories Reveal about the Mind.* Chicago: University of Chicago Press, 1987.
Lakoff, George and Mark Johnson. *Metaphors We Live By.* Chicago: University of Chicago Press, 1980.
Lao-Tzu. *Te-Tao Ching.* Translated by Robert Henricks. New York, Ballantine Books, 1989.
Laozi. *Daodejing: Making This Life Significant.* Translated by Roger T. Ames and David L. Hall. New York: Ballantine Bookis, 2003.
Lawton, Thomas, ed. *New Perspectives on Chu Culture During the Eastern Zhou Period.* Washington, D.C.: Smithsonian Institution, 1991.
Lear, Jonathan. *Aristotle: the Desire to Understand.* Cambridge: Cambridge University Press, 1988.
Lenk, Hans, and Gregor Paul. *Epistemological Issues in Classical Chinese Philosophy.* Albany: State University of New York Press, 1993.
Lewis, Ioan M. *Ecstatic Religion.* Harmondsworth: Penguin Books, 1969.
Li, Xueqin. *Eastern Zhou and Qin Civilizations.* Translated by Kwang-chih Chang. New Haven: Yale University Press, 1985.
— "Chu Bronzes and Chu Culture." In *New Perspectives on Chu Culture During the Eastern Zhou Period,* edited by Thomas Lawton, 1-22. Washington, D.C.: Smithsonian Institution, 1991.
Lieh-tzu. *The Book of Lieh-tzu.* Translated by Angus Charles Graham. New York: Columbia University Press, 1990.
Liu, Xiaogan. *Classifying the Zhuangzi Chapters.* Translated by Donald Munro. *Michigan Monographs in Chinese Studies, no. 65.* Ann Arbor, Michigan: The University of Michigan, 1994.
Lyotard, Jean-François. *Phenomenology.* Translated by Brian Beakley. Albany: SUNY Press, 1991.
Mair, Victor H., ed. *Experimental Essays on Chuang-tzu.* Honolulu: University of Hawai'i Press, 1983.
— *Wandering on the Way: Early Taoist Tales and Parables of Chuang Tzu.* New York: Bantam Books, 1994.
Makeham, John. *Name and Actuality in Early Chinese Thought.* Albany: State University of New York Press, 1994.

Maspero, Henri. *Les Religions Chinoises.* Vol. I, *Mélanges Posthumes sur les Religions et l'histoire de la Chine.* Paris: Civilisations du Sud S.A.E.P., 1950.

— *Le Taoïsme.* Vol. II, *Mélanges Posthumes sur les Religions et l'histoire de la Chine.* Paris: Civilisations du Sud S.A.E.P., 1950.

— *China in Antiquity.* Translated by Frank A. Kierman Jr. Amherst: University of Massachusetts Press, 1978.

Munro, Donald J. *The Concept of Man in Early China.* Stanford: Stanford University Press, 1969.

Murphy, John P. *Pragmatism: From Peirce to Davidson.* Boulder: Westview Press, 1990.

Needham, Joseph. *Science and Civilisation in China.* Vol. Volume 2, *History of Scientific Thought.* Cambridge: Cambridge University Press, 1956.

Ormiston, Gayle, and Alan D. Schrift, ed. *The Hermeneutic Tradition: from Ast to Ricoeur.* Albany, State Unversity of New York Press, 1990.

Palmer, Richard E. *Hermeneutics: Interpretation Theory in Schleiermacher, Dilthey, Heidegger, and Gadamer.* Evanston, Illinois: Northwestern University Press, 1969

Paper, Jordan. *The Spirits are Drunk: Comparative Approaches to Chinese Religion.* Albany: State University of New York Press, 1995.

Peerenboom, R. P. *Law and Morality in Ancient China: The Silk Manuscripts of Huang-Lao.* New York: State University of New York Press, 1993.

Peirce, Charles Sanders. *Reasoning and the Logic of Things.* Cambridge: University of Harvard Press, 1992.

Pi, Daojian 皮道坚. *Chu Yishu Shi* 楚艺术史. Chuguo Wenku. Wuhan: Hubei Jiaoyu Chubanshe 楚国文库. 武汉: 湖北教育出版社, 1995.

Piaget, Jean. *Structuralism.* Translated by Chaninah Maschler. New York: Basic Books, 1970.

Priest, Graham. *In Contradiction: A Study of the Transconsistent.* Vol. 39, *Nijhoff International Philosophy Series.* Dordrecht: Martinus Nijhoff, 1987.

Quine, W. V. *From a Logical Point of View.* Cambridge: Harvard University Press, 1953.

— *Word and Object.* Harvard: Massachusetts Institute of Technology, 1960.

Rae, Michael. *Material Constitution: A Reader.* Lanham: Rowman and Littlefield, 1997.

Raphals, Lisa. *Knowing Words: Wisdom and Cunning in the Classical Traditions of China and Greece.* Ithaca: Cornell University Press, 1992.

Rawson, Jessica. *Mysteries of Ancient China: New Discoveries from the Early Dynasties.* New York: George Braziller, 1996.

Rescher, Nicholas, and Robert Brandom. *The Logic of Inconsistency: A Study in Non-Standard Possible-World Semantics and Ontology.* Totowa: Rowman and Littlefield, 1979.

Rescher, Nicholas. *Process Metaphysics: An Introduction to Process Philosophy.* Albany: State University of New York Press, 1996.

Richards, Ivor Armstrong. *Mencius on the Mind: Experiments in Multiple Definition.* New York: Harcourt, Brace and Company, 1932.

Rosemont, Henry Jr. *Chinese Texts and Philosophical Contexts: Essays Dedicated to Angus C. Graham.* Vol. I, *Critics and Their Critics.* La Salle: Open Court, 1991.

Ryle, Gilbert. *Collected Papers.* Volumes I & II. New York: Barnes & Noble, 1971.

Sainsbury, Richard M. *Paradoxes.* 2nd ed. Cambridge: Cambridge University Press, 1995.

Saussure, Ferdinand. *Course in General Linguistics.* Translated by Wade Baskin. New York: McGraw-Hill, 1959.

Scheffler, Israel. *Beyond the Letter: A Philosophical Inquiry into Ambiguity, Vagueness and Metaphor in Language.* London: Routledge and Kegan Paul, 1979.

Schwartz, Benjamin. *The World of Thought in Ancient China.* Cambridge, Massachusetts: Harvard University Press, 1985.

Song, Gongwen 宋公文. *Chuguo Fengsu Zhi* 楚国风俗志. Chuxue Wenku. Wuhan: Hubei Jiaoyu Chubanshe 楚国文库. 武汉: 湖北教育出版社, 1995.

Song, Zhiqing 宋稚青. *Laozhuang Sixiang yu Xifang Zhexue* 老莊思想與西方哲學. Taibei: Sanmin Shuju 臺北: 三民書局, 1984.

Staten, Henry. *Wittgenstein and Derrida.* Lincoln: University of Nebraska Press, 1984.

Sun Yirang 孫詒讓. *Mozi Xiangu* 墨子閒詁. Huazheng Shuju. Taibei, 1987.

Takeuchi, Yoshio. *Rooshi to Sooshi.* Tookyoo: Iwanami Shoten, Shoowa 8. 1933.

Time-Life Books. *China's Buried Kingdoms: Lost Civilizations.* Alexandria: Time-Life Books, 1993.

Tu, Youguang 涂又光. *Chuguo Zhexue Shi* 楚国哲学史. Chuguo Wenku. Wuhan: Hubei Jiaoyu Chubanshe 楚国文库. 武汉: 湖北教育出版社, 1995.

Waissman, Friedrich. 'Verifiability.' *Proceedings of the Aristotelian Society* Supp. Vol. 19, 1945, pp 19—150.

Watson, William. *Early Civilization in China.* London: Thames and Hudson, 1966.

—— *Ancient China.* Connecticut: New York Graphic Society, 1974.

Wheeler III, Samuel C. *Deconstruction as Analytical Philosophy.* Stanford: Stanford University Press, 2000.

Wilhelm, Helmut, and Richard Wilhelm. *Understanding the I Ching: The Wilhelm Lectures on The Book of Changes.* Princeton: Princeton University Press, 1995.

Williamson, Timothy. 'Vagueness and Ignorance.' *Proceedings of the Aristotelian Society* Supp. Vol. 66, 1992.

— *Vagueness.* London: Routledge, 1994.

Wu, Fei Bai 伍非百. *Zhongguo Gu Mingjia Yan* 中國古名家言. Beijing, Zhongguo Shehui Kexue Chubanshe 北京: 中國社會科學出版社, 1983.

Wu, Kuang-ming. *The Butterfly as Companion: Meditations on the First Three Chapters of the Chuang Tzu.* Albany: State University of New York Press, 1990.

Wu, Kunru 邬昆如. *Zhuangzi yu Gudai Xila Zhexue Zhong de Dao* 莊子與古代希臘哲學中得道. Taibei: Taiwan Zhonghua Shuju 臺北:臺灣中華書局, 1976.

Zhang, Dainian. *Key Concepts in Chinese Philosophy.* Translated by Edmund Ryden. New Haven: Yale University Press, 2002.

Zhang, Zhengming. 张正明. *Chu Wenhua Shi* 楚文化史. *Zhongguo Wenhua Shi Congshu* 中国文化工史丛书. Shanghai: Shanghai Renmin Chubanshe 上海: 上海人民出版社, 1987.

Zhuang, Wanshou. 莊萬壽. *Zhuangzi Shilun: Zhuangzi zhi xin fangxiang: yuanliu, shengtai, pipan, yuyan* 莊子史論: 莊學之方向: 源流,生態,批,語言. Taibei: Wanquan Lou 臺北:萬卷樓, 2000.

Zhuangzi Yinde. 莊子引得 (A Concordance to Chuang Tzu). *Harvard-Yenching Institute Sinological Index Series.* Beiping: Harvard-Yenching Institute, 1947.

Index